Decolonising Intellectual Property is a momentous task: Its core foundations – such as progress, property and sovereignty – emanate from early European modernity and have long been universalised as part of colonial and neo-colonial enterprises. Taking an Afrocentric approach, Dr Jade Kouletakis and Dr Nkem Itanyi and their team of authors offer a rich account of alternative perspectives and visions for creativity and innovation in Africa – with their own takes on tailoring conventional IP protection tools to domestic needs, as well as substituting such tools for indigenous solutions.

Henning Grosse Ruse-Khan, *Fellow and Co-Director of the Centre for Intellectual Property and Information Law (CIPIL) at King's College, University of Cambridge*

The editors of this collection are to be congratulated for assembling such a tremendous range of scholarship and perspectives on intellectual property, producing a volume that is itself an instrument in the decolonisation of intellectual property scholarship and research. This collection of essays navigates the western mapping of intellectual property and reviews the full terrain of rights with fresh cartography. It is invaluable and imperative that intellectual property scholarship agitates the Anglocentric and anthropocentric lens within which much of that scholarship is compelled. And in doing so, it is important for scholarship to begin to interrogate not only its context but also the kinds of questions themselves and the reasons they are asked. This volume makes a critically important contribution to the re-mapping of intellectual property, its history and its cultures, and is a crucial addition to international intellectual property scholarship.

Johanna Gibson, *Herchel Smith Professor of Intellectual Property Law, Queen Mary, University of London, Editor-in-Chief, Queen Mary Journal of Intellectual Property*

This book contributes to the all-important epistemic debate over the evolution and jurisprudence of the Intellectual Property (IP) system as we know it today. Finding cogency in the rapid cross-cultural narratives that have animated IP landscape – narratives that are yet to come to a full circle given the predominance of Western worldview, the book reinforces existing Afrocentric scholarship on the geo-political currency of IP law. The editors, Jade Kouletakis and Nkem Itanyi and the authors, who are well-known in the field, offer a compelling voice to the redefinition of IP as a more dynamic and inclusive body of knowledge.

Adebambo Adewopo, *Professor, SAN Nigerian Institute of Advanced Legal Studies*

This book offers an interesting paradigm shift in intellectual property discourse, centering African perspectives and challenging Eurocentric norms. Essential reading for scholars, policymakers, and practitioners seeking a decolonized understanding of intellectual property rights in Africa and beyond.

Enrico Bonadio, *Professor of Intellectual Property Law, City St George's University of London (previously City, University of London)*

The book is timely, invaluable and highly relevant to the current need for a truly African-centred and decolonised intellectual property law. It is a must-read for students, IP specialists and policymakers in Africa and beyond.

Yeukai Mupangavanhu, *Associate Professor, University of the Western Cape, South Africa*

This book makes a unique contribution to the discourse on the interface between intellectual property and development. Employing an Afrocentric approach, the editors and the various authors engage with several topical issues relating to the role of intellectual property law in African development. The book offers useful insights and novel perspectives on issues such as African traditional communities and intellectual property rights, copyright and colonialism, patent rights and technological development, and the protection of traditional medicines via patent law. The book will therefore be of significant interest to those interested in the debates regarding the relationship between Africa, intellectual property rights, and development.

Dr Emmanuel Kolawole Oke, *Senior Lecturer in International Intellectual Property Law, Edinburgh Law School, University of Edinburgh*

Decolonising Intellectual Property Law: An Afrocentric Approach spotlights often overlooked aspects of intellectual property (IP) rights, presenting fresh insights from African scholars. By centring African narratives, it enriches the global IP discourse with diverse histories, cultural practices, and knowledge systems that have long been marginalised. Through its African centred lens, the timely book boldly challenges dominant Eurocentric narratives, offering alternative perspectives that reflect varied lived experiences from around Africa. In doing so, it expands the boundaries of IP scholarship, providing a richer, more inclusive, and dynamic understanding of IP.

Dr Titilayo Adebola, *Senior Lecturer and Theme Coordinator for International Intellectual Property and Information Law, University of Aberdeen*

Decolonising Intellectual Property Law

This book advocates for an Afrocentric approach to intellectual property (IP) law, using lessons from Nigeria's past to encourage reform for the future of Africa's legal IP landscape.

Highlighting the Eurocentric influence on the history of intellectual property law in Africa, the book demonstrates how this contradicts traditional African community culture. This book makes the case for legitimising cultural expressions of traditional communities despite the western legal framework within which they exist, reimagining a decolonised IP framework whereby African histories are centred. Questioning the fundamentals of the current IP landscape, such as the concept of eligibility in copyright which developed alongside European technological advances, the book also details the role of the courts in resolving IP disputes. It highlights Africa as a powerhouse of original, autonomous innovation, values, and traditions which predate the West's concept of intellectual property. It illustrates the African experience of intellectual property from a pro-African perspective as shared by African authors.

This book will be of interest to researchers in the field of intellectual property, copyright, and patent law, as well as African law.

Jade Kouletakis is an award-winning academic with experience teaching IP Law in multiple higher education institutions across two continents since 2014. She has been an invited keynote speaker at the University of Cambridge, the University of St Andrews, and the Scottish Law and Innovation Network. She has published one of the "most read" articles and the second "most read" article on the websites of the *Journal of World Intellectual Property* (for whom she peer-reviews) and *GRUR International: Journal of European and International IP Law*. For REF 2021, she produced a maximum number of REF-qualifying outputs and submitted an Impact Case Study.

Nkem Itanyi is an accomplished, experienced academic. She is a law lecturer and researcher specialising in intellectual property law. With over twenty years of research and teaching across two continents, she has an impressive record of scholarly achievement. As a TETFund scholar, she earned a doctorate from the prestigious School of Law at Queen's University Belfast, United Kingdom, an LLM in Corporate and Commercial Law from University College London, and an LLB (Hons) from Obafemi Awolowo University, Ile-Ife, Nigeria. Nkem's research activity is robust; she has an extensive publication record in law and has been cited in leading peer-reviewed academic journals indexed in Clarivate Web of Science, Scopus, and other databases. She has published one of the "most read" articles in the *Journal of World Intellectual Property* and received a certificate for it. Nkem is an invited and celebrated speaker at conferences who has been asked to share her research globally, including as a guest speaker at Harvard Law School, Harvard University, Cambridge, Massachusetts, Boston, United States of America,and as a Guest Lecturer at the School of Law, Queen's University Belfast, United Kingdom.

Routledge Research in Intellectual Property

Available:

Intellectual Property and Development
Geographical Indications in Practice
Barbara Pick

Collective Management of Music Copyright
A Comparative Analysis of China, the United States and Australia
Qinqing Xu

Intellectual Property Rights and Competition Law in India
Edited by Rajni Malhotra Dhingra and Nisha Dhanraj Dewani

Digitization, Copyright and the Law
Copyleft and the Future of Intellectual Property
Ettore M. Lombardi

Intellectual Property and Emerging Technologies
Generated Global IP Issues and Challenges
Tshimanga Kongolo

Innovation and Development of Knowledge Societies
Artificial Intelligence and Knowledge-Based Socioeconomic Growth
Nadia Naim, Alhanoof AlDebasi and David Price

Copyright Law in Photographic Works
Authorship, Originality and Protection
Faisal Alamri

Decolonising Intellectual Property Law
An Afrocentric Approach
Edited by Jade Kouletakis and Nkem Itanyi

For more information about this series, please visit https://www.routledge.com/Routledge-Research-in-Intellectual-Property/book-series/INTELLPROP

Decolonising Intellectual Property Law

An Afrocentric Approach

Edited by Jade Kouletakis and
Nkem Itanyi

Routledge
Taylor & Francis Group
LONDON AND NEW YORK

First published 2026
by Routledge
4 Park Square, Milton Park, Abingdon, Oxon OX14 4RN

and by Routledge
605 Third Avenue, New York, NY 10158

Routledge is an imprint of the Taylor & Francis Group, an informa business

British Library Cataloguing-in-Publication Data
A catalogue record for this book is available from the British Library

ISBN: 978-1-032-98571-8 (hbk)
ISBN: 978-1-032-99224-2 (pbk)
ISBN: 978-1-003-60298-9 (ebk)

DOI: 10.4324/9781003602989

Typeset in Times New Roman
by Deanta Global Publishing Services, Chennai, India

Contents

List of contributors

Adesoji Kolawole Adebayo is a lecturer in law at the School of Law and Security Studies, Babcock University. He obtained his law degree from Ekiti State University (EKSU) and was called to the bar in 2014. After practising law briefly, he proceeded to the University of Ilorin in Kwara State and obtained his LLM and PhD from Babcock University, Ogun State, Nigeria. He has several years of teaching, research, and consulting experience, focusing on Medical Law, Criminal Law, ADR, and Family Law. He has published in peer-reviewed journals, contributed to book chapters, and edited books.

Ikechukwu Chime earned his doctorate in digital economy from the University of Nigeria. He completed a master's degree with distinction in Petroleum Law and Policy, with a minor in International Business, at the Centre for Energy, Petroleum, Mining Law and Policy, University of Dundee in Scotland. Furthermore, he served as the editor of the CEPMLP Annual Review. Dr Chime was a visiting scholar at the School of Resource and Environmental Management at Simon Fraser University in Canada. He worked as an analyst at the Social Change Institute in British Columbia, Canada. He is currently a lecturer at the Faculty of Law at the University of Nigeria.

Nneka Chioma Ezedum obtained her bachelor's degree in law from the University of Nigeria, Nsukka (UNN). She earned her master's and doctorate degrees in Intellectual Property Law from Enugu State University of Science and Technology, Agbani, Enugu, Nigeria. She is a WIPO-Harvard Law School PatentX alumna and holds certifications in several Intellectual Property Law courses from the WIPO Academy. Currently, she is an IP Law lecturer at Enugu State University of Science and Technology, Agbani, Enugu, Nigeria. Additionally, she had a stint in corporate banking before venturing into academia.

Nkem Itanyi is an accomplished, experienced academic. She is a law lecturer and researcher specialising in intellectual property law. With over twenty years of research and teaching across two continents, she has an impressive record of scholarly achievement. As a TETFund scholar, she earned a doctorate from the prestigious School of Law at Queen's University Belfast, United Kingdom, an LLM in Corporate and Commercial Law from University College London, and an LLB (Hons) from Obafemi Awolowo University, Ile-Ife, Nigeria. Nkem's research activity is robust; she has an extensive publication record in law and has been cited in leading peer-reviewed academic journals indexed in Clarivate Web of Science, Scopus, and other databases. She has published one of the "most read" articles in the *Journal of World Intellectual Property* and received a certificate for it. Nkem is an invited and celebrated speaker at conferences who has been asked to share her research globally, including as a guest speaker at Harvard Law School, Harvard University, Cambridge, Massachusetts, Boston, United States of America,and as a Guest Lecturer at the School of Law, Queen's University Belfast, United Kingdom.

Jade Kouletakis is an award-winning academic with experience teaching IP Law in multiple higher education institutions across two continents since 2014. She holds a PhD in IP Law from Coventry University. She has been an invited keynote speaker at the University of Cambridge, the University of St Andrews, and the Scottish Law and Innovation Network. She has published one of the "most read" articles and the second "most read" article on the websites of the *Journal of World Intellectual Property* (for whom she peer-reviews) and *GRUR International: Journal of European and International IP Law*. For REF 2021, she produced the maximum number of REF-qualifying outputs and submitted an Impact Case Study.

Seun Lari-Williams is a PhD researcher at the University of Antwerp. His research focuses on dispute system design in the creative sector. He studied law at the University of Lagos, was called to the Nigerian bar in 2014, and subsequently worked as a litigation lawyer in Lagos and Abuja. In 2019, he was awarded a DAAD scholarship, enabling him to obtain a master's degree in intellectual property and competition law from the Max Planck Institute of Innovation and Competition in Germany. Seun is the 2021 winner of the ALAI European Authors' Rights Award.

Ayoyemi Lawal-Arowolo is a professor of law at the School of Law and Security Studies, Babcock University. She earned her law degree from Lagos State University (LASU) and was called to the bar in 1999. She obtained her LLM from Indiana University, Indianapolis, and her PhD from the University of Kent, Canterbury, UK. She was among the pioneer staff at the Nigerian Copyright Institute, the research and training arm of the Nigerian Copyright Commission. She has several years of teaching, research, and consulting experience, focusing on intellectual property rights, industrial law, data protection, and privacy law. She has published in peer-reviewed journals, book chapters, edited volumes, and books.

Regina Obiechine has been a senior associate and an integral member of the IP Team at Aluko & Oyebode for over a decade. She represents both local and international clients in a range of IP-related transactions, including trademarks, patents, industrial designs, and copyright prosecution and advisory. She is a member of the Academic Committee of the INTA, the Anti-Counterfeiting Collaboration (ACC) Nigeria, and the Intellectual Property Law Association of Nigeria (IPLAN). As a result of her work and contributions to knowledge, she has received several awards from Managing IP, IP Leader in the elite WIPR Leaders Guide, World Intellectual Property Review (WIPR), and others.

Foreword

As a non-African academic contributor to a book having an Afrocentric decolonial approach to intellectual property, I feel deeply honoured to be invited to write its opening words. My standpoint can only be one of humility and respect for the people of a continent that suffered generations of rapacious colonial rule, of which my own country (the United Kingdom) was a main perpetrator. Despite being more or less free of European colonialism for just a few decades, Africans have striven hard to transcend this awful legacy. Without a doubt they have made progress in doing so.

Admittedly, recent trends in international intellectual property law-making have barely gone Africa's way. The trade-related multilateral intellectual property framework, the design of which Africa had little influence over, completely failed Africa. This was most apparent when the HIV/AIDS crisis was at its worst and millions died for lack of access to medicines that would have kept them alive. Intellectual property law as we know it, including its global spread starting in the imperial age, is of course inherently colonial. Its origins are entirely European, and the textbook justifications for intellectual property rights' existence derive entirely from Western modes of thinking, from secularised formulations of natural rights to romantic authorship, utilitarianism, classical and neoclassical economics, and various combinations thereof.

Yet when it comes to intellectual property and intellectual property decolonisation, independent Africa has never been a sleeping giant. Its role in shaping the international law of intellectual property has for long been underestimated and deserves a great deal more recognition than it has been given. From the height of the 1960s decolonisation wave in Africa, the continent's involvement in intellectual property deliberations, including at the global level, has been a constant presence. Despite this, Africa has been assumed to be merely a rule-taker, depending on the guidance and advice of outsiders, rather than an actual, or potential, rule-maker able to make its own decisions and even to export innovative legal norms to other continents. While its rule-taker role largely reflects reality, change is in the offing, and history – surprisingly to some people perhaps – backs this up.

To provide a few examples of past African engagement and leadership, in 1969 the Organization of African Unity (OAU, now the African Union) called for the protection of African people's intellectual property in a document called the Pan African Cultural Manifesto. This interest in cultural protection and promotion was also reflected in newly independent African countries' efforts in promoting folklore (now referred to as traditional cultural expressions) at UNESCO and at what in 1970 became the World Intellectual Property Organization (WIPO).

Also in the 1960s, the OAU did much to promote the importance of traditional medicine in primary healthcare, first within that continent and then in international forums, especially the World Health Organization. While intellectual property was not apparently an immediate consideration here – nor elsewhere for that matter – Africans were probably the first to raise concerns about pharmaceutical corporations patenting inventions derived from freely-given plants used in traditional medicine ("biopiracy" as this was later known) and to suggest a response to it. A 1979 article in *Nature* noted that the OAU "has gone so far as to urge secrecy in herbal medicine research to prevent just this."

Despite the harm of TRIPS implementation of patents in all fields of technology, including medicines, the African Group was instrumental in the adoption of the Declaration on the TRIPS Agreement and Public Health at the 2001 Doha Ministerial Conference of the World Trade Organization. At the time of writing, much effort is being made to enable Africa to enhance its production of mRNA vaccines so as to become more self-reliant when the next global pandemic after COVID-19 emerges. The rest of the world, including those corporations that control the technologies and know-how, has been unhelpful in the main, but such is their determination that eventual success is assured.

In 2000, the African Union adopted its African Model Legislation for the Protection of the Rights of Local Communities, Farmers and Breeders, and for the Regulation of Access to Biological Resources. Admittedly, national implementation has been somewhat less than hoped for. Twenty-four years later, the African Group and African experts on official delegations played a decisive role in the adoption of the Treaty on Intellectual Property, Genetic Resources and Associated Traditional Knowledge. This was achieved by deploying high-quality and committed expertise that technically outmatched that of the United States, Europe, and other countries sceptical or opposed to the treaty, and a great deal of political skill that included positive relations with the WIPO secretariat and effective coordination with the Indigenous Caucus. African diplomats continue to be involved at WIPO in the drafting of a legal instrument on traditional cultural expressions.

But there is still far to go to achieve complete self-reliance. The flow of European missionaries bringing the Bible while their compatriots stole the land may have stopped. But true-believer intellectual property missionary work continues in various forms from we-know-better-than-you technical assistance programmes and professional persuaders including consultants, to those having more threat-power from the more aggressive and self-serving business associations and certain foreign governments. Despite my open scepticism towards "the more intellectual property the better" mantra that is frequently propagated by those who deploy it while disguising their personal interests in adherence to such faith-based assertions, I have been involved in the drafting of laws and regulations for countries I have visited but barely know. This needs to change.

Colonialism sinks deep roots. But just as new, perhaps better adapted, grape varieties can be grafted onto old rootstock, one can – metaphorically speaking – graft better adapted laws from underlying intellectual property structures. In other words, if the globalisation of European intellectual property norms is a form of globalised localism, these now globalised norms can be re-localised to be a better fit for African nations. Room for manoeuvre is, of course, less than it should be, and old dependencies have hardly vanished. But there remains scope for greater self-reliance. Intellectual property for Africa needs to be done by Africans, and the signs are that this is going to happen. When I became an intellectual property scholar and activist in the 1990s, the number of recognised African and diaspora intellectual property experts was not high. There is nothing inherently wrong with that having been the case. Intellectual property law is just one area of the law, and its importance relative to other areas of law will vary according to many factors I have no time to consider here. One hugely significant development, and this is one that the book you are holding bears testimony to, is the tremendous and rapid increase in the number of African and diaspora scholars on the intellectual property law scene. The world of intellectual property scholarship and legal innovation must now include Africans as a major presence.

Professor Graham Dutfield
Professor of International Governance, University of Leeds;
DPhil, University of Oxford;
MPhil, University of Cambridge

Introduction

Rewriting the history of intellectual property law in Africa – a decolonisation perspective

Nkem Itanyi

The African laws of intellectual property have usually been significantly influenced by the presence of the norms of the colonial legal systems, which do not give respect to the native forms of knowledge and traditional cultural expressions. This book is based on a critical review of the evolution of intellectual property laws in Africa, a continent known for its colonial inception, regarding the local effect on innovation and cultural heritage. The book demonstrates that the African continent needs a legal regime that strikes a fair balance between the interests involved, integrates traditional knowledge, upgrades local industries, and also fairly allows easy access to innovation.

The intellectual property rights system in Africa has its foundations in the period of colonialism. It was created primarily for the economic interests of the colonisers and not for the protection or encouragement of local inventions and knowledge about traditions. The colonial authorities in each African region sought to govern economic activities in the colony and provided for trademark and patent rights under rules suitable for European firms, paying no attention to local manufacturing and innovation. In Nigeria, for example, an established system, The Patents Ordinance 1900, imposed a notion of the West on individual possession and the act of registering something, which is entirely opposed to the communal knowledge sharing of the people of Nigeria.[1] The Trade Marks Ordinance of 1914 and the Copyright Act of 1970 did not consider or provide protection for communal innovation and folklore.[2] Consequently, Nigeria's intellectual

1 Alpha Alex Kwaya, "The Promulgation of Intellectual Property Law in Nigeria; Historical Overview, Challenges and the Way Forward" (2023) https://barristerng.com/the-promulgation-of-intellectual-property-law-in-nigeria-historical-overview-challenges-and-the-way-forward-by-alpha-alex-kwaya/ accessed 8 February 2025.

2 Inioluwa Olaposi, "Trademarks in Nigeria (Protection, Registration etc.)," *LawGlobal Hub*, 24 May 2022. https://www.lawglobalhub.com/trademarks-in-nigeria/ accessed 8 February 2025.

DOI: 10.4324/9781003602989-1

property regime continues to grapple with challenges that emanate from its colonial roots, notwithstanding legal reforms like the recently enacted Copyright Act 2022.

Colonial intellectual property laws key in on single ownership, formal registration, and commercial exploitation; they typically leave out indigenous innovation and artistic forms, which is the bedrock of the African system.[3]

This book examines the development of specific intellectual property laws in Africa from a decolonisation perspective, emphasising their role in legally protecting native creative expressions. It highlights that many of these laws introduced the notion of absolute rights and imposed a strict registration process, thereby failing to acknowledge indigenous creative systems.[4] The legal framework was designed to facilitate colonial administration and primarily serve the interests of foreign investors rather than supporting local craftsmen, creators, or communities. For example, the implementation of formal registration requirements created bureaucratic barriers that largely excluded most local creators who lacked access to essential legal information.

Generally, the body of laws did not recognise traditional artistic expressions or oral literature and the communal ownership of knowledge.[5] The features were of Western-style literary works, music, and artistic expressions, which were the focus of colonial governments, and through such, more marginalised forms of indigenous knowledge systems, which were orally transmitted, were marginalised. Under colonial rule, the legal system was designed to protect European commercial interests, leading to the economic exploitation of local resources and knowledge.[6] Indigenous textiles, carvings, medicinal practices, and oral traditions were widely used but lacked formal legal protection, leaving them vulnerable to biopiracy and commercial exploitation by foreign entities.[7]

At independence, African regions maintained the colonial statutes with little modification to suit present needs. This failure to carry out

3 Thomas Dreier, "Caught Between Post- and Neo-Colonialism: IP for Traditional Knowledge, Traditional Cultural Expressions and Indigenous Resources" in C. Godt and M. Lamping, (eds) *A Critical Mind. MPI Studies on Intellectual Property and Competition Law*, Vol. 30. Springer, Berlin 2023.

4 For example, the Patents Ordinance of 1900 was based on an act that was carried out in Britain, the Patents Act of 1852. See also, Shafiu Adamu Yauri, "'The Patent System in Nigeria"' (2021) World Patent Information. help_outline accessed 8 February 2025. , "" *Information*.

5 For example, the Copyright Act of Nigeria, 1911.

6 Owolade, F. "Writing a Colonial Legal History of Northern Nigeria: An Analysis of Methods and Sources". History in Africa, (2023) *Journal of African Law*.50, 73–98.

7 Ibid.

comprehensive intellectual property law reforms left indigenous knowledge and cultural expressions unprotected. Hence, misappropriations by foreign entities continued. For instance, under the Copyright Act of Nigeria, 1988, there was no express provision for the protection of traditional folklore; this loophole allowed foreign enterprises to pirate and profit from Nigerian cultural manifestations without any form of authorisation or compensation.[8] This legal gap created an opportunity for such misappropriation. Western fashion brands and entertainment industries borrowed heavily from African designs, motifs, and folk music without any mention of the origins – let alone sharing economic benefits with the creators. The lack of a unique framework for traditional knowledge and genetic resources further left Nigeria's indigenous innovation unsupported and without protection from unauthorised usage and misappropriation.[9] This was clear in the cases where Western pharmaceutical firms patented the medicinal values of Nigerian plant species like neem and kola without recognising the indigenous knowledge systems.

Our book gives a perspective from the lens of Africans on what traditional intellectual property rights were before colonialism. We argue that the basic structure of Western intellectual property law is individualistic.[10] Western intellectual property law focuses solely on rights and their commercial implications, which stands in stark contrast to the communal nature of African knowledge systems. This is particularly evident in areas such as medical knowledge, musical arts, and craftsmanship, where ownership is collective and information is shared orally. Western copyright laws did not take into account that cultural heritage is governed by communal rights, which led to numerous legal disputes whenever ownership claims were presented.

The authors individually do justice to these arguments. The discussions begin with Dr Kouletakis, who, in her chapter, argues that exclusive copyright ownership should be justified not solely on Western, capitalistic grounds of economic incentive and commercialisation, but within a broader framework rooted in socio-economic development, especially relevant to developing nations. She proposes a shift from the traditional individualistic and profit-driven justifications of copyright – like incentivisation and

8 Ibid.

9 Nneka Chioma Ezedum, "Protection of Traditional Knowledge and its Relevance to National Economic Growth and Development in Nigeria" (2022). *The Nigerian Juridical Review*, 17(1), 88–108.

10 Dreier, T. (2023). "Caught Between Post- and Neo-Colonialism: IP for Traditional Knowledge, Traditional Cultural Expressions and Indigenous Resources" in C. Godt and M. (eds) *A Critical Mind. MPI Studies on Intellectual Property and Competition Law*, Vol. 30. Springer, Berlin, 2023.

moral rights – to a model grounded in the United Nations' 2030 Agenda and its 17 Sustainable Development Goals.

Dr Itanyi, in the following chapter, explores the cultural, historical, and legal evolution of Nollywood, Nigeria's prolific film industry. She highlights its deep roots in communal oral storytelling traditions and the transformative impact of colonialism and modern technology. From moonlight tales and communal performances involving instruments like the Yoruba talking drum, Nigerian storytelling has long been a means of moral education and cultural preservation, noting that it all existed before the colonial era introduced Western education, print, and performance practices. She advocates for a hybrid legal approach – integrating modern frameworks with *sui generis* protections – to safeguard cultural heritage while enabling sustainable growth and innovation in Nigeria's creative industries.

The discussion continues with Professor Arolowo taking a deep dive into how African traditional communities historically developed and practised their own systems of knowledge protection through customary laws – long before the introduction of Western intellectual property regimes. She noted that indigenous systems included oral norms, communal customs, taboos, religious sanctions, and guild-based protections for intellectual and creative works. However, colonisation, foreign trade, and modern technological advances disrupted these traditions by introducing Eurocentric legal frameworks that disregarded and devalued African knowledge systems. She maintained that the imposition of Western intellectual property law, particularly copyright and patents, marginalised customary laws by treating African traditional knowledge as public domain and failing to recognise its intrinsic value.

Following closely in this line, Dr Ezedum, for her part, underscores the historical exclusion of indigenous knowledge (IK) from conventional intellectual property protection but notes a growing international recognition of its value. Central to her discourse is the Igbo Apprenticeship System (IAS), *or Igba boyi*, a traditional knowledge transfer model from Southeast Nigeria that facilitates skill acquisition, economic empowerment, and business incubation through mentorship and communal support. Her chapter draws a parallel between modern technology transfer under patent law and the indigenous method of skill transmission via apprenticeship. She argues that although traditional systems like IAS are informal and orally constructed, they deserve recognition and protection under a broader, more inclusive intellectual property framework. She advocates for the application of intellectual property principles – particularly those that uphold consent and benefit-sharing – to protect IK, ensuring its sustainable use, preventing exploitation, and recognising its communal ownership. Ultimately, she advocates for the formal integration of indigenous systems like apprenticeship into global intellectual property regimes as legitimate pathways for safeguarding cultural heritage and fostering indigenous economic development. Ms Obiechine, in her chapter, explores the evolution, current structure, and challenges of the patenting system in Nigeria and Africa at large. She acknowledges Africa's long history of innovation – highlighting remarkable African inventors such as Thomas L. Jennings, Seyi Oyesola, and Emeka Nelson – underscoring how colonial-era patent laws were not designed to promote indigenous innovation but rather to serve colonial interests. Her chapter concludes with a strong call for African countries to decolonise their patent laws, invest in indigenous innovation, and implement robust, independent intellectual property systems as key drivers for economic and technological advancement.

In their chapter, Professors Lawal-Arowolo and Adebayo critically explore the intersection of colonial legacy, traditional medicine, and intellectual property law in Nigeria, advocating for a decolonised mindset to elevate the role of indigenous healing practices in the national healthcare system. They highlight how colonialism introduced orthodox medicine and suppressed traditional medicine through stigma, legal marginalisation, and the entrenchment of a colonial mentality that still undermines indigenous knowledge today. Decolonisation, therefore, is presented not just as a political act but as a mental and cultural reawakening – one that challenges Eurocentric superiority and embraces the legitimacy, efficacy, and historical relevance of traditional medicine. Drawing parallels with China, India, and South Africa, they make a call for Nigeria to develop robust legal and institutional mechanisms that legitimise and support traditional medicine.

In his chapter, Seun Lari-Williams examines the differences between African and Western mediation cultures, focusing on their application in resolving disputes within the global music industry, particularly intellectual property conflicts. He highlights the African approach, which is rooted in communal values, elder-led directive mediation, spirituality, and reconciliation. He underscores how cultural factors, such as collectivism versus individualism and varying perceptions of justice, influence conflict resolution. Using the music industry as a case study, he illustrates the challenges in cross-cultural mediation, especially in intellectual property disputes. He, therefore, advocates for culturally intelligent mediation, recommending mediator training, the integration of local customs into dispute systems, and collaboration with copyright offices to bridge cultural and legal gaps.

Dr Chime completes the collection by looking at intellectual property in Nigeria from a forward-looking lens. His chapter explored the evolving role of technology in Nigeria's development, emphasising the potential of emerging technologies – such as artificial intelligence (AI), blockchain, and non-fungible tokens (NFTs) – to drive economic and social transformation. He observed that Nigeria's dynamic, tech-savvy youth present significant potential; however, the country's insufficient intellectual property frameworks impede innovation and investment. In his chapter, he critiques the current intellectual property laws in Nigeria, highlighting their inadequacy in addressing the challenges posed by emerging technologies and AI-generated content. He also emphasises the necessity for enhanced legal recognition and enforcement mechanisms.

Overall, this book and its contributions illustrate that Africans possess a unique perspective on intellectual property law, one that is distinct from that of their colonisers. It advocates for a re-evaluation of pre-colonial approaches to intellectual property law in Africa. This groundbreaking work captures the complexities and opportunities that could exist within Africa's intellectual property system, highlighting its uniqueness and distinctiveness from the frameworks operational in the Western world.

1 Decolonising copyright theory

Justifying copyright ownership through the prism of the United Nations' developmental agenda

Jade Kouletakis

1.1 Introduction

The existing paradigm of copyright creates a norm of exclusive ownership over an original work which is enjoyed by the copyright owner, who is usually the creator, for a limited period of time.[1] These rights may be limited within national legislation in certain special circumstances that are in accordance with international standards, such as the so-called "three-step test" in Article 13 of the Agreement on Trade-Related Aspects of Intellectual Property Rights 1994 (TRIPS Agreement). As limitations and exceptions diminish the copyright owner's private rights and deviate from the norm of exclusive ownership, the onus is on those calling for them to justify their creation. Speaking on the expansion of exclusive copyright ownership in the realm of software, Lessig famously warned that:

> Monopolies are not justified by theory; they should be permitted only when justified by facts ... Before [a] monopoly should be permitted, there must be reason to believe it will do some good – for society, and not just for monopoly holders.[2]

For Lessig, this "good" or "public interest" means furthering creativity and innovation – the capitalistic notion of economic or commercial development. There have been many who have sought to challenge the existing norm of exclusive copyright ownership and the monopolies it creates by putting forth alternative theories for the justification of exclusive copyright ownership. However, these alternative theories have all failed to adequately consider the socio-economic dimension of exclusive copyright ownership

1 Berne Convention for the Protection of Literary and Artistic Work (Berne Convention) as amended on 28 September 1979, Article 2(6); Agreement on Trade-Related Aspects of Intellectual Property Rights 1994, Article 1(1).

2 Lawrence Lessig, "May the Source Be with You," https://www.wired.com/2001/12/lessig/ accessed 14 October 2023.

DOI: 10.4324/9781003602989-2

and its potential to further the developmental goals of developing nations. As such, this chapter will argue that the copyright owner ought to justify their exclusivity with reference to the socio-economic developmental goals of developing nations. In other words, this chapter will argue that the norm of exclusive copyright ownership should exist within a culture of justification founded not merely upon capitalistic notions of economics or commercialisation, but upon the established link between intellectual property (IP) and its key role in furthering socio-economic developmental goals. This link between IP and socio-economic development has been explicitly recognised in the United Nations General Assembly *Transforming our world: the 2030 Agenda for Sustainable Development* A/RES/70/1 (UN 2030 Agenda) and 17 Sustainable Development Goals (SDGs). It will be argued within this chapter that the UN's 2030 Agenda and 17 SDGS ought to provide the new framework within which the norm of exclusive copyright ownership is justified. This chapter therefore brings together and builds upon a body of works by Kouletakis which have sought to highlight the shortcomings of the current international copyright framework pertaining to the application of exceptions and limitations to developing nations. Instead, this chapter will reinterpret the existing Eurocentric paradigm within a culture of justification founded upon the underlying public policy objectives of copyright ownership, namely the advancement of developmental goals. In this way, the chapter will offer a new theory for justifying exclusive copyright ownership which is premised not upon Western capitalistic notions of individual economic interest, but upon the collective need to see socio-economic transformation take place in the developing world. In doing so, a case will be made for communal copyright protection of traditional knowledge (TK) by indigenous communities, and the possibility of re-examining Western norms as they relate to the copyright regime.

In supporting this proposition, this chapter will first set out the status quo in copyright regarding exclusive ownership, unpacking the current paradigm which justifies exclusive copyright ownership by way of western economic or commercial interests and its shortfalls in relation to developing nations. It will then offer its own alternative justification theory for exclusive copyright ownership which is situated within a culture of justification premised upon the UN's 2030 Agenda and 17 SDGs. Focus will be placed on how this new justification theory may afford copyright protection to indigenous communities by way of a collective ownership claim regarding their traditional knowledge (TK), as well as providing opportunities for multi-level and multi-party collaborations to occur within the IP landscape. However, this chapter is not the first to offer an alternative justification theory for exclusive copyright ownership. Section 1.4 will analyse the shortcomings of the many competing alternative justification theories of exclusive copyright ownership that seek to challenge the current paradigm. This will be done with the aim of distinguishing the position of this chapter from those of competing theories; identifying the shortfalls of these competing theories which are better addressed by the position argued for herein; and highlighting the need for better representation of the socio-economic developmental goals of developing nations and their indigenous communities within the international IP framework, which can be best achieved by way of the position proposed herein.

1.2 The current copyright paradigm: the norm of exclusive ownership

IP owners enjoy a bundle of exclusive rights over their works. While the bundle of exclusive ownership rights in question differs according to the type of IP in question (including copyright), they generally include the right to reproduce or license the work in which legal protection vests. The copyright owner's rights vest automatically by virtue of the law. The historical rationale for giving copyright authors exclusive rights over their works is that in doing so it will incentivise creators to continue creating works. It will do this by rewarding them for their efforts with the potential to acquire financial or commercial interest in the work from third parties. In turn, this will inspire others to invest in the creation of similar works in the hope of seeing similar financial or commercial success. This is known as the "incentivisation" or "reward" theory, whereby the public interest in having the work protected by way of exclusive ownership is solely founded in financial or economic interests. It is therefore solely concerned with copyright and its capacity to reap economic and commercial gains as an end in itself.[3] This norm of exclusivity therefore relies upon a Western and capitalist understanding of "ownership," which views these exclusive rights as a largely individual benefit in the pursuit of capitalist ideals.[4]

In tandem with the economic rights, there exist "moral rights" which are independent of the authors' economic rights. Moral rights are only accorded to individual authors, and in many national laws, they remain with the authors even after the authors have transferred their economic rights.[5] The philosophy of moral rights was largely developed in 18th-century Germany. Most notably, this can be seen in the works of German philosophers Immanuel Kant and Friedrich Hegel who, building upon the

3 Graham Dutfield and Uma Suthersanen, *Dutfield and Suthersanen on Global Intellectual Property Law* (2nd edn, Edward Elgar 2020) 18.

4 Ibid.

5 World Intellectual Property Organization, "Understanding Copyright and Related Rights," https://www.wipo.int/edocs/pubdocs/en/wipo_pub_909_2016.pdf accessed 25 April 2023.

works of John Locke's natural rights model, posited that copyright works are expressions of the author's soul or personhood, which is why authors are assumed to have a deep personal interest in said works.[6] Moral rights protect the reputational and personality interests of the author. While the exact scope of moral rights can differ from one jurisdiction to the next, Article *6bis* of the Berne Convention for the Protection of Literary and Artistic Work (Berne Convention) as amended on 28 September 1979 requires its members to grant authors the following rights. First, the right to claim authorship of a work one has created (i.e. the right of attribution). Second, the right to object to any distortion or modification of one's work which may be prejudicial to one's honour or reputation (i.e. the right of integrity). It should be noted that while some novel approaches have been recommended – most notably that of Aplin and Mohamed who seek to borrow from the law of defamation – there has, in fact, been little commentary by courts or academics on what "honour" or "reputation" mean in the context of moral rights.[7] This reflects the reality that the primary incentive for creators in copyright is often financial gain, rather than the recognition of moral rights. While the recognition of moral rights can play a role in incentivising creators by fostering a sense of personal investment in their work and promoting a climate of respect for the creative works, it is generally agreed that economic incentives are more directly linked to the driving forces for creators to produce new works.[8] For this reason, the focus of the chapter will be on these economic rights. Furthermore, as is the case with economic rights and the incentivisation theory, the philosophical arguments in support of moral rights are individualistic and demand an idiosyncratic protection of the author's prerogatives.[9] Therefore many of the arguments made relating to economic rights may be equally applicable to those of moral rights.

The international IP framework recognises that co-existing – and sometimes conflicting – with the creator's privately held economic or commercial interests in the exploitation of their work lies a societal interest in the work as a means for achieving socio-economic development. According to

6 Mitchell Longan, "A System Out of Balance: A Critical Analysis of Philosophical Justifications for Copyright Law through the Lens of Users' Rights." (2023) 56 *University of Michigan Journal of Law Reform* 779.

7 Tanya Aplin and Ahmed Shaffan Mohamed, "The Concept of 'Reputation' in the Moral Right of Integrity." (2019) 14 4 *Journal of Intellectual Property Law & Practice* 268.

8 Martin Kretschmer, "Moral Rights and Incentives to Create: A European Perspective" in Michal Mejstřík and Eva Žáková (eds) *The Handbook of Intellectual Property Management* (Palgrave Macmillan 2020) 187.

9 Caterina Sganga, "Chapter 1: The Theoretical Framework of Copyright Propertization" in Caterina Sganga (ed) *Propertizing European Copyright: History, Challenges and Opportunities* (Edward Elgar 2018).

the WIPO Standing Committee on Copyright and Related Rights,[10] limitations to copyright are instances where no protection is required for the particular kind of subject matter in question. In other words, limitations exclude, or allow for the exclusion of, protection for particular categories of works or material. These include, for example, Article 2*bis*(1) (political speeches and speeches delivered in the course of legal proceedings) and Article 2(4) (official texts of a legislative, administrative and legal nature, and official translations of such texts). By contrast, exceptions can be termed "permitted uses," or "exceptions" to protection, in that they allow for the removal of liability that would otherwise arise. In other words, exceptions allow for the granting of immunity from infringement proceedings for particular kinds of use, for example, where this is for the purposes of news reporting or education, or where particular conditions are satisfied. These include Articles 9(2) (reproduction of the work in certain special cases), 10 (quotations and use of works by way of illustration for teaching purposes), 10*bis* (reproduction of newspaper or similar articles and use of works for the purpose of reporting current events), and 11*bis*(3) (ephemeral recordings for broadcasting purposes) of the Berne Convention. As noted by Samuelson, the distinction between "limitations" and "exceptions" is "somewhat murky" and "the two terms are often used interchangeably."[11]

This distinction between a private benefit expressed through exclusivity and society's interest in the work as a means of furthering socio-economic development expressed through exceptions and limitations can be seen in Articles 7 and 8 of the TRIPS Agreement. Article 7 takes cognisance of the competing interests of producers and users of technological knowledge and calls for an equitable balancing of these interests. It states that IP rights must be used "in a manner conducive to social and economic welfare, and to a balance of rights and obligations." This should be interpreted in line with Article 8, which "formulates the general guidelines to be observed by WTO members when they adopt exceptions to the exclusive rights conferred by IPRs."[12] It states the following principle:

> Members may, in formulating or amending their laws and regulations, adopt measures necessary to protect public health and nutrition, and to

10 WIPO Standing Committee on Copyright and Related Rights, Ninth Session, Geneva, 23–27 June 2003 SCCR/9/7: "Study on Limitations and Exceptions of Copyright and Related Rights in the Digital Environment."

11 Pamela Samuelson, "Chapter 1: Justifications for Copyright Limitations and Exceptions" in Ruth L Okediji (ed) *Copyright Law in an Age of Limitations and Exceptions* (Cambridge University Press 2018) 12.

12 Edson Beas Rodrigues Jr, *The General Exception Clauses of the TRIPS Agreement: Promoting Sustainable Development* (Cambridge University Press 2012) 45

> promote the public interest in sectors of vital importance to their socio-economic and technological development, provided that such measures are consistent with the provisions of this Agreement.

There are many examples of limitations to or exceptions from the creator's exclusive ownership rights due to society's interest in the work as a means for furthering socio-economic development. An example can be seen in Article 2*bis* of The Berne Convention which, as stated previously, includes the exception relating to the reproduction of political speeches and speeches delivered during legal proceedings. In this instance, society's interests in the work as they relate to freedom of information as well as access to open justice which underpins the rule of law and democracy, outweigh the creator's exclusive ownership right, thus justifying a limitation to or exception from the norm of exclusivity.[13]

More broadly, Article 13 of the TRIPS Agreement allows for limitations or exceptions that satisfy the so-called three-step test, stating:

> Members shall confine limitations or exceptions to exclusive rights to certain special cases which do not conflict with a normal exploitation of the work and do not unreasonably prejudice the legitimate interests of the right holder.

The three-step test has been compartmentalised and analysed by the Dispute Settlement Body of the World Trade Organisation (WTO DSB), which serves as the judiciary for the purpose of interpreting treaties such as the TRIPS Agreement. While the WTO DSB decisions or "reports" do not create binding precedent,[14] the Panel established to consider the United States – Section 110(5) Copyright Act case (WT/DS160/R) does provide an interpretation of Article 13 of the TRIPS Agreement. The WTO DSB in this case stated that the first step of the three-step test is "confin[ing] limitations or exceptions to exclusive rights to certain special cases." The term "certain" was interpreted as meaning "an exception or limitation in national legislation [that] must be clearly defined."[15] The term "special" was interpreted as meaning "limited in its field of application or exceptional in its scope."[16] The second step of the three-step test is ensuring

13 UN Office on Drugs and Crime, "Open Justice and Public Confidence," https://www.unodc.org/ji/en/knowledge-products/open-justice.html accessed 23 November 2022.

14 WTO, "Dispute Settlement System Training Module," https://www.wto.org/english/tratop_e/dispu_e/disp_settlement_cbt_e/c7s2p1_e.htm accessed 3 December 2023.

15 Report of the Panel, "United States – Section 110(5) of the US Copyright Act," https://libguides.wits.ac.za/ld.php?content_id=57786783 accessed 3 December 2023.

16 Report of the Panel (note 15).

that these "do not conflict with the normal exploitation of the work." The WTO DSB stated that this step will only be violated when the use of the work enters into economic competition with the ways in which the right-holders "normally extract economic value from the right at stake and thereby deprive them of significant or tangible commercial gains."[17] The term "normal exploitation" was deemed to involve consideration of the forms of exploitation that currently generate income for the right holder as well as those which, in the future, may have the potential to do so.[18] Lastly, the third step of the three-step test is that it must "not unreasonably prejudice the legitimate interests of the right holder." The WTO DSB found that legitimate interests can include, but are not limited to, economic interests.[19] However, in determining what degree of prejudice would be unreasonable, the WTO DSB chose to limit itself to considerations of economic interests. The WTO DSB stated that "if an exception or limitation causes or has the potential to cause unreasonable loss of income to the [rights holder]," such an exception or limitation would cause unreasonable prejudice unless he or she has been equitably compensated.[20]

An example of limitations to or exceptions from the creator's exclusive ownership drafted at an international level which falls within this three-step test can be found in relation to visually impaired members of society. This has been discussed in detail by Kouletakis.[21] In summary, Kouletakis posits that The Marrakesh Treaty to Facilitate Access to Published Works for Persons Who Are Blind, Visually Impaired or Otherwise Print Disabled (MS No. 25/2019) recognises society's interest in allowing visually impaired individuals to freely access literary works under certain special conditions so as to promote socio-economic development.[22] Members of the visually impaired community in signatory states are permitted to freely access a creator's literary works under certain special circumstances because doing so facilitates the furtherance of society's socio-economic developmental goals. An example used by Kouletakis is their legislative involvement in amending South African copyright legislation. This provides visually impaired individuals with free access to textbooks in accessible formats,

17 Report of the Panel (note 15).
18 Report of the Panel (note 15).
19 Report of the Panel (note 15).
20 Report of the Panel (note 15).
21 Jade Kouletakis, "A Critical Examination of Copyright Limitations and Exceptions for the Visually Impaired Pertaining to Literary Works in South Africa in the Local and Global Context." (2014) 2 *South African Intellectual Property Law Journal* 42–65; Jade Kouletakis, Tobias Schonwetter, Bram van Wiele, and Alexandra Akantorana Kisuul, "Marrakesh Treaty Implementation Guide for South Africa," http://ip-unit.org/wp-content/uploads/2015/05/IPUnit_MarrakeshGuideSA1.pdf (May 2015) accessed 22 November 2022.
22 Ibid.

which is central to realising the visually impaired community's right to have access to quality education, which is in turn central to realising their right to decent work, which is in turn central to realising the societal goal of eradicating poverty for all.[23]

It must be noted that the three-step test has long been heavily criticised.[24] A reason for this is that developing countries make poor use of exceptions and limitations because of their lack of infrastructure. Effective enforcement of copyright is dependent on factors such as political will, societal knowledge and perceptions, and the level of economic and technological development.[25] The same is true of exceptions and limitations. The existence of functioning legal and administrative infrastructures as prerequisites for the efficient application of international copyright norms and standards is taken for granted.[26] Minimum standards take time and money to adopt, and oftentimes require specialist skills lacking in the developing world.[27] Direct costs may involve administrative or legal fees along with the cost of training, reviewing, and drafting laws to implement the TRIPS Agreement. Indirect costs may include welfare costs such as increased prices, loss of jobs, and inhibition of competition and innovation due to heavy reliance on imported commodities.[28] Developing nations lack even the most basic infrastructure compared to their developed counterparts. For example, good road networks provide links to markets, as well as

23 OECD, "Education at a Glance 2022," https://www.oecd.org/education/education-at-a-glance/ accessed 22 November 2022; UN World Youth Report, "Youth and the 2030 Agenda for Sustainable Development – Chapter 4: Youth Education and Employment: Exploring the Nexus," https://www.un.org/development/desa/youth/world-youth-report/wyr2018.html accessed 22 November 2022.

24 Johan Rochel, "Intellectual Property and its Foundations: Using Art. 7 and 8 to Address the Legitimacy of the TRIPS." (2020) 23 *Journal of World Intellectual Property* 21; Pamela Samuelson and Kathryn Hashimoto, "Is the U.S. Fair Use Doctrine Compatible with Berne and TRIPS Obligations?" in Tatiana Synodinou (ed) *Universalism or Pluralism in International Copyright Law* (Kluwer Law International Information Law Series 2018).

25 Marisella Nabongo Ouma, "Enforcement of Copyright in the Music Industry: A Critical Analysis of the Legal and Institutional Framework on Enforcement in sub-Saharan Africa" (Queen Mary University PhD thesis 2010).

26 Veit Erlmann, *Lion's Share: Remaking South African Copyright* (Duke University Press 2022).

27 Bill Rosenblatt, "WIPO Webinar on Copyright Infrastructure: Lessons Learned, Challenges and Opportunities," https://www.wipo.int/meetings/en/details.jsp?meeting_id=80928 accessed 20 January 2024.

28 Alphonso B Kassor, "The World Trade Organization's Trade Related Aspects of Intellectual Property Rights (TRIPS) Agreement: The Compelling Challenges for Developing and Less Developed Member Countries – Implementation and Enforcement." (2018) 9 *Cybaris: An Intellectual Property Law Review* 107 at 114.

enhancing access to producer and consumer services.[29] Yet across Africa, only 43 per cent of roads are paved, of which 30 per cent are in South Africa.[30] Information and communications technology democratises access to information, thus strengthening governance and inclusion, as well as reducing transport costs.[31] Yet only 36 per cent of Africa's population has broadband internet access.[32] Africa also has one of the widest digital gender gaps worldwide, with the greatest disparity being between men and women using the internet.[33] Some argue that the international copyright system significantly raises the prices of important commodities, such as medicines, seeds, and educational materials, which reduces access to technological goods and further perpetuates the lack of infrastructure in the developing world.[34] This lack of infrastructure can lead to instances where so-called global minimum standards are unable to be met by developing nations, and exceptions and limitations are not fully utilised. An example of the latter is highlighted by Kouletakis in their research on the perceptions of South African documentary filmmakers about copyright clearance requirements and the effect of such requirements on their works.[35] In this example, research surveys and focus groups pertaining to filmmakers evidenced that the industry was dominated by a "clearance culture," that is, "a common law on the ground that everyone thinks is the law" requiring that every use of copyrighted material in a film be licensed. Nearly 70 per cent of the filmmakers interviewed reported that they did not know of any instances when they could use copyrighted content in their work without a licence of remuneration.[36] As a result, most of the filmmakers sought to obtain licences for things like incidental capture, even when they

29 Mthuli Ncube et al, "Introduction: Infrastructure in African Development" in Mthuli Ncube and Charles Leyeka Lufumpa (eds) *Infrastructure in Africa: Lessons for Future Development* (Cambridge University Press 2022).

30 Centre for Global Development, "Designing Roads for Africa's Future," https://www.cgdev.org/project/designing-roads-africas-future accessed 20 January 2024.

31 Mthuli Ncube et al., "Introduction: Infrastructure in African Development" (note 29).

32 The World Bank, "From Connectivity to Services: Digital Transformation in Africa," https://www.worldbank.org/en/results/2023/06/26/from-connectivity-to-services-digital-transformation-in-africa accessed 20 January 2024.

33 Ibid.

34 Walter G Park, "Averting a TRIPSxit from the Global Intellectual Property System" (note 27).

35 Jade Kouletakis et al., "Copyright Law Protection of Films in Nigeria (Nollywood) and South Africa (Sollywood): The Era of Covid." (2023) *Journal of World Intellectual Property* 1.

36 Sean Flynn, "Copyright Legal and Practical Reform for the South African Film Industry" (2015) 16 *AJIC* 38; Peter Jaszi and Sean Fiil-Flynn, "Untold Stories in South Africa: Creative Consequences of the Rights-Clearing Culture for Documentary Filmmakers." (December 2009) 20 *PIJIP Research Paper*.

could have used the content for free without a licence.[37] The experience of these documentary filmmakers is, according to Kouletakis, unsurprising as – given the lack of legislative or judicial clarity on exceptions and limitations – users in general are likely to err on the side of caution to their detriment.[38]

Others have criticised the Eurocentric or westernised focus and historical foundations of the TRIPS Agreement in general and the three-step test in particular, including Kouletakis, who has cautioned that the existing framework is not only unjust but untenable:

> It is important that … a paradigm shift takes place within the international community if it is to maximise global innovation, creativity and socio-economic developments. This is because it will need a stronger and more wide-ranging consensus on the importance of IP to every country in the world, regardless of economic or political positioning, if it is to make faster progress on commonly shared global challenges and aspirations such as economic growth, rights realisations and technological developments. All countries must see value in a shared framework that purports to reflect shared ideologies in order to "buy-in" to said structures.[39]

The global IP framework initially permeated developing nations through colonial implantation and subjugation, evidencing the fact that copyright at its inception was conceptualised from the point of view of the Westernised, developed world to the exclusion of the interest of developing nations.[40] Global power relationships evident at the negotiating table on the international arena since the end of colonialism still reflect longstanding global power hierarchies, particularly in relation to the cultural gatekeeping of the developing world by the developed world.[41] As a result, many have called for greater flexibility as it pertains to the three-step test and developing

37 Ibid.

38 Caroline Ncube, "Chapter 3: Fair is as Fair Does: Contractual Normative Regulation of Copyright User Contracts in South Africa" in Graeme B. Dinwoodie (ed) *Intellectual Property and General Legal Principles: Is IP a Lex Specialis?* (Edward Elgar 2015).

39 Jade Kouletakis, "Decolonising Copyright: Reconsidering Copyright Exclusivity and the Role of the Public Interest in International Intellectual Property Frameworks." (2022) 71 1 *GRUR International: Journal of European and International IP Law* 24 at 28.

40 Uma Suthersanen and Ysolde Gendreau (eds), *A Shifting Empire: 100 Years of the Copyright Act 1911* (Edward Elgar Publishing 2020).

41 Ibid.; Wanjiku Karanja, "The Legitimacy of Indigenous Intellectual Property Rights' Claims." (2016) 1 *Strathmore Law Review* 165.

nations.[42] For example, a group of prominent copyright scholars issued the Max Planck Institute Declaration where they criticised the WTO DSB decision for being "unduly narrow and restrictive" in viewing the three steps as independent of one another, especially in relation to developing nations and their socio-economic needs. The Declaration argues that instead an exception or limitation that fails to satisfy one of the three steps should not necessarily be deemed to violate the test. Rather, all three components of the test should be considered together in a "comprehensive overall assessment" that takes into account the threats that excessive levels of copyright protection pose to "human rights and fundamental freedoms," "interests in competition," and "other public interests, notably in scientific progress and cultural, social, or economic development."[43] Gana (later known as Okediji) positions the TRIPS Agreement as a form of passive coercion. This is because it requires developing nations to abide by the particular forms of protection for intellectual goods as a condition of membership in the new multilateral trading system despite this sometimes being to their cultural detriment.[44] Instead, the author argues that a "one-size-fits-all" view of IP limitations and exceptions is not appropriate in the context of developing nations which require a more responsive approach to societal needs. Gana/Okediji proposes the creation of "liberty-enhancing" limitations and exceptions that are mandatory on an international level yet still flexible in their domestic implementation, leaving some room for cultural autonomy and meeting the requirements of the so-called "three-step test" under the TRIPS Agreement.[45] Others, like Story, argue that the international copyright framework ought to be "repealed and a new framework be established on radically different grounds" in light of its "negative effects on countries of the South and its citizens."[46]

42 Margaret Chon, "Recasting Intellectual Property in Light of the U.N. Sustainable Development Goals: Toward Global Knowledge Governance" (2019) 34 4 *American University International Law Review* 763; Ruth L Okediji, "Does Intellectual Property Need Human Rights?" (2018) 51 *New York University Journal of International Law and* Politics 1–68.

43 The Max Planck Institute, "Declaration: A Balanced Interpretation of the 'Three-Step Test' in Copyright Law," https://www.jipitec.eu/issues/jipitec-1-2-2010/2621/Declaration-Balanced-Interpretation-Of-The-Three-Step-Test.pdf accessed 3 January 2024; Electronic Frontier Foundation, "Three-Step Test," https://www.eff.org/files/filenode/three-step_test_fnl.pdf accessed 6 January 2024.

44 Ruth L Gana, "Has Creativity Died in the Third World – Some Implications of the Internationalization of Intellectual Property." (1995) 24 *Denver Journal of International Law and Policy* 109.

45 Ruth L Okediji, "The Limits of International Copyright Exceptions for Developing Countries." (2019) 21 *Vanderbilt Journal of Entertainment and Technology Law* 689.

46 Alan Story, "Burn Berne: Why the Leading International Copyright Convention Must Be Repealed." (2003) 40 *Houston Law Review* 763.

1.3 A new copyright paradigm: centralising exclusive copyright ownership's legitimacy in furthering the United Nations' developmental agenda

Having highlighted the shortfalls in the current paradigm relating to exclusive copyright ownership, this section will seek to offer a new theoretical justification for copyright ownership found within the UN's developmental agenda. It will focus on the works of Kouletakis to argue that there ought to be a paradigm shift whereby instead of the onus being on users to evidence the need for access to the work, the onus should be shifted to *the copyright owner* needing to justify their exclusive ownership of the work in the first instance in relation to the UN's developmental agenda.[47] What this paradigm shift might look like in practice will be considered, with a focus on its potential to offer legal protection to TK and foster a culture of national, regional and international collaboration in the IP community.

The proposition that copyright and the furtherance of socio-economic development are intricately linked is nothing new. As noted by Kouletakis, in the Global South, indigenous justifications for the exclusivity of intangible property have long been considered inseparable from the communal interest, and this concept of the communal interest is not necessarily connected to capitalistic issues of economics or commercial exploitation.[48] In fact, according to the TRIPS Agreement, one of the main underlying public policy aims of the international IP framework is to assist in the furtherance of developmental objectives.[49] The Preamble to the Agreement Establishing the WTO – which administers the TRIPS Agreement – lists the objectives of raising standards of living and sustainable development. Despite this, human rights do not feature explicitly in the WTO mandate. In fact, the WTO has repeatedly been criticised by academics, civil society, and trade unions for ignoring the direct consequences of trade liberalisation on labour standards and human rights. It has been hailed as giving rise to the international "race to the bottom" in the area of labour standards and human rights, whereby developing countries relax labour standards and related rights in order to attract foreign investment from developed countries.[50]

The 2030 Agenda was adopted in 2015 and consists of an urgent call for action by all countries - developed and developing – to act in a global

47 Jade Kouletakis, "Decolonising Copyright: Reconsidering Copyright Exclusivity and the Role of the Public Interest in International Intellectual Property Frameworks" (note 39).

48 Ibid.

49 (Note 1).

50 Slade, "The Objectives and Principles of the WTO TRIPS Agreement: A Detailed Anatomy." (2016) 53 *Osgoode Hall Law Journal* 948.

partnership so as to achieve sustainable development.[51] The 2030 Agenda recognises that eradicating poverty in all its forms and dimensions, including extreme poverty, is the greatest global challenge and an indispensable requirement for sustainable development.[52] Of course, poverty does not exist in isolation from considerations such as access to education, access to healthcare, gender equality, and other human rights; nor does it exist in isolation from considerations of geography and birth. This web of interrelated considerations seeking to balance the three dimensions of sustainable development (i.e. the economic, social, and environmental) is represented within the UN's 17 SDGs. These consist of 17 interlinking and indivisible goals relating to topics such as quality education ("ensur[ing] inclusive and equitable quality education and promote lifelong learning opportunities for all"); good health and wellbeing ("ensur[ing] healthy lives and promot[ing] well-being for all at all ages"); and gender equality ("achiev[ing] gender equality and empower[ing] all women and girls"). All of this aims to end poverty in all its forms everywhere, with the focus being placed on doing so within the African continent. This is because Africa has been singled out as "a priority area" for concern in relation to achieving the SDGs. As per the 2030 Agenda, "progress made in the last 15 years has been uneven, particularly in Africa."[53] This can be demonstrated by examining the conditions in South Africa, the current chair of the African Union and the second largest and most industrialised economy on the African continent.[54] Despite this status, according to the UN Sustainable Development Cooperation Framework: South Africa 2020–2025 (developed through a participatory process between August 2019 and May 2020):

> More than half of South Africans live in poverty, nearly one third are unemployed and over a quarter of the population are food insecure. Economic growth is insufficient ... High levels of violence and crime, and persistent structural racial, economic, spatial, and gender inequalities impede social cohesion and undermine the national objective of

51 UN, "SDGs," https://sdgs.un.org/goals accessed 18 November 2022.

52 UN General Assembly, "Transforming Our World: the 2030 Agenda for Sustainable Development" A/RES/70/1.

53 UN, "Topics: Africa," https://sdgs.un.org/topics/africa accessed 18 November 2022.

54 UK Government, "Press Release: PM – UK and South Africa Will Turbocharge Growth Together," https://www.gov.uk/government/news/pm-uk-and-south-africa-will-turbocharge-growth-together accessed 1 December 2022; International Monetary Fund Blog, "Trade and Remittances Within Africa," https://www.imf.org/en/Blogs/Articles/2018/08/01/blog-trade-and-remittances-within-africa accessed 28 November 2022.

being a developmental state founded on the principles of equality and shared common values.[55]

A report on social mobility published by the Organisation for Economic Co-operation and Development in 2018 referred to South Africa as a country in which the people are "pessimistic about mobility prospects." It classed South Africa as a "high-inequality and low-mobility country," in which it would take at least nine generations for those born in low-income families to approach the mean income in their society if these probabilities of earnings mobility are not to change.[56]

The 2030 Agenda was adopted by all UN Member States and provides overlap with members of the WTO. Further overlap can be evidenced by the centrality of trade in achieving these SDGs. The 17th SDG ("partnerships for the goals") calls to utilise trade as a mechanism for strengthening the means of implementation and revitalising the Global Partnership for Sustainable Development. The 2030 Agenda defines international trade as "an engine for inclusive economic growth and poverty reduction, [that] contributes to the promotion of sustainable development." It specifically points to the WTO as "[a] major institutional stakeholder … on trade and the SDGs issues,"[57] with the TRIPS Agreement in particular being identified as a means by which the furthering of these SDGs can take place.[58] Indeed, the 2030 Agenda can be closely linked to the realisation of Article 7 of the TRIPS Agreement which states:

> The protection and enforcement of intellectual property rights should contribute to the promotion of technological innovation and to the transfer and dissemination of technology, to the mutual advantage of producers and users of technological knowledge and in a manner conducive to social and economic welfare, and to a balance of rights and obligations.

55 UN South Africa, "United Nations Sustainable Development Cooperation Framework: South Africa 2020 – 2025,"https://southafrica.un.org/en/180728-united-nations-sustainable-development-cooperation-framework-unsdcf-south-africa-2020-2025 accessed 8 October 2024; International Monetary Fund Blog, "Countries in the IMF Financial Stability Spotlight in 2022," https://www.imf.org/en/Blogs/Articles/2022/02/03/countries-in-the-imf-financial-stability-spotlight-in-2022 accessed 12 November 2022.

56 OECD, *A Broken Social Elevator? How to Promote Social Mobility: Overview and Main Findings* (OECD Publishing 2018).

57 UN, "Topics: Trade," https://sdgs.un.org/topics/trade accessed 5 November 2022.

58 WTO, "WTO's contribution to attaining UN Sustainable Development Goals: 2023 update to the High-Level Political Forum," https://www.wto.org/english/res_e/booksp_e/un_hlpf23_e.pdf accessed 9 September 2024.

The World Intellectual Property Organisation (WIPO) has also recognised that the IP framework "will be important for achieving the SDGs" and has initiated discussions on the implementation of the 2030 Agenda and the SDGs since April 2015.[59] It is therefore clear that, while the WTO is not a UN specialised agency, it has maintained strong relations with the UN and its agencies since its establishment and has been committed to the 2030 Agenda, with the IP framework expected to play an important role in helping to achieve the UN's SDGs.

The UN Declaration on the Right to Development 1986 established an inalienable human right to development. As per Article 1, this right entails that everyone is entitled to participate in, contribute to, and enjoy economic, social, cultural, and political development, in an environment in which human rights and fundamental freedoms can be fully realised. Article 6(2) reinforces that all human rights and fundamental freedoms are indivisible and interdependent. It places a duty on states to protect fundamental human rights to realise the right to development. However, it is the 2030 Agenda and 17 SDGs that this chapter uses as its basis for a new copyright paradigm rather than the UN Declaration on the Right to Development or the right to development for various reasons. First, the 2030 Agenda has expressly been informed by and integrated the right to development. Secondly, the 17 SDGs include rights that have been drawn from other later, human rights-focused, UN instruments. These include the UN Convention on the Rights of Persons with Disabilities 2016 and the UN Convention on the Rights of the Child 1989, both of which did not exist when the right to development was codified in 1986. As per the UN Declaration on the Right to Development, human rights are indivisible and as such ought not to be considered in isolation. Lastly, as already noted, the 17 SDGs – unlike the UN Declaration on the Right to Development – expressly recognise the TRIPS Agreement as a means by which to further the developmental objective, thereby highlighting the obligation IP frameworks have in furthering the broader developmental agenda. It is therefore entirely appropriate to shift the paradigm of exclusive copyright ownership from one in which the focus is on economic or commercial gains, to one in which the focus is on socio-economic developmental gains as expressed by the UN's 2030 Agenda and 17 SDGs.

However, instead of calling for greater flexibility to be afforded by the international IP community in relation to the exercise of limitations and exceptions,[60] a more fundamental paradigm shift which centralises the link between copyright ownership and socio-economic development is needed

59 UN, "WIPO," https://sdgs.un.org/node/24505 accessed 16 November 2022.

60 Margaret Chon, "Recasting Intellectual Property in Light of the U.N. Sustainable Development Goals: Toward Global Knowledge Governance" (note 42).

on a supranational level. The norm of exclusive ownership should exist within a culture of justification founded not merely upon capitalistic notions of economics or commercialisation as per the rewards or incentivisation theory, but upon the established link between IP and its key role in furthering socio-economic developmental goals. This link between IP and socio-economic development has been explicitly recognised within the TRIPS Agreement itself, and by the UN within its 2030 Agenda and 17 SDGs. The UN's 2030 Agenda and 17 SDGs can provide the new framework within which the norm of exclusive copyright ownership is justified. There ought to be a paradigm shift whereby instead of the onus being on third parties to evidence the need for access to the work being granted by way of limitations and exceptions, the onus should be shifted to *the copyright owner* needing to justify *their exclusive ownership of the work* for ownership to be justified in light of socio-economic developmental goals. In other words, copyright ownership should not compete with the public interest in furthering the developmental agenda for developing nations so that they may realise their socio-economic rights but seek to find its legitimacy within the furtherance of this public interest.[61] This is important because, as per Kouletakis:

> By reassessing the nature of copyright exclusivity rather than delegating conversations about non-commercial communal needs to limitations and exceptions, the Global South is no longer seen as mere passive receptors of Western norms and values, but as active participants with inherent value in the creation of a truly global IP framework.[62]

It should also be noted that this new paradigm does not necessitate the taking away of what is currently protected by copyright – in many instances, it might justify the continuation of copyright protection or even the extension of copyright protection. An example of such a case has been highlighted by Kouletakis et al.[63] In this article, the authors critique South Africa's Draft Sports Broadcasting Services Amendment Regulations 2018 within the context of socio-economic development. According to the South African Copyright Act 1978, broadcasts are protected as works under copyright. Exclusive ownership of a broadcast vests in the first broadcasting corporation, which may include the licensing of the broadcast to subscription services. The Regulations sought to change this by prohibiting exclusive

61 Jade Kouletakis, "Decolonising Copyright: Reconsidering Copyright Exclusivity and the Role of the Public Interest in International Intellectual Property Frameworks" (note 39).
62 Ibid. at 24.
63 Jade Kouletakis et al., "Exclusivity in the 6th edition of the Nigeria Broadcast Commission (NBC) Code and a glimpse of the practice in South Africa and the United Kingdom." (2021) 43 6 *European Intellectual Property Review* 388.

licensing of the most popular sporting events in South Africa – such as National Netball – so that they may be broadcast on free-to-air services and thus be more accessible to the public. However, as argued by the authors, the norm of copyright exclusivity was able to meet the burden of justification in this instance as it could be argued that exclusivity in this instance was a means for furthering society's socio-economic developmental goals. An example of one such argument put forth by the authors pertained to Netball South Africa (Netball SA), the only body responsible for the administration, control and governance of netball in South Africa. It is also the biggest women's sports organisation in South Africa, with netball being the most popular participation sport for women in South Africa and the second most participated in team sport in South Africa, with well over two million participants all over South Africa. Netball SA relies almost entirely upon the income stream generated through the exclusive licensing of events such as the Netball Provincial Premier League.[64] Using this income, Netball SA is able to pay its predominantly female sportspeople a liveable wage of ZAR 5,000 per month in a country where the labour market is more favourable to men than it is to women, and men are more likely to be in paid employment than women.[65] According to Statistics South Africa, the expanded unemployment rate – which does not take job searching into account – increased from 30.9 per cent in 2008 to 37.2 per cent in 2018, with both the official and expanded definitions of unemployment rates being higher among women than men.[66] The report concludes that "the labour market position of women hasn't changed much over the last decade; in fact, it has deteriorated in some respects."[67] The same can be said about women and gender-based violence. President Ramaphosa has stated that South Africa is "one of the most unsafe places in the world to be a woman, with levels of violence that are comparable to countries that are at war."[68] The South African Medical Research Council has reported

64 Netball South Africa, "Netball SA Submission on Draft Sports Broadcasting Services Amendment Regulations 2018," https://www.icasa.org.za/legislation-and-regulations/netball-sa-submission-on-the-draft-sports-broadcasting-services-amendment-regulations accessed 31 March 2021.

65 Statistics South Africa, "How Do Women Fare in the South African Labour Market?," http://www.statssa.gov.za/?p=11375&gclid=CjwKCAjw19z6BRAYEiwAmo64LfXOuzOgYMuEu6IDs1T1ff3tgFUIsBuEZQIXwEzBC-VaFPKsZs_OMBoCbPwQAvD_BwE accessed 31 March 2021.

66 Statistics South Africa, "How do Women Fare in the South African Labour Market?," https://www.statssa.gov.za/?p=11375 accessed 2 December 2023.

67 Statistics South Africa, "General Household Survey 2018," http://www.statssa.gov.za/publications/P0318/P03182018.pdf accessed 31 March 2021.

68 Mava Lukani, "Violence against Women in South Africa Comparable to Countries That Are At War – Ramaphosa," https://www.parliament.gov.za/news/violence-against-women-sa-comparable-countries-are-war-ramaphosa accessed 31 March 2021.

that more women are murdered by their partner or ex-partner in South Africa than anywhere in the world.[69] A key factor that works to mitigate against such violence against women is financial independence and economic empowerment among women.[70] It is widely accepted that promoting women's participation in sport and providing them with a liveable wage decreases their risk of falling victim to gender-based violence in the first instance and increases their likelihood of successfully coming out of an abusive environment.[71] In this way, the authors were able to justify the continuance of exclusive copyright ownership in this instance of sports broadcasting by drawing upon key considerations reflective of the UN's 17 SDGs such as gender equality, reduced inequalities, and access to decent work.

While there may be instances where the status quo needs to continue unchanged insofar as it can be justified within these parameters, there may also be instances where copyright protection could justifiably be *expanded* because doing so is in the public good. A prime example of this can be seen with regard to TK and its protection within the sphere of copyright. WIPO defines TK as "knowledge, know-how, skills and practices that are developed, sustained and passed on from generation to generation within a community, often forming part of its cultural or spiritual identity."[72] These indigenous communities – who mainly, although not exclusively, come from the developing world – from which TK stems have long been left without legal recourse to protect their interests against third parties. Famous examples of this include the lack of collective action afforded to the Zulu tribe (an indigenous people of Southern Africa) for the protection of its song "The Lion Sleeps Tonight," which was exploited by Disney in "The Lion King," and the sacred chants of the Ami tribe (an indigenous people of Taiwan) being copied by the German rock group Enigma in its song "Return to Innocence." In both cases, the indigenous communities were left with no legal recourse in which they could assert their interests

69 Naeemah Abrahams and Bianca Deke, "South African Medical Research Council Research on Femicide and Child Homicide," https://www.samrc.ac.za/research-for-our-people/samrc-research-femicide-and-child-homicide accessed 31 August 2021.

70 R Jewkes et al., "Effective Design and Implementation Elements in Interventions to Prevent Violence against Women and Girls: What Works to Prevent Violence?" https://whatworks.co.za/documents/publications/373-intervention-report19-02-20/file accessed 30 September 2021.

71 Cassandra Ogunniyi, "The Effects of Sport Participation on Gender Relations: Case Studies of Female Footballers in Johannesburg and Cape Town, South Africa." (2015) 46 1 *South African Review of Sociology* 25.

72 WIPO, "Traditional Knowledge," https://www.wipo.int/tk/en/tk/#:~:text=Traditional%20knowledge%20(TK)%20is%20knowledge,its%20cultural%20or%20spiritual%20identity accessed 9 August 2024.

in the musical works in question. WIPO recently sought to change this lack of legal recourse afforded to indigenous communities with its adoption of the first Treaty on Intellectual Property, Genetic Resources and Associated Traditional Knowledge. However, this Treaty deals exclusively with genetic resources and patents rather than copyright. At Article 31(1) of the UN Declaration on the Rights of Indigenous Peoples (adopted by the General Assembly on 13 September 2007), the UN recognises that indigenous people have the right to maintain, control, protect and develop their intellectual property over their TK. However, the position as it relates to TK and copyright remains unresolved.

Some have suggested that this exercise might be attempting to fit a square peg into a round hole and that, instead, alternative means of offering protection to indigenous communities ought to be explored. One such alternative protection that has been posited is stewardship. However, this concept is neither fully explained nor is it supported by a clear, normative legal framework.[73] For example, Okediji proposes a theological framework of "biblical stewardship" replacing that of copyright ownership insofar as TK is concerned. This concept is founded in Judeo-Christian understandings of human nature and social interaction and is based upon moral obligations as they relate to property.[74] According to Okediji, property rights include the right to exclude others from accessing said property, which is absent in the case of biblical stewardship. Biblical stewardship is not to be confused with the public domain, as access is not justified because of the need to incentivise creativity, but because there exists a deontological requirement to obtain "moral righteousness," a term which is legally ambiguous.[75] This moral righteousness is seen as being in direct conflict with the IP framework:

> As things stand currently, [the IP framework offering adequate protection to indigenous communities] seems implausible, with stiff resistance by leading industrialized countries to [recognize] proprietary rights in traditional knowledge ... Fundamentally, the legal systems, political arrangements, and institutions that govern interaction between indigenous peoples and other citizens, perpetuate and perfect a set of disabling

73 Kristen A Carpenter et al., "In Defense of Property." (2009) 118 *Yale Law Journal* 1022 at 1079–1087; Stephen R Munzer and Kal Raustiala, "The Uneasy Case for Intellectual Property Rights in Traditional Knowledge" (2009) 27 *Cardozo Arts & Entertainment Law Journal* 37 at 65 –68.

74 Ruth Okediji, "Is the Public Domain Just?: Biblical Stewardship and Legal Protection for Traditional Knowledge Assets" (2022) 45 *Columbia Journal of Law and Arts* 461.

75 Ibid. at 581.

conditions that make it implausible to secure a progressive path to the sustained flourishing of indigenous peoples.[76]

The sentiment expressed by Okediji that the current IP framework is, at present, incompatible with the way in which TK has been developed and is maintained is one that is accepted within this chapter. Indeed, indigenous people themselves frequently state that for IP rights to afford them adequate protection of their TK, the framework must include two elements which are hitherto omitted: collective or communal property rights, and custom.[77] However, it is the position of this chapter that the paradigm shift proposed herein is able to incorporate both these elements.

With regard to collective or communal property rights, the paradigm shift proposed within this chapter would enable collective copyright ownership claims by indigenous communities. This is because the active involvement of indigenous communities and adequate protection of TK are instrumental in the achievement of all 17 SDGs. In fact, the 2030 Agenda makes six specific references to indigenous peoples, which includes a commitment to ensure equal access to education for indigenous children and to empower and engage indigenous peoples in the implementation of the 17 SDGs.[78] The UN Permanent Forum on Indigenous Issues has recognised that the protection of TK is "of central importance to indigenous peoples" and vital for "the attainment of their human rights [and] the implementation of the 2030 Agenda."[79] The link between TK and the furtherance of socio-economic development has long been recognised by all, from the World Bank and OECD to academics alike.[80] In this shifted paradigm,

76 Ibid. at 510–511.

77 Mat Callahan, "Distinguishing Friend from Foe in the Intellectual Property Debate." (2010) 24 2 *Socialism and Democracy* 191.

78 UN, "Traditional Knowledge – An Answer to the Most Pressing Global Problems?" https://www.un.org/uk/desa/traditional-knowledge-%E2%80%93-answer-most-pressing-global-problems accessed 7 September 2024.

79 UN Permanent Forum on Indigenous Issues, "UNPFII Eighteenth Session: 22 April–3 May 2019," https://social.desa.un.org/issues/indigenous-peoples/unpfii/unpfii-eighteenth-session-22-april-3-may-2019 accessed 19 September 2024.

80 World Bank Group, "Indigenous Knowledge for Development: Opportunities and Challenges (English)," https://documents.worldbank.org/en/publication/documents-reports/documentdetail/574381468765625385/indigenous-knowledge-for-development-opportunities-and-challenges accessed 7 August 2024; OECD Global Education Monitoring Report, "Background Paper Prepared for the 2016 Global Education Monitoring Report: Indigenous Knowledge and Implications for the Sustainable Development Agenda" https://unesdoc.unesco.org/ark:/48223/pf0000245623 accessed 7 August 2024; Sanchita Bansal, "Indigenous Communities and Sustainable Development: A Review and Research Agenda." (2023) 43 4 *Global Business and Organizational Excellence: A Review of Research & Best Practices* 65.

it is for the copyright owner to justify their exclusive rights with reference to socio-economic developmental goals. If it is accepted that these socio-economic developmental goals seek to benefit indigenous communities by, for example, reducing inequalities (SDG 1) and eradicating poverty (SDG 10) through obtaining fair representation in governance structures and benefiting equitably from their intangible resources respectively, then it logically follows that indigenous communities must be afforded an ownership claim in copyright to realise these benefits. An example of this can be seen in the South African Intellectual Property Laws Amendment Act 2013 (IPLAA), which extended the Copyright Act 1978 to recognise and protect TK; established a National Council in respect of indigenous knowledge; provided for national databases for recording indigenous knowledge; and established a National Trust Fund for indigenous knowledge. Section 28B states that works may be protected where they are "capable of substantiation from the collective memory of the relevant indigenous community." The IPLAA has yet to come into force as it awaits the passing of enabling regulations. Significant portions of the IPLAA remain ambiguous and underdeveloped (e.g. what is the regulatory framework for the aforementioned National Council and National Trust Fund and how will TK be recorded in the national database?). Be that as it may, the IPLAA is important because it demonstrates (a) that developing nations identify the protection of their TK as being an issue that needs to be addressed *within* the realm of copyright, and (b) that developing nations are willing and able to think creatively about the protection of their TK *within* the realm of copyright despite the current international framework being unfavourable to this.

With regard to custom, this can be acknowledged and appreciated as it relates to indigenous communities through the paradigm shift proposed within this chapter. It must be noted at the outset that customs and TK, while related in the indigenous context, are not the same. WIPO defines customs as comprising practices, beliefs, and values that are accepted as obligatory rules of conduct by indigenous peoples.[81] While customs may exist in relation to TK insofar as they govern the context within which TK is utilised within the indigenous community, custom is not the same as TK. This distinction is important because the protection of custom is outside the scope of this chapter. The issues relating to whether custom ought to be afforded greater safeguarding than the 2003 UNESCO Convention for

81 WIPO, "Customary Law, Traditional Knowledge and Intellectual Property: An Outline of the Issues" https://www.wipo.int/export/sites/www/tk/en/docs/resources/overview_customary_law.pdf accessed 01 November 2024; Ulia Gosart and Wend Wendland, "Indigenous Intellectual Property Rights: An Interview with Wend Wendland." (2023) 84 5–8 *The Serials Librarian* 66.

the Safeguarding of the Intangible Cultural Heritage affords it are of no concern. The focus of this chapter is exclusively on the protection of TK. However, it must be acknowledged that for an indigenous community to make an ownership claim under copyright, they would necessarily draw upon the customs relating to the TK to evidence that the subject matter in question belongs to them. For example, the Xhosa tribe of South Africa has a ceremony called *Intlombe.* This ceremony incorporates dancing, singing, and playing drums as a way of connecting with and invoking the spirits of the Xhosa tribe's ancestors during the initiation of a new traditional medical practitioner or "healer" (*amagqira*).[82] While the dances, songs, and musical compositions associated with the *Intlombe* ceremony would be protected as TK under copyright and owned by the Xhosa tribe under this paradigm shift, such a communal claim would necessarily involve evidencing that the TK is associated with their customs relating to traditional healing, spiritual connections with tribal ancestors, and social connections within the community. By affording copyright protection to the Xhosa tribe for their dances, songs, and musical compositions relating to the *Intlombe* ceremony, the importance of the associated customs that exist alongside the TK is acknowledged and appreciated despite being a deviation from Western norms. This is the case regardless of whether the customs are themselves legally protected.

In some jurisdictions, like South Africa, customs relating to indigenous communities are afforded legal protection and act as a source of law. One such example of this is the principle or value of *ubuntu*, which is often expressed through the Zulu phrase, *umuntu ngumuntu ngabantu* (tentatively translated as "a person is a person through other people").[83] While *ubuntu* is not expressly mentioned in the Constitution of South Africa 1996 (the supreme source of law in the country), section 211 of the Constitution does refer to custom "as one of the primary sources of law under the Constitution." It is therefore accepted by the Constitutional Court – the highest court in post-Apartheid South Africa – the legislature, and academia that *ubuntu* is a foundational constitutional principle or value which *must* be used in interpreting the Constitution as a whole and the Bill of Rights in particular.[84] In *S v Makwanyane and Another*, the first-ever case to be heard by the Constitutional Court, the court was tasked with considering

82 M Buhrmann, "The Xhosa Healers of Southern Africa: 1. Intlombe and Xhentsa: A Xhosa Healing Ritual." (1981) *Journal of Analytical Psychology* 26.

83 *MEC for Education: KwaZulu-Natal v Pillay* 2008 1 SA 474 (CC) para 53.

84 Serges Djoyou Kamga, "Cultural Values as a Source of Law: Emerging Trends of Ubuntu Jurisprudence in South Africa." (2018) 18 *African Human Rights Law Journal* 625; Chuma Himonga et al., "Reflections on judicial views of ubuntu." (2013) 16 5 *Potchefstroom Electronic Law Journal* 369; *S v Makwanyane and Another* 1995 (3) SA 391 at para 237–306.

the constitutionality of the death penalty. Central to the court's reasoning and judgement was the constitutional and customary value of *ubuntu*. This is because an outstanding feature of *ubuntu* in a community sense is the value it places on human life and dignity. The dominant theme of the value of *ubuntu* is that the life of another person is at least as valuable as one's own.[85] This can be contrasted with the Western centrality of individual human dignity and the pursuit of happiness, instead focusing on the inherent dignity and happiness of all within the community. However, whether a country chooses to give legal weight to custom, like South Africa, is of no concern to this chapter and has no impact on the proposed paradigm shift. As previously stated, the legal protection of a communal copyright claim to TK will necessarily require evidence relating to associated customs and an appreciation of the same as they relate to indigenous communities. Regardless, the legal protection of TK argued for within this chapter may exist independent of any protection (or lack thereof) of custom.

Another difficulty in extending copyright protection to TK in some jurisdictions is the fact that most TK is not fixed in a material form. However, it must be noted that fixation is a requirement and therefore a barrier for copyright protection extending to TK only within those countries that expressly provide for it. Article 2(2) of the Berne Convention allows for national legislatures to prescribe that works shall not be protected under copyright unless they have been fixed in some material form. There is therefore no requirement of fixation in the international framework for copyright to subsist, and many countries do not incorporate such a requirement in their national laws relating to copyright.[86] However, there are some countries – like the UK and South Africa – that do make use of the Article 2(2) option to require that a work be fixed in some material form to be afforded copyright protection. Much has been written in these jurisdictions about the difficulties of reconciling this fixation requirement with forms of expression that are not traditionally fixed in a material form, such as dance.[87] Some argue that fixation ought to be reconsidered as an essential element of copyright protection in these jurisdictions for this reason.[88]

The implementation of the paradigm shift relating to copyright ownership proposed within this chapter presupposes extensive collaboration at

85 *S v Makwanyane and Another* 1995 (note 85) at para 225.

86 Daniel J Gervais, "Chapter 4: Protection Thresholds: Originality and Fixation" in *(Re) structuring Copyright: A Comprehensive Path to International Copyright Reform* (Edward Elgar 2017) 94–102.

87 Mathilde Pavis et al., "Who Can Profit from Dance?: An Exploration of Copyright Ownership." (2017) 35 1 *Dance Research: The Journal of the Society for Dance Research* 96.

88 Enrico Bonadio and Nicola Lucchi, "How Far Can Copyright Be Stretched? Framing the Debate on Whether New and Different Forms of Creativity Can Be Protected." (2019) *Intellectual Property Quarterly* 115.

numerous levels. This collaboration may take place on a national, regional or international level; it may include collection agencies, authors, users, NGOs, and multinational bodies. On a national level, it is envisioned that authors upon whom the duty to justify ownership based on socio-economic developmental goals would lie will collaborate – either directly or indirectly e.g. through collection agencies or interest groups – with the community to identify and address developmental needs as per the 17 SDGs. For example, the Authors' Licensing and Collecting Society in the UK might wish to collaborate with organisations such as the Royal National Institute of Blind People or the British Dyslexia Organisation, which represent users with print disabilities to better understand the challenges faced by users in terms of access and ensure the industry more meaningfully addresses the developmental goals impacting said portion of society. This may result in reporting to government on steps taken to, e.g. increase the number of publications that have been translated into accessible formats and how this relates to the goals of reducing inequalities and increasing access to quality education. With regard to indigenous communities as beneficiaries of the SDGs, it will be crucial that these communities are represented at every stage of governance so that their interests in intangible property are fully understood and reflected. This will require interest groups comprising experts in various specialised areas relating to art and law in order to meaningfully engage with these communities at a grassroots level and assist in advocating for said interests at all levels of governance. Indigenous communities must be placed front and centre, actively participating in any law-making process which seeks to better reflect and protect their rights to TK.

On a regional level, the member states of the African Continental Free Trade Area (AfCFTA) adopted the Protocol on Intellectual Property Rights in February 2023 during the 36th African Union Summit in Addis Ababa, Ethiopia. One of the primary objectives, consistent with the aspirations of the UN SDGs, is to promote inclusive growth and sustainable development underpinned by a continental market that facilitates the free movement and indiscriminate treatment of persons, capital, goods, and services between member states. Article 41 of the Protocol mandates the state parties to negotiate and adopt an Annex on TK which will be binding upon them once it has been adopted. This opportunity provides impetus for the development of a continent-wide regulatory and cooperation framework on IP in general and TK in particular.[89] In this way, it may promote the

89 Caroline B Ncube, "The Protection of Traditional Knowledge, Traditional Cultural Expressions, Expressions of Folklore and Genetic Resources Within the African Continental Free Trade Area – Alignment with International and Regional Developments." (2024) 263 *Southviews* 1.

linkage between IP and socio-economic development policies through a collaborative, continent-wide effort.

On an international level, collaborations between NGOs and multinational bodies will enable the international framework to better give weight to the import of socio-economic development as it relates to copyright and provide ways in which this may be facilitated on a regional or national level. For example, the protection of culture and related human rights largely falls under the "jurisdiction" of UNESCO. Article 2(1) of the 2003 Convention for the Safeguarding of the Intangible Cultural Heritage commits to safeguarding oral traditions and expressions, performing arts, social practices, knowledge and practices concerning nature and traditional craftsmanship. The preamble expressly considers intangible cultural heritage as being a "guarantee of sustainable development." The overlap in terms of works protected and membership of UNESCO and the WTO means the scope for collaboration is rife. The 2007 UNESCO Convention on the Protection and Promotion of the Diversity of Cultural Expressions makes specific reference in its preamble to the precursor of the 2030 Agenda and its SDGs such as gender equality and eradicating poverty. It centralises TK and its positive contribution to sustainable development, calling for nations to adopt measures that protect and promote the diversity of cultural expressions and strengthen international cooperation. To this end, the WTO – in its administration of the TRIPS Agreement – may collaborate with UNESCO to better reflect the right to intangible culture and the importance of cultural diversity within the framework of copyright protection, such as extending copyright protection to TK. A successful example of such a multi-layered collaborative approach occurring can be seen in the Marrakesh Treaty, which is addressed in detail by Kouletakis.[90]

Adopting the new paradigm posited within this chapter does not necessitate abandoning copyright owners' right to economically exploit their works or even their right to determine what should be done with their works. It does not necessarily threaten the norm of exclusive ownership rights where this may be founded upon the furtherance of socio-economic developmental goals. Instead, this new approach seeks to justify the norm of exclusive copyright ownership within a framework which explicitly and directly acknowledges the link between copyright ownership and the serving of socio-economic developmental goals. This novel approach requires copyright owners to justify their position of privilege in holding these exclusive ownership rights within the context of Article 7 of the TRIPS Agreement as reflected in the 2030 Agenda's 17 SDGs. Of course, this

90 Jade Kouletakis, "A Critical Examination of Copyright Limitations and Exceptions for the Visually Impaired Pertaining to Literary Works in South Africa in the Local and Global Context" (note 21).

chapter is not the first to challenge the existing copyright paradigm. The inequalities and shortfalls of the current framework have given rise to many academics eager to offer an alternative theory of justification for copyright exclusivity. The next section will consider some of these alternative theories, highlighting their shortcomings when held against the one proposed within this chapter.

1.4 Competing copyright paradigms: alternative theories for justifying exclusive copyright ownership

As highlighted in Section 1.2 , the shortfalls of the current copyright paradigm and its application to predominantly developing nations have long been well documented. This has given rise to academics proposing new theories within which to situate copyright exclusivity and its place in relation to society. Some of these theories, such as the labour theory, seek to draw on Enlightenment-era philosophies and remodel them for a 21st-century copyright landscape; others, such as the democratic theory, seek to draw on more modern concepts such as human rights and socio-political freedoms to reconsider the economic or commercial "public interest" justification for copyright exclusivity. Having considered each of these in turn, it will be demonstrated that what all these theories have in common are two major shortfalls. First, there is a lack of a normative legal framework within which to situate their theoretical approach to justifying exclusive copyright ownership. Second, there is a failure to adequately centralise the importance of exclusive copyright ownership as a means to furthering socio-economic development in developing nations, or – in some theories – a failure to even acknowledge the copyright framework's inherent obligation to do so, as evidenced within the previous section.

It is a common shortfall of alternative theories of justification for exclusive copyright ownership that they lack a normative legal framework within which to situate their theoretical approach to copyright exclusivity. The first, and oldest, such theory which has been expanded to include copyright is Locke's labour theory which is premised upon so-called natural rights. According to Locke, one has an unlimited divine right to the fruits of one's labour. By "mixing" one's labour with land or other tangible property that is either unowned or communal, a "natural right" to the property is, according to Locke, acquired. However, Locke provides the *proviso* that this natural right applies "only if, after the acquisition, there is enough and as good left in common for others." This *proviso* means that as long as another's position is not worsened by one's appropriation of a resource, ownership based on labour is permitted. Of course, Locke speaks in the language of tangible property and unlimited monopolies, which raises issues as to Locke's theory being applied to intangible property, such as copyright. For example, if X created a work that was worthy of copyright and Y subsequently but independently created a work that was substantially similar or identical to X's, Locke's theory would support Y also having ownership in their creation. To do otherwise would leave Y worse off, and thus arguably violate Locke's *provisio*.[91] This would, of course, undermine the limited monopoly X expects from having acquired copyright in their work in the first place. More evidence of Locke's theory having been borrowed and applied to the realm of copyright can be uncovered when considering works that were created with more than one "labourer," such as TK,[92] or works which have no labourer at all, such as in the case of AI generated works.[93] Most importantly for the purpose of this chapter, Locke's deontological approach to intellectual property lacks a normative legal framework within which to situate modern ownership rights. As previously stated, Locke's theory was never intended to be applied to copyright and to date there has not been anyone able to find the theory within a modern, comprehensive legal framework.

Another – and more modern - theory used to justify copyright is cultural theory.[94] It was first developed by Carpenter et al., who argue that certain lands, resources, and expressions should be entitled to legal protection as cultural property belonging to the group rather than the individual because they are integral to the group identity and cultural survival of indigenous people.[95] To this end, the concept of property law is reimagined to include a culturally connected collective as a potential rights-holder, rather than the Western norm of individual ownership. Per Carpenter et al.:

> The classic view of property law focuses on the predictability and certainty of protecting the individual owner's rights of exclusion and alienation primarily for wealth-maximization purposes. Yet a more relational vision of property law honours the legitimate interests of both owners and nonowners, in furtherance of various human and social values, potentially including nonmarket values.[96]

The justification for copyright, according to Carpenter et al., should not merely be the protection of the rights-holder's economic interests, but also

91 John Locke, "Second Treatise of Civil Government," https://www.gutenberg.org/files/7370/7370-h/7370-h.htm accessed 3 October 2023.

92 Stephen R Munzer and Kal Raustiala, "The Uneasy Case for Intellectual Property Rights in Traditional Knowledge" (note 73) at 59–61.

93 Aviv H Gaon, *The Future of Copyright in the Age of Artificial Intelligence* (Edward Elgar 2021).

94 Kristen A Carpenter et al., "In Defense of Property" (note 73) at 1028.

95 Kristen A Carpenter et al., "In Defense of Property" (note 73) at 1028.

96 Ibid. at 1027.

the various public goods copyright policy seeks to achieve.[97] However, a major downside of Carpenter et al.'s position is that it too lacks a normative framework provided to support the author's otherwise abstract position.[98] Fisher has attempted to provide Carpenter et al.'s work with such a normative framework, and in doing so offers the position that copyright law ought to be organised so as to promote "human flourishing."[99] Fisher suggests eight conditions that are essential for human flourishing and argues that a copyright framework ought to be organised in such a way as to promote these eight conditions. These conditions are not a closed list and include a normal length of life; good health; public engagement (in employment, politics, and culture); personal autonomy; self-expression; competence to succeed in life; sociability; and privacy.[100] However, while Fisher has sought to provide an otherwise absent normative framework for Carpenter et al.'s cultural theory, Fisher's framework is still at best ambiguous and unfounded in law, much less human rights.

While other alternative theories, like relational and democratic theory, are, unlike labour and cultural theory, founded within the law relating to freedom of expression, they still lack a comprehensive normative framework for which to justify the granting of exclusive copyright ownership. Instead, these alternative theories utilise freedom of expression as a means to justify the *limiting* of exclusive copyright ownership rather than to justify the granting of exclusive copyright ownership in the first instance.

For example, relational theory focuses on freedom of expression as a means of limiting the monopoly enjoyed by copyright-holders in the interest of the creative commons and users' interests or rights.[101] In other words, relational theory builds upon the idea that users benefit not from the existence of exclusive copyright ownership, but from exceptions and limitations to the exclusive rights owned by copyright-holders. It seeks to better understand the role of users and their rights or interests in relation to copyright-holders, thus focusing on questions pertaining to the *scope*

97 J Janewa OseiTutu, "Emerging Scholars Series: A Sui Generis Regime for Traditional Knowledge: The Cultural Divide in Intellectual Property Law." (2011) 15 *Intellectual Property Law Review* 147 at 207.

98 Michael F Brown, "Culture, Property, and Peoplehood: A Comment on Carpenter, Katyal, and Riley's 'In Defense of Property'." (2010) 17 *International Journal of Cultural Property* 569.

99 William Fisher, "The Puzzle of Traditional Knowledge." (2018) 67 *Duke Law Journal* 1511 at 1549–1554.

100 Ibid.

101 Carys J Craig, "Putting the Community in Communication: Dissolving the Conflict Between Freedom of Expression and Copyright." (2006) 56 1 *The University of Toronto Law Journal* 75 at 76.

of copyright ownership and the nature of limitations and exceptions.[102] Craig, the original proponent of this theory, states that the overarching theme of relational theory is "regarding copyright from a public interest perspective and recognising the social value of discursive engagement" so that one "can appreciate the system's incentivisation of cultural production as a means by which to enhance relations of communication."[103] In other words, relational theory seeks to view users of works protected by copyright not as trespassers upon the author's exclusive rights, but as participants in a process of cultural dialogue and exchange which ought to be protected by way of freedom of expression and an obligation on the part of copyright-holders to make their works available to the public or community as a whole.[104] As per Craig:

> [Copyright] structures relationships between authors and users, allocating powers *and responsibilities* amongst members of cultural com munities … The importance of copyright lies in its capacity to structure relations of communication, and also to establish the power dynamics that will shape these relations. Its purpose is to maximize communication and exchange by putting in place incentives for the creation *and dissemination* of intellectual works [emphasis added].[105]

Craig therefore argues that for copyright to remain legitimate, the granting of exclusive rights must be balanced against freedom of expression and a duty to make works accessible to the public to facilitate cultural participation. This view is shared by Shi, another proponent of the relational theory, who states that there is an obligation in today's digital age for authors or copyright-holders to make their content accessible and available to the public under fair circumstances.[106] In fact, proponents of the theory are highly critical of exclusive copyright ownership *in toto*. Pappalardo contends that one ought to be rather sceptical of "business models or technological restrictions that are designed primarily to make it more difficult or

102 Cary J Craig, "Gripe Sites and Trademark User Rights: Lessons from Canada's Cooperstock Case" in Haochen Sun and Barton Beebe (eds) *Charting Limitations on Trademark Rights* (Oxford University Press 2023) 79.

103 Carys J Craig, *Copyright, Communication and Culture: Towards a Relational Theory of Copyright Law* (Edward Elgar 2011).

104 Carys J Craig (note 103) at 3 and 261; Carys J Craig and Ian R Kerr, "The Death of the AI Author." (2021) *Ottawa Law Review* 31; Carys J Craig, "Putting the Community in Communication: Dissolving the Conflict Between Freedom of Expression and Copyright" (note 101).

105 Carys J Craig (note 103) at 261.

106 Xiaoxiang Shi, "Towards a Relational Theory of Copyright Law" (Queensland University of Technology PhD thesis, 2010).

more expensive for users to access and use copyrighted works."[107] This is because users should be seen as having a right or an interest in autonomy, self-expression, personal connection, education, community, and play; therefore, copyright *exceptions or limitations* should be interpreted more broadly to support passive consumption, active consumption, cultural engagement, and ongoing creative acts.[108] Shi even questions the connection between exclusive copyright ownership and economic development, instead arguing that a thriving and diverse economy does not depend upon a copyright regime.[109] This is because, they contend, evolutionary economics suggests that the free flow of information and "the variations generated from the flow" are "the core ingredients of the growth of knowledge and thus the evolution of economy."[110] Meese too chastises the "common presumption ... that copyright is vitally necessary legal technology for any innovative sector populated by creative practitioners," instead arguing that there exist a number of "highly creative" fields which are "either not protected by copyright or essentially ignore copyright laws that do exist."[111]

Like relational theory, democratic theory also finds its legal weight in arguing that freedom of expression ought to be utilised to limit exclusive copyright ownership, rather than concerning itself with a justification for the granting of exclusive copyright ownership in the first place. Democratic theory concerns copyright as a means of furthering cultural democracy and distributive justice.[112] According to Netanel,[113] the main proponent of the theory, it emphasises that copyright exclusivity is a state measure that uses market institutions to enhance the democratic character of civil society. It acts as an "engine for free expression" in three ways. First, copyright serves a "production function." It does this by acting as an economic incentive for original expression on a wide array of social, political and aesthetic issues. Second, copyright serves a "structural function." It supports a sector of authors who produce works that are free of state involvement or subsidy, instead relying on the free market. In this way, the works within the copyright system are independent from government control. Third, copyright has an "expressive function." By encourag-

107 Kylie Pappalardo, "A Tort Law Framework for Copyright Authorisation" (Australian Catholic University PhD thesis, 2016).

108 Ibid.

109 Xiaoxiang Shi, "Towards a Relational Theory of Copyright Law" (note 106).

110 Ibid.

111 James Meese, "Chapter 5: Reimagining the Pirate: Approaching Infringement Relationally" in James Meese (ed) *Authors, Users, and Pirates: Copyright Law and Subjectivity* (Cambridge 2018) 121.

112 Neil Weinstock Netanel, "Copyright and a Democratic Civil Society." (1996) 106 2 *The Yale Law Journal* 283.

113 Ibid.

ing authors, it symbolically reinforces the social and political importance of original contributions to public discourse. Democratic theory therefore looks at freedom of expression as it relates to copyright as a means with which to promote democratic deliberation about public issues in a decentralised environment free from state control.[114] Balkin stresses that democratic culture as furthered by copyright within the democratic theory is not about democratic governance but about democratic participation.[115] Democratic theory thus seeks to use freedom of expression as a means of broadening public participation in the creative commons free from state control.[116] As per Balkin:

> The theory of free speech as democratic culture ... argues that intellectual property rights must facilitate broad cultural participation ... To make intellectual property consistent with the idea of free speech as democratic culture, there must be a robust and ever-expanding public domain with generous fair use rights. Intellectual property also must not be permitted to create chokepoints or bottlenecks in the spread of knowledge and the distribution of culture.[117]

As with relational theory, democratic theory seeks to utilise freedom of expression as a means to rationalise the dichotomy which this chapter seeks to undermine, namely that original works and interests of authors are protected through the granting of limited monopolistic control over their works, whereas the public interest (in democratic theory, this would be synonymous with public participation in democratic discourse) is protected through the limitation of these rights. Democratic theory is concerned with the challenge of continuing to ensure that copyright strikes a balance between the need to incentivise authors to create original works through exclusivity and the desire to make certain that those creative works are widely disseminated to the populace – which it deems as being the public interest - through exceptions and limitations.[118] In other words, democratic theory operates within the existing status quo that sees authors' interests as justifying their limited rights over their works, and – competing with this – the public's interest as justifying limitations and exceptions to these limited rights. By contrast, this chapter is concerned with turning said

114 Neil Weinstock Netanel, "Is Copyright "the Engine of Free Expression"?" in Neil Weinstock Netanel (ed) *Copyright's Paradox* (Oxford University Press 2008) 81.
115 Ibid.
116 Jack M Balkin, "Digital Speech and Democratic Culture: A Theory of Freedom of Expression for the Information Society." (2004) 79 1 *New York University Law Review* 50.
117 Ibid.
118 Ibid.

status quo on its head, arguing that the public interest in socio-economic development within developing nations can and should be repositioned as a central justification for maintaining the exclusive ownership rights held by copyright owners under the current framework.

Like alternative theories such as relational and democratic theory, Geiger's promotion of cultural and scientific progress theory is also concerned with limiting the expansion of exclusivity in copyright and broadening its exceptions and limitations, rather than justifying exclusive ownership. Geiger argues that there currently exists the erroneous perception that the primary objective of copyright exclusivity is to reward right owners rather than to promote cultural or scientific progress.[119] Geiger insists that copyright has, since its inception in the Statute of Anne 1710, had a "social function" in addition to an economic one posited by the rewards or incentivisation theory.[120] According to Geiger, copyright has always had the goal of ensuring cultural and social development even though it might have been forgotten over the years.[121] What makes Geiger's position distinct from other theories is that it *does* seek to provide a normative legal framework. Geiger calls for a return to the "social function" of copyright by way of constitutional or quasi-constitutional means so as to "help ... the general public to accept and respect IP rights more willingly' and thus aid in the legitimacy of IP during modern times "of piracy and disillusion."[122] To this end, Geiger proposes amending either Article 17 (right to property), Article 13 (freedom of arts and sciences) or Article 11 (freedom of expression and information) of the EU Charter.[123]

However, the circumspect approach to the relationship between human rights and copyright taken by Geiger is suboptimal. As has been demonstrated previously within this chapter, copyright interplays with many human rights in so far as it enables their realisation. Human rights are subject to the indivisibility principle, with the international and academic community frequently referring to human rights as "universal, indivisible and interrelated."[124] The UN General Assembly Resolution 32/130 states that:

119 Christophe Geiger, "Chapter 35: Implementing Intellectual Property Provisions in Human Rights Instruments: Towards a New Social Contract for the Protection of Intangibles" in Christophe Geiger, *Research Handbook on Human Rights and Intellectual Property* (Edward Elgar 2015).

120 Ibid.

121 Christophe Geiger, "Chapter 35" (note 119).

122 Ibid.

123 Ibid.

124 Jan Essink et al., "The Indivisibility of Human Rights: An Empirical Analysis." (2023) 23 3 *Human Rights Law Review* 1.

> [A]ll human rights and fundamental freedoms are indivisible and interdependent; equal attention and urgent consideration should be given to the implementation, promotion, and protection of both civil and political, and economic, social, and cultural rights.[125]

The Committee on Economic, Social and Cultural Rights states that, in relation to everyone's right to take part in cultural life, "[c]ultural rights are an integral part of human rights and, like other rights, are universal, indivisible and interdependent."[126] The African Charter on Human and Peoples Rights adopts a similar approach, with the Preamble stating that "the satisfaction of economic, social and cultural rights is a guarantee for the enjoyment of civil and political rights."[127] Indeed, that this indivisibility principle forms a key tenet of international human rights law "speaks to a firmly held belief that human rights, as fundamental and necessary for human dignity, constitute an organic and inviolable whole."[128] While some challenge the effectiveness of the indivisibility principle as it relates to economic, social and cultural rights,[129] this has rarely led to a challenge on the existence of the indivisibility principle itself.[130] The indivisibility principle refers to the unity of purpose of human rights protections, so that they are interpreted and applied not as separate entities, but as parts of an integrated and coherent commitment to recognising one's inherent dignity. In other words, all rights are of equal importance, and none can be fully enjoyed without the others.[131] For this reason, this chapter argued in Section 1.3 that the justification for individual (and potential for collective) ownership rights in the realm of copyright ought to be anchored within socio-economic developmental goals found within the UN's 2030 Agenda

125 UN, "Alternative Approaches and Ways and Means within the United Nations System for Improving the Effective Enjoyment of Human Rights and Fundamental Freedoms," https://digitallibrary.un.org/record/188376?ln=en&v=pdf accessed 5 October 2024.

126 "General Comment No 21: Right of Everyone to Take Part in Cultural Life," available at https://www.ohchr.org/en/resources/educators/human-rights-education-training/i-general-comment-no-21-right-everyone-take-part-cultural-life-article-15-para-1-international accessed 6 December 2023.

127 Organization of African Unity, "African Charter on Human and Peoples' Rights," available at https://www.refworld.org/docid/3ae6b3630.html accessed 6 December 2023.

128 Jack Donnelly and Daniel J Whelan, "Chapter 4: The Unity of Human Rights" in Jack Donnelly and Daniel J Whelan (eds) *International Human Rights* (Routledge 2020) at 70.

129 Alberto Quintavalla and Klaus Heine, "Priorities and Human Rights." (2019) 23 4 *The International Journal of Human Rights* 679.

130 Jan Essink et al., "The Indivisibility of Human Rights: An Empirical Analysis" (note 124).

131 UN Population Fund, "Human Rights Principles," available at https://www.unfpa.org/resources/human-rights-principles accessed 6 December 2023.

and 17 SDGs. A key benefit of favouring this approach over Geiger's is that it offers a less circumspect framework within which to reconsider copyright ownership than merely assessing its ability to further "cultural or scientific progress." Considerations which would fall outside the scope of Geiger's "cultural or scientific progress" model but which are directly related to the furtherance of the UN's 17 SDGs such as gender equality and access to decent work, are central to the furtherance of socio-economic development and – as is the position of this chapter – ought to be considered when justifying exclusive copyright ownership.

Another shortfall with the existing alternative theories is that they fail to assist in the furtherance of copyright's underlying developmental objectives. As detailed in Section 1.3, according to the TRIPS Agreement and WTO, one of the main underlying public policy aims of the international IP framework is to assist in the furtherance of developmental objectives and achieving sustainable development. However, the alternative justifications fail to do so, instead "othering" the interests of developing nations when it comes to justifying the granting of exclusive ownership rights. By "othering" it is meant that the theories either are not intended to be applied in the context of developing nations as exclusive copyright owners, or that applying them in this context is not intended to further the realisation of their socio-economic developmental goals.

For example, while labour theory and relational theory make no mention of developing nations, cultural and democratic theory only do so in order to argue that copyright is either not capable of or ought not to be concerned with protecting the interests of developing nations. For cultural theory, this comes in the form of stewardship. For democratic theory, Netanel, the most prominent democratic theorist, and Mbuka caution that democratic theory will be of little use to the developing world and might even have a negative impact upon their interests:

> Copyright holder exclusive rights would appear to have only marginal effect on, or even to impair, democratic transition and democratic consolidation where such support is lacking or where government is otherwise able to exert concerted pressure on commercial media … [This] belie[s] the notion that requiring authoritarian and developing countries to implement proprietary copyright regimes modelled on those of the West will, as a matter of course, engender global democracy.[132]

Proponents of democratic theory have therefore recognised that there is a disconnect between the pursuance of public participation in the creation of

132 Neil Weinstock Netanel, "Asserting Copyright's Democratic Principles in the Global Arena." 51 *Vanderbilt Law Review* 217 at 277.

culture and the realisation of basic socio-economic needs held by developing nations. They have acknowledged that members of developing nations will likely choose not to participate in the creation and consumption of culture due to a preoccupation with failing to have their basic needs met, making democratic theory of little to no practical effect in the developing world unless said needs are met first.[133] Democratic theory is not concerned with the interests of developing nations, nor is it concerned with wider socio-economic rights. Instead, democratic theory centres upon protecting the prized notion of an individual's freedom of expression within the developed Western world to the exclusion of concerning itself with the interests of developing nations, thus ignoring copyright's underlying public policy objective.

Both Craig's relational theory and Geiger's promotion of cultural and scientific progress theory take a different approach. These theories *do* recognise the interests of developing nations, but only in relation to exceptions and limitations rather than exclusive copyright ownership itself. For example, Geiger references the need for developing nations to have better access to generic drugs in order to combat epidemics,[134] and Craig makes the case for developing nations requiring open access in order to achieve gender equality.[135] This chapter is not concerned with copyright limitations and exceptions *per se*, but with the exclusive ownership rights afforded to authors and how these rights ought to be justified at a global level. Where both Craig and Geiger take the stance that users of works in the developing world benefit only from exceptions and limitations to the copyright owner's exclusive rights, this chapter supports the idea that entire communities within the developing world can and should benefit from the copyright owner's exclusive rights. Instead of arguing for an expansion of exceptions and limitations to copyright ownership, this chapter has made the novel argument for the copyright regime – including the maintenance of the norm of exclusive copyright ownership enjoyed by the rights-holder – being renegotiated within a culture of justification founded upon the role of copyright in furthering socio-economic developmental goals. It has argued that copyright ownership itself ought to be reimagined within a culture of justification premised upon the realisation of human rights found in the

133 John Mukum Mbaku, "Copyright and Democratization in Africa." (2011) 7 *Brigham Young University International Law & Management Review* 51 at 91; Neil Weinstock Netanel, "Asserting Copyright's Democratic Principles in the Global Arena" (note 132).

134 Christophe Geiger, "Chapter 35" (note 119) at 5.

135 Carys J Craig, "Intellectual Property and Gender Inequality: Towards Sustainable Development—or Sustaining the Status Quo?" in Bita Amani et al. (eds) *The Elgar Companion to Intellectual Property and the Sustainable Development Goals* (Edward Elgar 2023); Carys J Craig, "What is Feminist About Open Access?: A Relational Approach to Copyright in the Academy." (2011) 11 *Feminists@law* 1.

UN's 2030 Agenda and 17 SDGs so as to assist in the furtherance of copyright's developmental objectives.

1.5 Conclusion

This chapter has set out to achieve the ambitious aim of turning the current copyright paradigm upon its head. In doing so, Section 1.2 of this chapter has set out the current position of exclusive copyright ownership as furthering economic or commercial interests, competing with limitations to or exceptions from this exclusivity which seek to further the non-economic or non-commercial interests of the wider public. This has included highlighting the well-documented shortfalls of this status quo, in particular its treatment of the interests of developing nations and their indigenous communities. In Section 1.3, this chapter has provided an alternative copyright paradigm or justification theory for exclusive copyright ownership which seeks to better represent these interests of developing nations with reference to the UN's 2030 Agenda and 17 SDGs. This theory requires the norm of exclusive copyright ownership to exist within a culture of justification whereby copyright owners must justify their rights with reference to the developmental goals found within the 17 SDGs. In doing so, this new paradigm seeks to give better representation to the oft-ignored interests of developing nations and their indigenous communities alike; refocus attention upon the foundational principles of the international copyright framework as expressed within the TRIPS Agreement and Berne Convention regarding utilising copyright to further developmental goals; and centralise the established link between copyright and socio-economic development acknowledged by the UN, WTO and WIPO in justifying exclusive copyright ownership. While competing alternative theories of justification for exclusive copyright ownership exist, Section 1.4 has evidenced that these theories either lack a comprehensive, normative legal framework or fail to adequately consider the interests and realities of developing nations and their indigenous communities. In this sense, Section 1.4 has evidenced that – despite competing theories to justify exclusive copyright ownership – the position proposed within this chapter is the only one in which a normative legal framework (the UN's 2030 Agenda and 17 SDGs) is put forth with which to reimagine the justification for copyright exclusivity as being centred upon the socio-economic developmental interests of developing nations and their indigenous communities who have historically been ignored. In adopting this novel theory, it will enable TK to be afforded copyright protection despite the current challenge of collective ownership claims; foster a culture of collaboration in the IP community at a national, regional and international level; better reflect the core principles of the TRIPS Agreement; and encourage others to critically re-examine the so-called core tenements of copyright law in the West.

2 From moonlight tales to town halls to cinemas

Customary copyright practices and performances that led to Nollywood in Nigeria

Nkem Itanyi

2.1 Introduction

The Nigerian film industry, Nollywood, stands as a remarkable cultural and economic force, producing over 2,500 films annually and capturing audiences both domestically and internationally.[1] Behind Nollywood's success lies a deep connection to Nigeria's storytelling traditions, which span centuries and are rooted in community practices, cultural preservation, and moral education. In pre-colonial Nigerian societies, "moonlight tales" – evening storytelling sessions held under the moonlight – served as a communal activity that connected generations. Elders would narrate folklore, myths, and legends to children and adults alike, using music, dance, and drama to enrich the stories. Instruments like the Yoruba talking drum played a vital role, mimicking tonal inflexions and enhancing the interactive nature of the sessions. These oral traditions were dynamic and fluid, allowing storytellers to adapt narratives to suit the context and audience, fostering both education and entertainment. This communal aspect of storytelling is a key part of Nollywood's cultural roots, connecting it to the shared history and values of the Nigerian people.

The colonial era brought significant changes, introducing Western education, Christianity, and new forms of artistic expression, including theatre and print media. Town halls, public squares, and missionary schools became venues where indigenous performance arts blended with Western theatrical techniques, paving the way for travelling theatre troupes like the Alarinjo Theatre of the Yoruba region.[2] These troupes adapted tradi-

1 Martin Armstrong, "Nollywood is Booming" (31 January 2022) https://www.statista.com/chart/26728/nollywood-films-produced-and-censored-timeline/ accessed 17 December 2024

2 Dennis Eluyefa, "The 'Alarinjo' Theatre in Yoruba Nigeria: Fact or Fiction?" in *New Directions in African Theatre and Performance* (Adonis and Abbey 2020) https://bgro.repository.guildhe.ac.uk/id/eprint/787/ accessed 17 December 2024.

DOI: 10.4324/9781003602989-3

tional stories into dramatised performances, reaching wider audiences and formalising aspects of indigenous storytelling. The hybridisation of oral traditions with colonial influences laid the groundwork for what would eventually become Nollywood in the 20th century.

Affordable video technologies and informal distribution systems catalysed the emergence of Nollywood in the 1980s and 1990s.[3] Filmmakers drew heavily on traditional narratives, folktales, and moral themes, blending them with contemporary issues to create relatable and engaging content. However, this transition from oral storytelling to commercial film production highlighted critical tensions between customary copyright practices and modern intellectual property frameworks. In traditional settings, stories were communally owned, and storytellers were custodians rather than exclusive owners. This principle of collective authorship conflicted with modern copyright laws, which emphasise individual ownership, exclusive rights, and economic benefit.

The Nigerian Copyright Act 2022 represents a milestone in bridging these gaps by providing protections for traditional cultural expressions (TCEs) and recognising their cultural and economic value.[4] This act, which marks a pivotal step toward safeguarding traditional cultural expressions (TCEs) while offering creators protection in an increasingly digital and commercialised media environment, is a significant development for Nollywood. Despite challenges such as piracy, enforcement difficulties, and the lack of mechanisms to ensure that communities benefit from the commercialisation of their heritage, the Nigerian Copyright Act 2022 provides a framework for addressing these issues. Nollywood's ability to preserve its cultural roots while adapting to modern legal and technological realities, as supported by this Act, is crucial for its sustained success. This chapter explores the historical, cultural, and legal trajectories that shaped Nollywood, highlighting its reliance on storytelling traditions, its evolution through colonial and technological influences, and the role of copyright laws in protecting Nigeria's creative output. By examining these elements, the chapter underscores the need for a balanced approach that respects cultural heritage while fostering innovation and economic growth in Nigeria's creative industries.

3 Giovanna Santanera and Paul Ugor, "Media Globalization, African Popular Culture, and History from Below: Nigerian Video Films." (2012) 3 *Journal of African Media Studies* 45, 48.

4 Chukwunye Augusta Ojeih and Olumide Ogidan, "Content Creators: Rights under the Nigerian Copyright Act 2022." (2024) 4 *Redeemer's University Journal of Jurisprudence and International Law* 82.

2.2 Historical context: the roots of Nollywood

The thriving Nigerian film industry, known as Nollywood, has its roots in the rich storytelling customs and performance arts that have long been ingrained in Nigerian culture.[5] This historical context, which spans from moonlight storytelling gatherings to the advent of cinema, demonstrates the evolution of cultural practices as well as the complex interplay between traditional copyright norms and modern legal frameworks. These "moonlight tales" were more than just entertainment; they were a vital means of preserving history, imparting moral lessons, and reinforcing community values. The Yoruba talking drum, for instance, played a significant role in these gatherings, with its rhythms and tones enhancing the narrative and engaging the audience.[6]

2.2.1 Traditional storytelling (oral literature)

Nollywood, Nigeria's vibrant film industry, has deep roots in the nation's rich tradition of oral storytelling.[7] In pre-colonial Nigeria, storytelling was not just a critical medium for preserving history, imparting moral lessons, and fostering community cohesion. It was a communal activity that engaged multiple generations. The community collectively owned these stories, and their transmission was a communal activity that engaged various generations. While the creators of such works received some recognition, the creations belonged to the community, and everyone was allowed to use them. Therefore, songs, poetry, stories, architecture, creations of artisans, and textile design, amongst others, produced by members of a community were available free for use by its members, and such use of the author's creative effort was viewed as a great compliment.[8] In many Nigerian cultures, storytelling sessions took place in the evening under the moonlight, known as "tales by moonlight."[9] These sessions were not

5 Adesina Lukuman Azeez, "History and Evolution of Nollywood: A Look at Early and Late Influences" in *Nollywood in Glocal Perspective* (Springer, 2019) 3–24. https://link.springer.com/chapter/10.1007/978-3-030-30663-2_1 accessed 17 December 2024.

6 Uchenna Onuzulike, "Nollywood: Nigerian Videofilms as a Cultural and Technological Hybridity." (2009) 1 *Journal of African Cinemas* 1–20.

7 Joshua Usman, "Indigenous Narratives as Experimental Cinematic Texts in Nigerian Films." (2019) 29 *Southern African Journal for Folklore Studies* 21.

8 Bankole Sodipo, *Piracy and Counterfeiting: GATT, TRIPS and Developing Countries* (Kluwer Law International Ltd 1997) 48.

The indigenous system was based on a communal mode of ownership, which was different from the modern system of individual ownership under modern intellectual property and copyright law.

9 Sam Omotoso, "Storytelling: A Cherished Cultural Heritage in Nigeria." (1978) 55 *Language Arts* 724, https://www.jstor.org/stable/41404699 accessed 17 December 2024

merely for entertainment; they were an informal education system where elders passed down knowledge, values, and traditions to younger members of the community.

The Yoruba talking drum, for instance, played a significant role in these storytelling sessions.[10] It was capable of mimicking the tonal inflexions of the Yoruba language, thereby adding layers of meaning and emotion to the narratives. This musical element was integral to the storytelling tradition, enhancing the performative aspect and making the stories more engaging.

The narratives themselves were diverse, ranging from myths and legends to historical accounts and moral tales. The stories were dynamic, allowing each storyteller to adapt and embellish them based on the audience and the context.[11] This fluidity ensured that the stories remained relevant and resonant across different times and settings. Significantly, these stories were not attributed to any single author but were seen as the collective creation of the community. This concept of collective authorship stands in stark contrast to modern copyright laws, which emphasise individual ownership and exclusive rights.

2.2.2 *Performances in town halls and public squares*

The advent of colonial rule in the late 19th and early 20th centuries introduced significant changes to Nigerian society, including its storytelling traditions.[12] While colonial authorities often sought to suppress indigenous cultural practices, they also introduced new forms of entertainment and education that influenced traditional performance arts.[13] Schools and churches, established by colonial administrators and missionaries, became new venues for cultural expression. These institutions often incorporated elements of traditional storytelling into their activities, blending them with Western theatrical forms.

During this period, town halls and public squares emerged as important venues for performances. These spaces hosted masquerades, plays, and dramatised folklore, maintaining the interactive essence of traditional storytelling. The 1950s and 1960s saw the rise of travelling theatre troupes,

10 Adeyemi Oluwole, "The Role of the Talking Drum in Yoruba Oral Tradition." (2023) 12 *African Music Journal* 45.

11 Ibid., n 9.

12 Shaman Roy, "Colonial Legacy in Nigeria: Impacts on Society And Culture" (2024) https://www.afrodiscovery.com/country/nigeria/nigeria-history/colonial-legacy-in-nigeria-impacts-on-society-and-culture/ accessed 17 December 2024.

13 Afro Discovery, "Colonial Legacy in Nigeria: Impacts on Society And Culture" (2024) https://www.afrodiscovery.com/country/nigeria/nigeria-history/colonial-legacy-in-nigeria-impacts-on-society-and-culture/ accessed 17 December 2024.

such as the Alarinjo Theatre in the Yoruba region.[14] These troupes adapted traditional stories for larger audiences, using the new performance spaces provided by colonial infrastructure.[15] The performances were rich with music, dance, and drama, reflecting the multifaceted nature of Nigerian storytelling traditions.

Colonial influence also led to the formalisation of these performances. The introduction of Western education and Christian missionary activities brought new ideas and techniques that were integrated into traditional performances.[16] For example, the stagecraft, costumes, and narrative structures of Western theatre were incorporated into indigenous performances, creating a unique hybrid form of cultural expression.[17] This period marked the beginning of a cultural renaissance that laid the groundwork for the emergence of Nollywood.

2.2.3 Indigenous copyright practices

In traditional Nigerian societies, the concept of copyright was not formalised in the way it is today. Instead, there were customary practices that governed the ownership and dissemination of stories and performances. These practices were deeply rooted in the communal nature of storytelling and the collective ownership of cultural expressions.[18] One of the key principles of indigenous copyright practices was the recognition of the storyteller or performer as the custodian of the tale.[19] While stories and performances were considered communal assets, the custodian had the exclusive right to tell the story or perform the piece. This right was often passed down through generations, ensuring the continuity and preservation of the oral tradition.[20]

14 Smithsonian Institution, "Alarinjo: The Traditional Yoruba Travelling Theatre" (1978) https://www.si.edu/object/siris_sil_751517 accessed 17 December 2024.

15 Ibid., n. 13.

16 AZ Research Consult, "Role of Christian Missionaries in Shaping Early Formal Education in Nigeria" (2023) https://azresearchconsult.com.ng/project-role-of-christian-missionaries-in-shaping-early-formal-education-in-nigeria/ accessed 17 December 2024.

17 Adeyemi, Sola, "Aspects of Intercultural Performance Aesthetics in Femi Os` ofis ´ an's Drama." (2021) 11 *African Performance Review* 2, 7–27.

18 Shehu Ali, "Understanding the Nature of Folklore and Neighbouring Rights as Copyright Works in Nigeria" (2018) https://www.academia.edu/36615348/Understanding_The_Nature_Of_Folklore_And_Neighbouring_Rights_As_Copyright_Works_In_Nigeria accessed 18 December 2024.

19 Michael C. Ogwezzy, "Protection of Indigenous or Traditional Knowledge Under Intellectual Property Laws: an Examination of the Efficacy of Copyright Law, Trade Secret." (2012) *International and Comparative Law Review* 12(1), 5-34.

20 Kunle Ola, "Evolution and Future Trends of Copyright in Nigeria" in Brian Fitzgerald and John Gilchrist (eds), *Copyright Perspectives: Past, Present and Prospect* (Springer International Publishing 2015)

Customary copyright practices also included a form of moral rights, where the original creator of a story or performance was acknowledged and respected within the community.[21] If someone else wanted to tell the story or perform the piece, they needed to seek permission and give credit to the original creator.[22] This practice helped maintain the integrity of the cultural expression and ensured that the original creator's contribution was recognised. Another critical aspect of indigenous copyright practices was the communal responsibility to protect and preserve cultural heritage. Communities had mechanisms in place to safeguard their stories and performances from external appropriation or misuse. These mechanisms included oral agreements, communal sanctions, and social ostracism for those who violated the norms.[23] Such practices ensured that cultural expressions were respected and protected within the community.[24] However, as Nigerian society evolved and came into contact with Western legal systems, the need for formal copyright protection became increasingly apparent. The introduction of Western education and the influence of colonial rule brought about a shift in the perception of intellectual property.[25] This shift necessitated the development of legal frameworks to protect the rights of creators in a more formalised manner.[26]

The Nigerian Copyright Act, enacted in 1988 and subsequently amended, provides the legal framework for the protection of intellectual property in Nigeria. The Act defines the scope of copyright protection,[27] the rights of copyright owners,[28] and the remedies available for infringement.[29] It recognises both the economic and moral rights of authors and performers,[30] allowing them to control the use of their works and receive compensation for their use while also protecting their personal and reputational interests.[31] The Nigerian Copyright Act is significant for the

21 Ehusani Abel Simpa, "The Role of the Customary Court in Protecting Traditional Knowledge and Cultural Intellectual Property in Nigeria." (2022) 12 *Nigerian Journal of Intellectual Property* 34
22 Ibid.
23 Kunle Ola, "Evolution and Future Trends of Copyright in Nigeria," n. 20.
24 Ibid.
25 Oriakhogba Desmond, Oyewunmi Adejoke, Kur Joseph, Olubiyi Ifeoluwa, and Ayanleye Oluwakemi, "Intellectual Property Teaching and Research in Nigeria: Emerging Issues and Future Directions." (2023) 12 *Nigerian Journal of Intellectual Property* 45.
26 Ibid.
27 The Nigeria Copyright Act 2022, s 2.
28 The Nigeria Copyright Act 2022, s 28.
29 Nigeria Copyright Act 2022, s 37.
30 Nigeria Copyright Act 2022, s 66.
31 Nigeria Copyright Act 2022, s 16.

protection of traditional stories and performances.[32] It acknowledges the importance of safeguarding cultural heritage and provides a legal basis for protecting traditional cultural expressions. The Act also aligns with international conventions, such as the Berne Convention for the Protection of Literary and Artistic Works, to which Nigeria is a signatory.[33] This alignment ensures that Nigerian cultural expressions receive protection both domestically and internationally.[34]

Despite the existence of legal frameworks, challenges remain in effectively protecting traditional cultural expressions. One major challenge is the difficulty of enforcing copyright protection for oral traditions and communal performances. Unlike written works or recorded media, oral stories and live performances are often ephemeral and intangible, making it challenging to establish authorship and ownership. Additionally, the collective nature of traditional storytelling means that multiple individuals or communities may have a stake in a single work, complicating the issue of copyright ownership.

Another challenge is the tension between customary practices and formal legal systems. While the Nigerian Copyright Act provides a framework for the protection of intellectual property, it does not always align with the customary norms and practices of traditional societies. For example, the concept of individual authorship may conflict with the communal ownership of stories and performances in some cultures. This tension necessitates a nuanced approach to copyright protection that respects and integrates customary practices while providing formal legal recognition.

To address these challenges, there have been efforts to develop *sui generis* systems of protection for traditional cultural expressions. These systems are designed to complement existing copyright laws and provide tailored protection for traditional works. The World Intellectual Property Organization (WIPO) has been actively involved in promoting the development of such systems. Nigeria has participated in various international discussions on the protection of traditional knowledge and cultural expressions.[35]

32 S.P.A. Ajibade & Co, "A Review of the Nigerian Copyright Act 2022" (S.P.A. Ajibade & Co, 2024) https://spaajibade.com/a-review-of-the-nigerian-copyright-act-2022/ accessed 18 December 2024.

33 Sandra Eke, Franklin Okoro, and Kelson Emmanuel, "A Review of the Nigerian Copyright Act 2022" (Mondaq, 2023) https://www.mondaq.com/nigeria/copyright/1356178/a-review-of-the-nigerian-copyright-act-2022 accessed 18 December 2024.

34 Nigeria Copyright Act 2022, s 16.

35 World Intellectual Property Organization, "Intellectual Property and Traditional Cultural Expressions/Folklore" (2023) https://www.wipo.int/edocs/pubdocs/en/tk/913/wipo_pub_913.pd accessed 17 December 2024.

A *sui generis* system for the protection of traditional cultural expressions would involve recognising the collective ownership of cultural heritage and providing mechanisms for communities to assert their rights over their cultural assets. This could include the establishment of community registers, where traditional stories and performances are documented and recorded, providing a legal basis for their protection. Additionally, such a system could include provisions for benefit-sharing, ensuring that communities receive compensation for the use of their cultural expressions.

The Nigerian government and various cultural organisations have also made concerted efforts to support and promote traditional storytelling and performances. The National Council for Arts and Culture (NCAC), for instance, organises annual festivals and competitions that celebrate traditional arts and encourage the younger generation to engage with their cultural heritage.[36] These initiatives play a crucial role in preserving and revitalising Nigeria's rich cultural traditions.[37]

Moreover, educational institutions have integrated the study of traditional storytelling and performances into their curricula, ensuring that these practices are passed down to future generations.[38] Universities and cultural centres offer courses and workshops on traditional arts, providing students with opportunities to learn and appreciate their cultural heritage. These educational initiatives help bridge the gap between traditional and modern practices, fostering a deeper understanding and appreciation of Nigeria's cultural diversity.[39]

2.3 Transition to modern media

Colonialism and the advent of Western media and education had a major impact on Nigeria's shift to contemporary media. Indigenous Nigerian cultural practices were merged with Western forms of education, writing, and performance brought by British colonialists. Nigerian media was transformed by the advent of the printing press and radio broadcasting, which made it possible for ideas and stories to be shared more widely.

36 Just U Magazine, "The National Council for Arts and Culture (NCAC) Hosts the 2024 Edition of the National Festival of Arts and Culture (NAFEST)" (2024) https://justumagazine.com/events/the-national-council-for-arts-and-culture-ncac-host-the-2024-edition-of-the-national-festival-of-arts-and-culture-nafest/ accessed 17 December 2024.

37 Ibid., n. 33.

38 Nkechi Madubuko, "Integrating Traditional Storytelling in Nigerian Education: A Cultural Heritage Perspective." (2022) 14 *International Journal of Education and Development* 88.

39 Nigeria Copyright Act 2022, s 16.

2.3.1 *Early influences*

The transition from traditional oral storytelling and communal performances to modern media in Nigeria was significantly influenced by colonialism and the introduction of Western education and media. During the colonial period, British colonialists brought with them Western forms of education, literature, and performance, which began to merge with indigenous Nigerian cultural practices.[40] This period saw the establishment of schools and missionary activities that introduced new ways of thinking and new forms of artistic expression. One of the key influences during this period was the introduction of the printing press and the dissemination of printed literature.

The establishment of printing presses in Nigeria, such as the CMS (Church Missionary Society) Bookshop, facilitated the production and distribution of books, newspapers, and magazines.[41] This development allowed for the wider dissemination of stories and ideas, bridging the gap between oral traditions and written literature.

The introduction of radio broadcasting in the 1930s further revolutionised the landscape of Nigerian media.[42] Radio provided a platform for reaching a broad audience, transcending the limitations of literacy and geography. It became a powerful tool for education, information dissemination, and entertainment. Radio dramas and storytelling programmes became popular, blending traditional narratives with modern formats. For instance, the government-established Nigerian Broadcasting Service (NBS) aired programmes that featured local folklore and music, which helped to preserve and promote Nigerian cultural heritage.[43]

2.3.2 *Emergence of theatre and film*

The emergence of theatre and film in Nigeria marked a significant shift from live, communal performances to recorded media that could be distributed and consumed by a wider audience. The first Nigerian films were produced in the 1960s and 1970s, during the post-independence era, which was a time of national reawakening and cultural pride. Pioneers such as

40 Folasade R. Sulaiman, "Internationalization in Education: The British Colonial Policies on Education in Nigeria 1882–1926." (2012) 3 *Journal of Sociological Research* 22.

41 David Okunola, "The Oldest Bookshop in Nigeria: CMS Bookshop" (2023) https://blog-davidokunola.com/the-oldest-bookshop-in-nigeria/ accessed 17 December 2024.

42 AbdulWasiu Kuforiji, "History of Radio Broadcasting in Nigeria" (2022) https://nigerian-finder.com/history-of-radio-broadcasting-in-nigeria/ accessed 17 December 2024.

43 Mary Madaki, "Folktales Essential for Shaping the Younger Generation, Preserving Cultural Heritage" (2024) https://nbs.na.gov.ng/2024/11/07/folktales-essential-for-shaping-younger-generation-preserving-cultural-heritage/ accessed 17 December 2024.

Hubert Ogunde, Ola Balogun, and Moses Olaiya (Baba Sala) used film to tell Nigerian stories and address social issues.[44]

Hubert Ogunde, often referred to as the father of Nigerian theatre, established the Ogunde Theatre Party in the 1940s, which laid the foundation for modern Nigerian theatre and film.[45] Ogunde's productions were known for their rich cultural content and political themes, which resonated with the Nigerian audience. His work paved the way for other filmmakers and theatre practitioners to explore the medium of film. Ogunde's film "Aiye" (1979) was a significant milestone in Nigerian cinema, blending traditional storytelling with modern filmmaking techniques.[46] Ola Balogun, a prominent Nigerian filmmaker, was instrumental in the development of the Nigerian film industry.[47] His films, such as "Ajani Ogun" (1976) and "Ija Ominira" (1978), were among the first to gain widespread recognition.[48] Balogun's work highlighted the potential of film as a medium for cultural expression and social commentary. His collaboration with French filmmakers and the use of 16mm film technology introduced new techniques and standards to Nigerian cinema.

The Yoruba travelling theatre tradition, known as the "Alarinjo" theatre, also played a crucial role in the evolution of Nigerian cinema.[49] These travelling theatre troupes, which performed in various towns and villages, began to adapt their stage performances into film. This transition was driven by the desire to reach a larger audience and preserve their performances for posterity. The Alarinjo Theater's emphasis on improvisation, music, and dance influenced the storytelling style of early Nigerian films.[50] The establishment of the National Theatre in Lagos in 1976 provided a significant boost to the Nigerian performing arts.[51] The National Theatre became a hub for cultural activities, hosting theatrical performances, film screenings, and other artistic events. It served as a platform for Nigerian

44 Afrocritik, "Moses Olaiya's Mosebolatan Heralded an Age for Comedy in the Nigerian Film Industry" (2023) https://www.afrocritik.com/moses-olaiyas-mosebolatan-heralded-an-age-for-comedy-in-the-nigerian-film-industry/ accessed 17 December 2024.

45 Oluwatosin Enesi, "Ogunde, The Father of Nigerian Theatre" (2022) https://broadcastersint.com/ogunde-the-father-of-nigerian-theatre/ accessed 17 December 2024.

46 Aduku, Armstrong Idachaba, "Elements of Traditional African Drama in Contemporary Nigerian Video-Film. The Performer." (2018) *Ilorin Journal of the Performing* Arts 9.

47 Akoroko, "Ola Balogun: Where Are the Nigerian Cinema Pioneer's Films?" (2023) https://akoroko.com/ola-balogun-where-are-his-films/ accessed 17 December 2024.

48 Ibid.

49 Ibid.

50 Ibid.

51 The Cable, "National Arts Theatre: The Rebirth of a National Monument by Bankers' Committee" (2024) https://www.thecable.ng/national-arts-theatre-the-rebirth-of-a-national-monument-by-bankers-committee/ accessed 17 December 2024

artists to showcase their talents and connect with audiences, further promoting the growth of theatre and film in the country.[52]

2.3.3 *Informal copyright norms*

In the early days of Nigerian theatre and film, there were no formal copyright laws in place to protect the intellectual property of creators.[53] Instead, informal norms governed the use and distribution of creative works. These norms were rooted in traditional practices, where stories and performances were communal assets rather than individual property. However, as the film industry began to grow, the need for formal copyright protection became increasingly apparent.

Customary practices in traditional Nigerian society played a crucial role in the management of intellectual property. Storytelling was a communal activity, and the ownership of stories was often collective.[54] This communal approach to intellectual property posed challenges when traditional stories and performances began to be adapted into modern media formats, which required more formalised copyright protection to prevent unauthorised use and ensure that creators received fair compensation.

Before the enactment of formal copyright laws, Nigerian filmmakers and theatre practitioners relied on community recognition and respect to protect their works.[55] For example, it was customary for performers and storytellers to acknowledge the original creator of a story or performance when retelling or adapting it. This practice served as a form of moral rights, ensuring that the original creator received credit and recognition for their work.[56] However, as the Nigerian film industry began to grow and attract commercial interest, the limitations of these informal copyright norms became evident. Filmmakers and theatre practitioners faced challenges in protecting their works from unauthorised copying and distribution. The absence of formal copyright protection meant that creators had limited legal recourse in cases of infringement.[57]

52 Ibid.
53 Chudi Ojukwu, "The Role of Copyright in the Protection of the Nigerian Entertainment Industry" (2022) https://sabilaw.org/the-role-of-copyright-in-the-protection-of-the-nigeria-entertainment-industry/ accessed 17 December 2024.
54 Nneka Chioma Ezedum, "Protection of Traditional Knowledge and its Relevance to National Economic Growth and Development in Nigeria." (2022) 17 *The Nigerian Juridical Review.*
55 Gloria Ernest-Samuel, "A Historical Study of the Nigerian Film Industry and Its Challenges" (2021) https://www.academia.edu/73128390/A_Historical_Study_of_the_Nigerian_Film_Industry_and_Its_Challenges accessed 17 December 2024.
56 Ibid.
57 Ibid.

The need for formal copyright protection became more pronounced with the advent of video technology in the 1980s. The introduction of affordable video cameras and VHS tapes revolutionised the Nigerian film industry, leading to the proliferation of home video production. This period marked the birth of what is now known as Nollywood, the Nigerian film industry. Nollywood films, often produced on low budgets and distributed directly to consumers through video cassettes, became immensely popular.

The informal distribution networks, known as "marketers," played a crucial role in the growth of Nollywood. These marketers financed film productions and distributed the finished products to a wide audience.[58] To address the challenges posed by the lack of formal copyright protection, the Nigerian government enacted the Nigerian Copyright Act in 1988.[59] The Act provided a legal framework for the protection of intellectual property rights, including the rights of filmmakers and other creative artists. The Nigerian Copyright Commission (NCC) was established to administer and enforce copyright laws, ensuring that creators received fair compensation for their works.[60]

The Nigerian Copyright Act of 1988 was later replaced by the Copyright Act of 2022, which provides a more comprehensive and updated legal framework for the protection of intellectual property in Nigeria.[61] The 2022 Act defines the scope of copyright protection, the rights of copyright owners, and the remedies available for infringement.[62] It recognises both the economic and moral rights of authors and performers, allowing them to control the use of their works and receive compensation for their use, while also protecting their personal and reputational interests.[63] The Act also includes provisions for the protection of traditional cultural expressions, ensuring that Nigeria's rich cultural heritage is safeguarded.[64]

Despite the existence of formal copyright laws, challenges remain in effectively enforcing copyright protection in the Nigerian film industry. Piracy continues to be a significant issue, with pirated copies of Nollywood

58 Jade L. Miller, "Nollywood Central: The Nigerian Videofilm Industry." (2016) 13 *Journal of Communication*, 771–773.

59 Isochukwu, "A Brief History of Copyright Law" (2018) https://isochukwu.com/2018/06/19/a-brief-history-of-copyright-law/ accessed 17 December 2024.

60 Ibid.

61 Templars Law, "A New Dawn for Copyright Protection in Nigeria" (2023) https://www.templars-law.com/app/uploads/2023/06/A-New-Dawn-for-Copyright-Protection-in-Nigeria-Final.pdf accessed 17 December 2024.

62 The Nigeria Copyright Act 2022, s 37.

63 Oriakhogba Desmond, Oyewunmi Adejoke, Kur Joseph, Olubiyi Ifeoluwa, and Ayanleye Oluwakemi, "Intellectual Property Teaching and Research in Nigeria: Emerging Issues and Future Directions." (2023) 12 *Nigerian Journal of Intellectual Property* 45.

64 The Nigeria Copyright Act 2022, s 74.

films widely available both in Nigeria and internationally.[65] The NCC has implemented various measures to combat piracy, including public awareness campaigns, enforcement actions, and collaboration with international organisations. However, the pervasive nature of piracy in Nollywood and the informal distribution networks make it difficult to fully eradicate the problem.[66]

2.4 Reconciling cultural heritage and copyright: challenges and opportunities

The Copyright Act 2022 serves as a cornerstone for intellectual property regulation in Nigeria, particularly in its efforts to reconcile traditional cultural expressions with modern copyright law.[67] Customary practices, including storytelling, communal performances, and folklore, form the foundation of much of Nigeria's creative output.[68] However, the transition of these practices into the regulated framework of copyright law presents unique challenges, especially as these works increasingly inspire Nollywood productions. The Act recognises the importance of safeguarding cultural heritage while providing avenues for creators and communities to benefit from their contributions.[69] This analysis explores the Act's provisions, highlighting its protections, limitations, and areas for improvement in addressing customary practices.

Section 74 of the Copyright Act 2022 explicitly acknowledges expressions of folklore as a category of protected works.[70] Folklore, defined as literary, artistic, and musical creations rooted in traditional culture and collectively owned by a community, is afforded legal recognition and

65 Obinna Tony-Francis Ochem, "How the Nigerian Government Loses Money Annually Due to Intellectual Property Rights Violations in the Music and Film Industry" (2024) https://nairametrics.com/2024/12/18/how-nigerian-government-loses-money-annually-due-to-intellectual-property-rights-violations-in-the-music-and-film-industry/ accessed 17 December 2024.

66 Niyi Akimolayan, "Piracy in Nollywood: Accessibility and the Industry's Real Challenge" (2024) https://www.pulse.ng/articles/entertainment/movies/piracy-in-nollywood-niyi-akimolayans-take-on-accessibility-and-the-industrys-real-challenge-2024120907132835036 accessed 18 December 2024.

67 Nigerian Copyright Commission, "Copyright Act 2022: Bridging Traditional and Modern Intellectual Property Laws" (2023) https://www.copyright.gov.ng/CopyrightAct/CopyrightAct2023FinalPublication1.pdf accessed 18 December 2024.

68 Kelechi C. Samuel, "Authentic Creativity: How Two Segments of Nigeria's Cultural and Creative Economy are Promoting and Redefining Nigeria." (2022) *Journal of Creative Industries Studies*, https://jocis.org/wp-content/uploads/2022/02/JOCIS_5_Samuel.pdf accessed 18 December 2024.

69 Nigeria Copyright Act 2022, s 74.

70 Ibid.

protection.[71] Section 74 of the Act provides the means through which folklore can be expressed to include:

a. Folklore, folk poetry, and folk riddles;
b. Folk songs and instrumental folk music;
c. Folk dances and folk plays; and
d. Productions of folk arts, in particular, drawings, paintings, carvings, sculptures, pottery, terracotta, mosaics, woodwork, metalware, jewellery, handicrafts, costumes, and indigenous textiles.

The Act stipulates that expressions of folklore are safeguarded against unauthorised use, with any commercial exploitation requiring prior approval from the Nigerian Copyright Commission (NCC) or other designated authorities. This provision signifies an important shift in Nigeria's legal landscape, emphasising the economic and cultural value of traditional works. By criminalising unauthorised exploitation under Section 75, the Act also establishes a deterrent against the misappropriation of cultural heritage. However, while these provisions are commendable, the Act leaves critical gaps in implementation. For example, the mechanisms for determining the rightful custodians of folklore and distributing royalties remain underdeveloped. When Nollywood producers adapt traditional tales into commercial films, there is often no clear legal pathway for compensating the originating communities. This creates a scenario where folklore is commercialised without ensuring that the benefits flow back to its cultural custodians.

Customary practices in Nigeria operate on principles fundamentally different from those underlying modern copyright law. Traditional storytelling, moonlight tales, and other communal performances are typically seen as collective creations with no single author or owner.[72] These works are part of the cultural commons, shared freely within and between communities. In contrast, the Copyright Act 2022 emphasises individual or corporate ownership.[73] Section 28 of the Act provides that copyright initially vests in the author of a work or, in cases where the work is created under a contract, in the entity commissioning it. This framework does not easily accommodate the communal and collaborative nature of traditional creative expressions.

Although Section 29 addresses collective works, its application is limited to those created under the direction or supervision of an individual or

71 Ibid.
72 Adebola Y. Adebajo, 'Revisiting Moonlight Storytelling for Reclaiming Foundational Traditional Yoruba Culture in Nigeria' (2022)_LASU Journal of African Studies 60..
73 Nigeria Copyright Act 2022, s 28.

entity. This definition excludes the organic and iterative processes through which folklore and other traditional works are developed. Consequently, traditional expressions may fall outside the protective scope of copyright law, leaving them vulnerable to misappropriation. These limitations underscore the need for a more nuanced approach that recognises communal authorship and provides specific mechanisms for protecting such works.

Another critical distinction between traditional and statutory frameworks lies in the duration of protection. Copyright protection for literary, musical, and artistic works under Section 19 of the Act typically lasts for 70 years after the author's death. In contrast, expressions of folklore are protected perpetually under Section 74, reflecting their status as intergenerational cultural assets. This perpetual protection ensures that traditional works cannot be freely exploited long after their original custodians have passed, preserving their cultural significance for future generations.

While perpetual protection is a step forward, the Act does not establish a clear process for cataloguing or registering folklore. Without such systems, enforcement of protections becomes difficult, especially in cases where traditional works inspire commercial adaptations. For instance, Nollywood producers often draw on folktales, proverbs, and traditional music for their films.[74] The absence of a formal registry or database of folklore complicates efforts to monitor and regulate these uses, potentially leaving communities without recourse for unauthorised adaptations. A structured approach to documenting folklore would strengthen the Act's ability to safeguard these works.

The Copyright Act also introduces comprehensive measures to address infringement, which are critical for protecting traditional expressions. Section 36 prohibits the unauthorised reproduction, distribution, or adaptation of copyrighted works, including folklore. These provisions provide legal remedies for communities and other rights holders when their works are exploited without permission. However, enforcement remains a significant challenge, particularly for folklore. Many traditional works have already been adapted into films, music, and other media without authorisation, often due to a lack of awareness among both creators and communities about their rights under the Act.[75]

74 Usman Joshua, "Folktale as Material Resources for Movie Production in Selected Nollywood Movies." (2013) *International Journal of English and Literature* https://academicjournals.org/journal/IJEL/article-full-text-pdf/097291A5228 accessed 18 December 2024.

75 1st Attorneys, "Critical Analysis of the 2022 Nigeria Copyright Act" (2024) https://1stattorneys.com/articles/2024/10/24/critical-analysis-of-the-2022-nigeria-copyright-act/ accessed 18 December 2024.

The Nigerian Copyright Commission plays a pivotal role in administering the protections outlined in the Act. Section 74 grants the NCC authority to regulate the use and licensing of folklore, ensuring that benefits derived from these works are equitably distributed. Additionally, the NCC is tasked with promoting collective management organisations (CMOs) under Section 88, which can facilitate the administration of royalties and licensing fees for folklore. While CMOs offer a potential solution for managing the commercial use of traditional works, their operations are often limited to urban centres, leaving many rural communities excluded. Strengthening the NCC's capacity to reach underserved areas and ensuring that communities are actively involved in the management of their cultural assets are critical for the effective implementation of these provisions.

The Act also provides exceptions to copyright under Section 20, allowing certain uses of protected works without prior authorisation. These exceptions include fair dealing for purposes such as education, research, and private use. However, the application of these exceptions to folklore remains ambiguous. For example, Nollywood filmmakers might argue that adapting a folktale for a film constitutes fair dealing, particularly if the adaptation is intended for educational or cultural preservation purposes. Such interpretations could undermine the protections afforded to folklore under the Act. Clear guidelines on the scope of exceptions, particularly in relation to traditional works, are necessary to prevent misuse while allowing legitimate uses.

While the Copyright Act 2022 makes significant strides in protecting expressions of folklore,[76] it falls short in several areas. One major limitation is the lack of specific provisions for ensuring that communities benefit financially from the commercial use of their cultural expressions. The Act's reliance on the NCC to oversee licensing and royalties is a positive step, but without explicit mechanisms for identifying and compensating communities, these protections remain theoretical. Moreover, the Act does not address the challenges of enforcing copyright protections for folklore at the international level. Nollywood films based on Nigerian folktales are often adapted or distributed abroad without proper authorisation, highlighting the need for stronger international agreements and collaboration.[77]

To address these gaps, several reforms are recommended. First, the development of a formal registry or database for expressions of folklore would provide a clear record of protected works and their communities of origin. This would facilitate the licensing process and ensure that benefits

76 Ibid., n. 68.

77 Babatunde Stephen Maku & Edith Ugochi Ohaja, "Adoption of Foreign Production Aesthetics in Nigerian Films as a Form of Cultural Imperialism: Evidence from Three Selected Nollywood Movies." (2024) 2 *IJSSAR* 1.

are distributed equitably. Second, the NCC should prioritise community education initiatives to raise awareness about copyright protections and the rights of communities under the Act. By empowering communities with knowledge, the NCC can enhance their ability to advocate for fair compensation. Third, the adoption of a *sui generis* legal framework for folklore would provide tailored protections that better align with the communal nature of these works. Such a framework could draw on international examples, such as India's protection of traditional knowledge and Brazil's indigenous cultural heritage laws.[78] Finally, the Nigerian government should strengthen its engagement with international copyright organisations to advocate for the inclusion of folklore in global intellectual property treaties.

The Copyright Act 2022 represents a significant step forward in recognising and protecting Nigeria's cultural heritage. Its provisions for expressions of folklore highlight the importance of safeguarding traditional works while enabling their commercial potential. However, the Act's effectiveness depends on addressing the practical challenges of enforcement, community involvement, and international collaboration.[79] By building on the foundation established by the Act and implementing targeted reforms, Nigeria can ensure that its rich cultural traditions are preserved and fairly compensated in the modern creative economy.

2.5 Comparative analysis: Hollywood, Nollywood, and Bollywood

The emergence of the film industries of Hollywood, Bollywood, and Nollywood represents different trajectories of cultural and economic development. Hollywood is renowned for its global dominance in high-budget films,[80] Bollywood for its cultural integration with music and traditions,[81] and Nollywood for its grassroots-driven, fast-paced

78 Maria Laura Viveiros de Castro Cavalcanti, "The Legal Protection of the Intangible Cultural Heritage in Brazil" (2019) https://link.springer.com/chapter/10.1007/978-3-319-72983-1_2 accessed 18 December 2024.

79 1st Attorneys, "Critical Analysis of the 2022 Nigeria Copyright Act" (2024) https://1stattorneys.com/articles/2024/10/24/critical-analysis-of-the-2022-nigeria-copyright-act/ accessed 17 December 2024.

80 John Wihbey, "The Changing Role of Hollywood in the Global Movie Market." (2013) *Journal of Media Economics* https://journalistsresource.org/economics/changing-role-hollywoodglobal-movie-market/ accessed 17 December 2024.

81 Rashmi Sharma, "Bollywood Music Industry: Evolution, Trends, and Cultural Impact." (2021) 4 *IJAMSR* 11, 28 https://ijamsr.com/issues/6_Volume%204_Issue%2011/20240712_071328_Dr.%20Rashmi%20Sharma%202021.pdf accessed 17 December 2024

production.[82] This comparative analysis evaluates their production and distribution systems, copyright regulations, and the cultural roles they play, with particular reference to Nigeria's Copyright Act, 2022.

2.5.1 Production and distribution

Hollywood is characterised by large-scale productions, extensive use of advanced technology, and vast resources. Films such as *Avatar* or *The Avengers* have budgets exceeding $200 million.[83] The United States' robust legal frameworks, including the Copyright Act of 1976 and amendments under the Digital Millennium Copyright Act (DMCA), provide mechanisms for protecting intellectual property through strict copyright terms, usually extending up to 70 years posthumously for creators.[84] Distribution involves global marketing campaigns and reliance on cinema chains, streaming platforms, and merchandise sales.

Conversely, Bollywood, India's Hindi-language film industry, blends high-volume productions with cultural storytelling.[85] While Bollywood produces over 1,600 films annually, its budgets often fall short of Hollywood's, averaging $1.5–$15 million per film.[86] Bollywood relies heavily on domestic markets, where music rights alone can generate 5–10% of a film's revenue.[87] India's Copyright Act of 1957, modernised by amendments in 2012, includes provisions that protect creators from exploitation by production houses.[88] However, Bollywood remains vulnerable to piracy, with losses estimated at $2.8 billion annually.[89]

82 Jade L. Miller, "Nollywood Central: The Nigerian Videofilm Industry." (2016) 13 *Journal of Communication*, 771–773.
83 Y.M. Cinema Magazine, "Hollywood's Future: How AI and New Technology Are Transforming the Industry" (2024) https://ymcinema.com/2024/10/31/hollywoods-future-how-ai-and-new-technology-are-transforming-the-industry/ accessed 17 December 2024
84 US Copyright Office, "Copyright Law of the United States" (2022) https://www.copyright.gov/title17/ accessed 17 December 2024.
85 Moments Log, "Indian Cinema: Bollywood's Impact and Regional Film Industries" (2023) https://www.momentslog.com/culture/indian-cinema-bollywoods-impact-and-regional-film-industries accessed 17 December 2024.
86 Evonne Leanna Davids, "The Evolution of Film Genres: A Comparative Analysis of Hollywood and Bollywood." (2023) 2 *Art and Society* 15 https://www.paradigmpress.org/as/article/download/736/628 accessed 18 December 2024.
87 Soundcharts, "Indian Music Industry: Market Stats, Analysis, & 2020 Trends" (2022) https://soundcharts.com/blog/india-music-market-overview accessed 17 December 2024.
88 India Copyright Act, 1957, s 18
89 EY and the Internet and Mobile Association of India (IAMAI), "The Rob Report" (2023) https://economictimes.indiatimes.com/industry/media/entertainment/indian-entertainment-industry-lost-rs-22400-cr-to-piracy-in-2023-ey-iamai-report/articleshow/114503950.cms accessed 17 December 2024

Nollywood, Nigeria's film industry, produces over 2,500 films annually, making it the most prolific globally.[90] Unlike Hollywood's blockbuster model or Bollywood's cultural extravagance, Nollywood emphasises rapid, low-budget production, with films often made for $10,000–$25,000.[91] Initially distributed via DVDs and VCDs, the industry now increasingly relies on digital platforms like Netflix and IrokoTV. The recent Copyright Act 2022 aims to modernise protection mechanisms by addressing issues such as online piracy and performers' rights. Notably, Section 19(1) of the Act sets the copyright duration for audiovisual works at 50 years post-publication, aligning Nigeria with global standards.[92]

2.5.2 Copyright laws

Copyright legislation in Hollywood, Bollywood, and Nollywood reflects their economic and cultural priorities. In the United States, copyright protection is enshrined in the Constitution (Article I, Section 8) and further developed under the United States Copyright Act of 1976. The law grants creators exclusive rights to reproduce, distribute, and perform their works. The DMCA (1998) introduced anti-circumvention measures for digital works, which became critical with the rise of streaming platforms such as Netflix and Disney+. Enforcement mechanisms include statutory damages ranging between $750 and $30,000 per infringement, with provisions for higher penalties in cases of wilful infringement.[93]

India's Copyright Act 1957 includes protections for artistic, literary, and cinematographic works.[94] Amendments in 2012 strengthened moral rights for creators, mandating that authors receive royalties when their works are adapted or performed. However, Bollywood faces challenges in enforcement, as piracy persists despite strict provisions, such as imprisonment of up to three years and fines of up to INR 200,000 for copyright violations.[95] Nollywood's growth has been hampered by weak enforcement of copyright laws and widespread piracy.

90 Ibid.

91 Destiny M. George, "How Nollywood Is Shaping the African Film Industry" https://kashgain.net/blog/how-nollywood-is-shaping-the-african-film-industry/ accessed 18 December 2024.

92 The Nigerian Copyright Act, 2022.

93 Ayush Tiwari, "The Digital Millennium Copyright Act, 1998" https://blog.ipleaders.in/the-digital-millennium-copyright-act-1998/ accessed 18 December 2024.

94 The Copyright Act, 1957, India Code, s 13.

95 Gururaj D. Devarhublia and Anjani Singh Tomarb, "A Critical Study on Copyright Violations in the Indian Entertainment Industry in the Internet Age." (2021) 12 *Turkish Online Journal of Qualitative Inquiry* 1, 1084–1092 https://tojqi.net/index.php/journal/article/download/1342/654/1484 accessed 18 December 2024.

The Copyright Act of 2022, however, introduces several reforms aimed at modernising the legal landscape. Section 15 addresses equitable remuneration for the broadcasting of sound recordings, while Section 50 tackles technological protection measures to prevent unauthorised copying or distribution. Moreover, Section 74 emphasises the protection of expressions of folklore, ensuring that Nigeria's cultural heritage, deeply embedded in Nollywood narratives, is safeguarded.

2.5.3 Cultural expression and storytelling

Hollywood represents Western ideals of individuality and heroism, often catering to a global audience by universalising themes.[96] Its cultural export, driven by "soft power," influences global perceptions of the United States. For example, superhero franchises like Marvel dominate international box offices while subtly promoting American values.[97] Bollywood, by contrast, serves as a cultural anchor for the Indian diaspora. Themes of family, religion, and morality dominate narratives, often delivered through musicals that reflect India's diverse traditions. Bollywood's success in reaching over 90 countries, including Africa, highlights its role in preserving and promoting Indian culture globally.[98]

Nollywood distinguishes itself by prioritising local narratives rooted in African traditions and contemporary societal issues. Films like *Living in Bondage* (1992) and *The Wedding Party* (2016) explore themes of corruption, love, and cultural identity.[99] Folklore and oral storytelling traditions, historically performed in town halls and moonlit gatherings, heavily influence Nollywood's scripts.[100] The Copyright Act of 2022, particularly Section 74, ensures that these expressions of folklore are protected from exploitation.

Hollywood, Bollywood, and Nollywood represent three distinct models of filmmaking, each shaped by unique cultural, economic, and legal contexts. While Hollywood epitomises commercial success and technological

96 Scott R. Olson, "The Globalization of Hollywood." (2000) XVII *International Journal on World Peace* 4, 3–12.

97 Danielle Han, "The MCU: A Tale of American Exceptionalism" https://daily.jstor.org/the-mcu-a-tale-of-american-exceptionalism/ accessed 18 December 2024.

98 Lorna Stevens, "Bollywood Cinema's Global Reach: Consuming the 'Diasporic Consciousness'." (2012) *Journal of Macromarketing* https://www.academia.edu/107676483/Bollywood_Cinema_s_Global_Reach accessed 18 December 2024.

99 Jonathan Haynes, "Living in Bondage: Money and Values" in *Nollywood: The Creation of Nigerian Film Genres* (Chicago Scholarship Online, 2016) 18–58.

100 Joshua Usman, "Indigenous Narratives as Experimental Cinematic Texts in Nigerian Films." (2019) *Southern African Journal for Folklore Studies* https://journals.co.za/doi/pdf/10.25159/2663-6697/4228 accessed 18 December 2024.

advancement, Bollywood celebrates cultural resilience, and Nollywood exemplifies innovation born of necessity. As Nollywood matures, the Copyright Act 2022 positions it to address longstanding challenges such as piracy and copyright enforcement while safeguarding Nigeria's cultural identity. By learning from the successes and failures of Hollywood and Bollywood, Nollywood can chart a path towards sustainable growth on the global stage.

2.6 Current developments and future directions

Nollywood, the Nigerian film industry, has experienced significant technological advancements in recent years, transforming the way films are produced, distributed, and consumed.[101] These advancements have had a profound impact on copyright practices and enforcement, addressing longstanding challenges while also introducing new complexities.

The advent of digital technology has revolutionised film production in Nollywood. High-definition digital cameras, sophisticated editing software, and improved sound recording equipment have elevated the quality of Nollywood films, making them more competitive on the global stage. The use of advanced technology, such as drones for aerial shots and digital effects, has further enhanced production standards. Digital technology has also democratised filmmaking, allowing independent filmmakers to create high-quality content with relatively low budgets.[102]

The proliferation of internet and mobile technology has facilitated the online streaming of Nollywood films, extending their reach to a global audience. Platforms like Netflix, YouTube, and IROKOtv have provided wider distribution networks and created new revenue streams for filmmakers through subscription services and advertising. Netflix, in particular, has made substantial investments in Nollywood, commissioning original Nigerian content and acquiring distribution rights for popular films. This shift to digital distribution has necessitated changes in copyright practices to protect the intellectual property of filmmakers in the digital age.[103]

101 Disciplines NG, "The Impact of Technology on the Nigerian Film Industry" (2024) https://disciplines.ng/impact-of-technology-on-film-industry/ accessed 17 December 2024.

102 Gourav Gill and Rahul Tiwari, "The Impact of Digital Technology on Film Production & Distribution." (2023) *International Journal of Novel Research and Development*, https://www.ijnrd.org/papers/IJNRD2306628.pdf accessed 18 December 2024.

103 Deborah Dan-Awoh, "Top Nigerian Producers That Worked with Netflix's Over $23M Funding in 8 Years" (2024) https://nairametrics.com/2024/12/08/top-nigerian-producers-that-worked-with-netflixs-over-23m-funding-in-8-years/ accessed 18 December 2024.

One notable technological advancement is the use of digital piracy detection tools. These tools help filmmakers identify and take down pirated copies of their films from the internet, thereby protecting their intellectual property rights. Blockchain technology is also being explored as a means to secure film distribution and ensure that filmmakers receive fair compensation. Blockchain provides a transparent and immutable ledger of film transactions, making it easier to track the distribution and ownership of digital content. Despite these advancements, piracy remains a significant challenge for Nollywood.[104]

2.6.1 *Policy recommendations*

To address the ongoing challenges faced by Nollywood and support its growth, several policy recommendations can be considered:

2.6.1.1 *Enhanced enforcement mechanisms*

The NCC should be equipped with modern tools and sufficient resources to combat piracy effectively. This includes training personnel in digital forensics and increasing collaboration with international copyright enforcement agencies. The establishment of specialised courts to handle copyright infringement cases could expedite the legal process and ensure that justice is served swiftly. Additionally, the NCC should work closely with law enforcement agencies to conduct raids and crack down on street vendors selling pirated copies of Nollywood films. Given the global nature of digital piracy, international cooperation is crucial. Collaborating with organisations like WIPO and Interpol can help Nigeria adopt best practices and benefit from global intelligence and enforcement strategies.[105]

2.6.1.2 *Public awareness campaigns*

Educating the public about the impact of piracy on the film industry and the importance of respecting intellectual property rights can help reduce piracy. Awareness campaigns can be conducted through traditional media, social media, and community outreach programmes. These campaigns should emphasise the economic and cultural importance of Nollywood, highlighting how piracy undermines the industry and affects the livelihoods of those involved. Partnerships with schools, universities, and community organisations can also help in spreading the message more effectively.

104 Ibid.
105 World Intellectual Property Organization, "Nigeria Validates National IP Policy and Strategy (NIPPS)" (22 September 2022) https://www.wipo.int/about-wipo/en/offices/nigeria/news/2022/news_0002.html accessed 18 December 2024.

Celebrities and influencers within the film industry can play a significant role in raising awareness and promoting anti-piracy messages.[106]

2.6.1.3 *Support for filmmakers*

Government and private sector initiatives can provide financial support and incentives for filmmakers to adopt new technologies and improve the quality of their productions. This includes grants, low-interest loans, and tax incentives. Establishing film development funds and incubation centres can foster innovation and creativity, helping filmmakers to experiment with new ideas and techniques without the immediate pressure of commercial success. Additionally, providing training and capacity-building programmes can help filmmakers stay abreast of the latest technological advancements and best practices in the industry. Partnerships with international film schools and organisations can facilitate knowledge transfer and expose Nigerian filmmakers to global standards and trends.

2.6.1.4 *Collaboration with international platforms*

Partnering with global streaming platforms can provide Nollywood films with wider distribution and greater protection against piracy. These platforms often have sophisticated anti-piracy measures that can help safeguard Nigerian films. Collaborations can also extend to co-productions, where Nigerian filmmakers work with international counterparts to create content that appeals to a global audience. Nollywood's global reach necessitates international cooperation to protect Nigerian filmmakers' rights abroad. Nigeria should leverage bilateral agreements and multilateral treaties, as recognised under Sections 8 and 78 of the Copyright Act 2022, to secure protection in international markets.

2.6.1.5 *Innovation and technology integration*

Encouraging the integration of new technologies in film production and distribution can drive Nollywood's growth. Innovations such as virtual reality (VR), augmented reality (AR), and artificial intelligence (AI) can create immersive storytelling experiences and attract a broader audience.[107]

106 "Funke Akindele Urges Fans to Fight Piracy Ahead of New Film Release" (2024) https://punchng.com/video-funke-akindele-urges-fans-to-fight-piracy-ahead-of-new-film-release/ accessed 18 December 2024

107 Valentina Nisi et al., "Inclusive Digital Storytelling: Artificial Intelligence and Augmented Reality to Re-Centre Stories from the Margins" (Interactive Storytelling Conference, 2023) https://link.springer.com/chapter/10.1007/978-3-031-47655-6_8 accessed 18 December 2024.

Government and industry stakeholders should invest in research and development to explore the potential of these technologies and provide the necessary infrastructure and support for their adoption. Additionally, the establishment of tech hubs and innovation centres can facilitate collaboration between filmmakers and tech experts, leading to the development of cutting-edge solutions for the film industry.[108]

2.6.2 *Cultural preservation: balancing innovation with respect for traditional storytelling*

As Nollywood continues to grow and evolve, it is essential to balance innovation with the preservation of traditional storytelling practices. Many Nollywood films draw on Nigerian folklore, myths, and cultural heritage, which are valuable aspects of the nation's identity. Efforts should be made to document and archive traditional stories and performances to ensure they are not lost in the digital age. Institutions like the National Film and Video Censors Board (NFVCB) and the Nigerian Film Corporation (NFC) can play a pivotal role in this regard by establishing digital archives and encouraging filmmakers to explore and reinterpret traditional narratives.[109]

Additionally, filmmakers should be encouraged to incorporate cultural elements into their productions, promoting a sense of national pride and identity. This can be supported through initiatives that recognise and reward films that celebrate Nigerian culture and traditions. Awards and festivals that focus on culturally significant films can help promote this agenda, while educational programmes and workshops can inspire the next generation of filmmakers to appreciate and preserve their cultural heritage.[110]

Education plays a critical role in cultural preservation. By integrating the study of Nigerian folklore, history, and traditional arts into school curricula, young Nigerians can develop a deeper appreciation for their cultural heritage. Film schools and training institutes can also incorporate modules on traditional storytelling techniques, encouraging students to

108 Camoin Associates, "The Role of Technology Hubs in Fostering Innovation and Economic Development" (2023) https://fastercapital.com/content/Innovation-and-Technology-Hub--The-Role-of-Technology-Hubs-in-Fostering-Innovation-and-Economic-Development.htmlaccessed 18 December 2024.

109 Adediran Kayode Ademiju-Bepo and Solomon Idyo, "Nollywood and the Challenge of Digital Archiving and Preservation in the Digital Era." (2023) 23 *Nigerian Theatre Journal* 1 https://www.ajol.info/index.php/ntj/article/download/266545/251520 accessed 18 December 2024.

110 Vejune Zemaityte et al., "Quantifying the Global Film Festival Circuit: Networks, Diversity, and Public Value Creation." (2024) *PLOS ONE* https://journals.plos.org/plosone/article?id=10.1371/journal.pone.0297404 accessed 18 December 2024.

experiment with blending these methods with modern filmmaking practices. Collaborations between educational institutions and the film industry can lead to the development of programmes and projects that celebrate and preserve Nigeria's cultural legacy.[111]

Community engagement is another critical aspect of cultural preservation. By involving local communities in the filmmaking process and giving them a platform to tell their stories, filmmakers can create authentic representations of Nigerian culture. Community-based film projects can provide opportunities for local talent to participate in film production and help preserve traditional knowledge and practices. These projects can also promote social cohesion and create a sense of ownership and pride among community members.

Furthermore, partnerships between Nollywood and cultural institutions such as museums, cultural centres, and heritage sites can enhance efforts to preserve traditional storytelling practices. Collaborative initiatives can include film screenings, exhibitions, and workshops that highlight the cultural significance of traditional narratives. These partnerships can also facilitate the exchange of knowledge and resources, ensuring that both the film industry and cultural institutions work together to safeguard Nigeria's rich heritage.

Finally, the Nigerian government can play a significant role in cultural preservation by enacting policies and providing funding to support initiatives that celebrate and preserve traditional storytelling practices. This includes investing in infrastructure and resources for cultural institutions, supporting research and documentation efforts, and providing grants and scholarships for students and researchers focused on Nigerian folklore and cultural heritage.

2.7 Conclusion

Nollywood's emergence as a global powerhouse is a testament to Nigeria's cultural resilience and adaptability. Rooted in centuries-old oral traditions, moonlight tales, and communal performances, Nollywood represents an evolution that bridges traditional storytelling with modern filmmaking. This rich heritage has not only defined Nollywood's unique identity but also positioned it as a significant contributor to Nigeria's economy and global cultural landscape. However, as the industry grows, it faces critical challenges in protecting traditional cultural expressions and ensuring fair compensation for creators and originating communities.

111 Ibid.

The Nigerian Copyright Act 2022 provides a vital legal foundation for addressing these issues, particularly by recognising and safeguarding expressions of folklore. While the Act introduces important protections, gaps remain in enforcement, equitable distribution of royalties, and mechanisms for cataloguing traditional works. Piracy remains a persistent challenge, undermining the revenue potential of Nollywood and the efforts of creators. To overcome these obstacles, a multi-pronged approach is essential: strengthening enforcement mechanisms, introducing *sui generis* protections tailored for folklore, and leveraging technological innovations to combat piracy. As Nollywood continues to evolve in an increasingly digital and globalised world, the industry must strike a balance between innovation and cultural preservation. By integrating traditional storytelling practices into modern creative processes and ensuring legal protections for cultural heritage, Nigeria can safeguard its stories for future generations. Nollywood's success lies not only in its economic potential but also in its ability to honour the cultural roots that make it uniquely Nigerian.

3 Traditional peoples in Africa and intellectual property rights

Losing the status of their jurisprudence and knowledge systems

Ayoyemi Lawal-Arowolo

3.1 Introduction

African Jurisprudence is unwritten, but it is indestructible and ineffaceable.[1] Customary law is unique, and many traditional communities were regulated solely by it prior to the introduction of received English laws, French laws and laws from other European countries in various parts of Africa.[2] Islamic law plays a role in some parts of Africa as well,[3] where it is observed substantially in its pure form in some areas, and in others it is mixed.[4] This chapter focuses on customary law and does not perceive Islamic law as practised in some jurisdictions as customary law. Both laws are viewed as separate and distinct. In customary law, there were ways that

1 Remigius N. Nwabueze, "The Dynamics and Genius of Nigeria's Indigenous Legal Order." (2002) 1 *Indigenous Law Journal* note 24; "non-literacy did not prove fatal to the preservation of customary doctrine. Apart from the elders, who were deemed to be natural repositories of the law, there were traditional functionaries, well versed in forensic science and learned in the law, who had special responsibilities in directing the proceedings in the courts and acted generally as legal experts … The institution of legal specialization facilitated the process of transmitting the legal heritage from generation to generation by oral tradition"; S. K. B. Asante, "A hundred Years of a National Legal System in Ghana: A Review and Critique" in *Proceedings and Papers of the Sixth Commonwealth Law Conference*, Lagos, Nigeria 17–23 August (Academy Press 1980) 152.

2 Adegoke A. Olanrewaju, *Indigenous African Law: A Comparative Study in Epiphany Azinge and Animi Awah, Legal Pluralism in Africa: A Compendium on African Customary Law* (Nigerian Institute of Advanced Legal Studies 2012) 36. "Customary law was the principal system of law in African communities. However, this exclusivity was broken in the nineteenth century when European colonialists introduced their own metropolitan law and systems into their colonies, but retained so much of customary law and the African judicial process that they did not deem contrary to basic justice or morality."

3 Ayoyemi Lawal-Arowolo, "Science and Art in Islam: The Protection of Traditional Intellectual Property Rights in Muslim Communities in Africa." (2018) 40(11) *European Intellectual Property Review* 736.

4 Ibid. "In other jurisdictions, Islamic law is observed only in some aspects of legal relationships, and other laws are applied in different aspects of such relationships."

DOI: 10.4324/9781003602989-4

creations of the mind were protected; even though it was then predominantly an oral society, there were some forms of fixation in certain areas of creativity in artistic works (sculpting, carving, pottery, textile designs, rock art, and more).[5]

Traditional intellectual property rights in the form of accepted customs protect African knowledge systems as the foundation of their emerging creative and innovation industries. The acceptance of a community gives a custom its obligatory nature, supported by sanction and made enforceable.[6] African traditional knowledge systems and protection mechanisms within the African environment prior to colonial laws and knowledge systems introduced to and accepted in Africa are examined in this chapter.[7]

Intellectual property law was established for the protection of Western knowledge systems brought into African traditional communities as they were then. Angela Riley depicted the situation aptly in reference to the Indigenous peoples in the United States and their relationship with intellectual property rights and their knowledge systems. This perspective is similar to the situation in Africa regardless of the absence of their independence and the physical absence of the colonisers.

> The lack of legal protection for indigenous peoples under current intellectual property systems is a complicated and multi-faceted problem. For example, under the U.S. regime (which has become the dominant regime in the world), songs are protected, if at all, largely by federal copyright law. However, the "Beauty Way" song – a traditional Navajo "curing" song that has existed for thousands of years-simply does not fit within the parameters of federal copyright law. Because the "Beauty Way" song is an inter-generational creation, formed as a living work within Navajo culture, the song is not "original," it does not have a known author or author(s), nor is it "fixed in any tangible medium of expression." As a result, it is ineligible for protection under federal copyright laws.[8]

Conversely, viewing the same issue from the perspective of the suitability of customary law with intellectual property, it is apparent that traditional

5 Ayoyemi Lawal-Arowolo, "African Traditional Intellectual Property Rights, Customary Law, and Legal Pluralism." (2019) *African Journal of Legal Studies* 300.

6 Remigius N. Nwabueze, "The Dynamics and Genius of Nigeria's Indigenous Legal Order." (2002) 1 *Indigenous Law Journal* 156.

7 Annie Patricia Kameri-Mbote and Philippe Cullet, Law, "Colonialism and Environmental Management in Africa." (1997) 6 (1) *Environment Management in Africa* (Blackwell Publishers Ltd) 25–31.

8 Angela Rilley, "'Straight Stealing': Towards an Indigenous System of Cultural Property Protection." (2005) 80(1) *Washington Law Review* 74.

peoples' ways of protecting their knowledge systems are not easily reconcilable with the law of intellectual property.[9] For the benefit of and from the perspectives of traditional peoples, the implementation of customary law is perhaps the most effective means of protecting their knowledge systems and possibly preventing misappropriation.[10] Law was intended in the first place for the local European and legal aspects of economic activities with Western patterns and later became operative for Africans who participated directly in such economic activities. Many literatures depict Africa as helpless prior to the coming of colonisation, while others have a perspective that the people of Africa were perfectly well, had viable economic activities that were on par with the West if not better, and the problems in Africa are due to post-colonial transition.[11]

Foreign products of creativity and inventions were introduced to traditional communities with the required protection mechanisms. This action relegated traditional practices in Africa to the background. At that time, African ways were unknown to foreigners, and perhaps the intention then was to substitute what existed in those communities with what was familiar to the foreigners.[12] Language, custom, clothing, modes of worship, and entertainment in existence in traditional communities did not appear to be of interest to foreigners and were perceived to be activities for the public domain. However, significant implications for the survival of traditional people, both economic and social in Africa, are apparent in perceiving

9 Nopera Dennis-McCarthy, "Indigenous Customary Law and International Intellectual Property: Ascertaining an Effective Indigenous Definition for Misappropriation of Traditional Knowledge." (2020) 51 *VUWLR* 598.

10 Ibid.

11 Emmanuel Kwesi Boon and Charles Takoyoh Eyong, "History and Civilizations: Impacts on Sustainable Development in Africa." *AREA STUDIES – AFRICA (Regional Sustainable Development Review) – Vol. II, Encyclopedia of Life Support Systems* (EOLSS) 2. "Some scholars assert that Africa had experienced a level of development that was at par with the West if not more advanced in some aspects prior to the arrival of Europeans. For instance, 'during the Middle Ages – when most of the people of Europe suffered disease, fear, ignorance, and oppression – the Soninke people of the Empire of Ghana enjoyed a world that was rich in culture and famous as a center of learning and trade.' A historical review of some great empires of Africa such as the empires of Mali, Mwanemutapa, Songhai and the Swahili Kingdoms also reveals that pre-colonial Africa had a rich history, culture, economy, politics and governance structures. These former centres of trade, culture, tradition and politics are largely failed states today."

12 Deborah Wassel, "From Mbube to Wimoweh: African Folk Music in Dual Systems of Law." (2009) 20 *Fordham Intellectual Property Media and Entertainment Law Journal* 296. "Customary law can be a concept foreign to those trained in the Western tradition, and therefore, to understand the traditional concept of intellectual property within African traditions, it is necessary to provide an overview of the nature and role of musical composition as well as the relevant principles of customary law."

traditional knowledge as an extension of the public domain.[13] Ironically, traditional knowledge perceived to be in the public domain became a den of resources for creativity and innovation by foreigners.

Protecting traditional knowledge from the outside world was not necessary until colonisation, foreign trade, and technology, particularly biotechnology in recent times, put at stake the economic returns to African societies.[14] Colonisation increased access to African resources for industrial development in Europe to the detriment of knowledge and economic development in Africa.[15] This chapter focuses on the effect of intellectual property rights and Western knowledge on traditional legal systems and traditional knowledge during and after colonisation, proposing that the colonial legacy still in existence contributed significantly to the disregard and lack of protection for traditional knowledge systems by favouring dominant Western knowledge systems and legal mechanisms. The advocacy for a *sui generis* system that does not take customary law into consideration as a protective mechanism deepens the problem of finding a suitable legal mechanism to protect African traditional knowledge systems.

Both traditional and Western legal systems are applicable in African countries as part of African jurisprudence. These systems are applicable to intellectual property issues relating to African traditional knowledge systems, depending on the parties concerned and the level of occurrence (communal, national, regional, and international). This chapter suggests Africa should be in control of its knowledge system and determine the way forward in how it should be protected, which can be in multiple forms based on its cultural and historical background. Ignoring customary law in this journey has not and will not help the situation. Africa must look inwards and backwards to move forward with its traditional knowledge systems in various industries for social, cultural, and economic development.

3.2 The status of traditional peoples prior to colonisation

Traditional peoples in Africa were not familiar with how the introduced intellectual property system operated or the rights they possessed beyond

13 Ruth L. Okediji, "Traditional Knowledge and the Public Domain." (June 2018) 176 *Center for International Governance Innovation (CIGI)* Papers 2, https://www.cigionline.org/sites/default/files/documents/Paper%20no.176web.pdf accessed 10 October 2024.

14 "European colonialist engaged in unprecedented robbery of Africa," *Lagos Observer*, 19 February 1885, quoted in U.O. Umozurike "International Law and Colonialism." (1970) 3 *East African Law Review* 47.

15 Patricia Kameri-Mbote and Philippe Cullet, 'Law, colonialism and environmental management in Africa' (1997) *Review of European Community and International Environmental Law* 23.

customs or customary law.[16] However, proprietary rights in intangibles were not new to traditional communities, based on cultural practices.[17] These communities had their own means of protection.[18] In the area of creativity, sanctions were derived from magical beliefs; ostracism, fines, and death were attached to the copying of art. Traditional leadership also played a key role in customary law and regulating the use of traditional knowledge. In Zimbabwe, reflecting what occurred in the past and is still acceptable in the present, Chapter 15 of the Constitution recognises the role of traditional leaders under customary law as responsible for performing cultural, customary, and traditional functions of a chief, head person, or village head for his or her community.[19]

Bankole Sodipo is of the view that there are two main classes of customary law: royal decrees and taboos.[20] There were also ways in which belonging to a family, age group, or clan served as a protection mechanism; other members of the community who did not belong to the group could not participate in an activity or claim a work.[21] Members of a trade belong to a guild, and the protection mechanism was of a spiritual nature, with a

16 The term traditional peoples is adopted to reflect a wider group of people in Africa, including indigenous peoples as defined by international law. Every individual of African origin is a traditional person, and as a group, they are traditional peoples. See Deborah Wassel, Deborah Wassel, "From Mbube to Wimoweh: African Folk Music in Dual Systems of Law." (2009) 20 *Fordham Intellectual Property Media and Entertainment Law Journal* 296. "In much of sub-Saharan Africa, most people "belong to tribes and have roots in traditional communities, [regardless of] whether they live in villages or cities." These traditional roots influence much of their day-to-day lives, including particular rituals that may be performed."

17 Bankole Sodipo, "Overview of Intellectual Property Rights Protection for Traditional Knowledge, Innovation and Traditional Medicine Practice in Nigeria" (paper delivered at the International Workshop on Intellectual Property Rights (IPR) for Traditional Medicine Knowledge and Practice held Wednesday 30 November 30–Saturday 3 December 2005 at Sheraton Hotel and Towers, Abuja). Based on the research previously conducted by the author, it is demonstrated that the recognition and protection of proprietary rights in intangibles were not uncommon in pre-colonial Nigeria prior to the advent of modern intellectual property. It is, however, noted that authors of the materials relied on did not have intellectual property concepts in mind when they carried out their research.

18 Ibid.

19 Gabriel Muzah, "The Role of Traditional Leadership and Customary Law under a Sui Generis System of Intellectual Property Rights in Traditional Knowledge." (2021) *Raoul Wallenberg Institute of Human Rights and Humanitarian Law* 62.

20 The king and elders had the power to make and repeal laws, among other roles. A taboo classified certain peoples, resources, and places as sacred and prohibited, and if breached, attracts the wrath of the gods. Though often embedded in superstitions, it instilled fear in the people in comparison to being fined or going to prison. Bankole Sodipo, *Copyright Law: Principles, Practice and Procedure* (SWAN 2017) 28.

21 Ibid., 29.

god capable of protecting and punishing erring members.[22] Cultural works included drama, which is often linked to religious activities; folktales and folksongs to build "the African character"; music for religious festivals; and artworks on pottery, rocks, sculptures, and more.[23] Religious beliefs were also a type of protection mechanism, as those who breached them were punished by the gods.[24] Trade secrets were common in areas similar to industrial properties, and they were passed across generations to members of a group, family, or family or apprentice.[25] "For their own purposes and until recent times, this system of protection was sufficient and perhaps more effective than the patent system in terms of protecting works."[26] Traditional symbols carved into farming products, including hoes and cutlasses, denoted source in similarity to trademarks.

Traditional peoples understood the norms that guided them at the communal level, and they abided by them. Customary law protection of folklore in Africa is identifiable by comparing similarities in creations and inventions by traditional peoples and modern intellectual property.[27] Customary law protection of folklore relies on norms and sanctions which seem to make sense only to members of the groups. Within the groups, there is pressure to recognise and respect the rights and privileges associated with folklore in the common interest of members of the community. Inherent in this system, however, is a defect that may limit the usefulness of customary law in tackling the problems of unauthorised uses, since many of the individuals engaged in the unauthorised use of folklore are foreigners.[28] The application of customary law to foreigners is seen as one of the challenges facing its application.

Intellectual property rights as a system of private rights were alien to Africa's human social organisation and traditional legal systems. Intellectual

22 Ibid., 30.

23 Bankole Sodipo, *Copyright Law: Principles, Practice and Procedure* (SWAN 2017) 27.

24 Ibid., 31, some musical instruments and attire were used mainly by certain cults.

25 Bankole Sodipo, "Overview of Intellectual Property Rights Protection for Traditional Knowledge, Innovation and Traditional Medicine Practice in Nigeria" (paper delivered at the International Workshop on Intellectual Property Rights (IPR) for Traditional Medicine Knowledge and Practice held Wednesday 30 November–Saturday 3 December 2005 at Sheraton Hotel and Towers, Abuja).

26 Bankole Sodipo, "Overview of Intellectual Property Rights Protection for Traditional Knowledge, Innovation and Traditional Medicine Practice in Nigeria" (paper delivered at the International Workshop on Intellectual Property Rights (IPR) for Traditional Medicine Knowledge and Practice held Wednesday 30 November –Saturday 3 December 2005 at Sheraton Hotel and Towers, Abuja).

27 P. Kuruk, "Protecting Folklore under Modern Intellectual Property Regimes: A Reappraisal of the Tensions between Individual and Communal Rights in Africa and the United States." 48 *American Law Review* (1999) 786.

28 Ibid.

property was introduced to African communities during colonisation, and there was pressure on members of these communities to recognise the intellectual property rights of foreigners. Even though such rights were alien to these communities, they accepted and practised them. The struggle for protection mechanisms designed to protect different knowledge systems in Zimbabwe were apparent.[29] Each protection system recognises the rights of individuals or groups to gains arising from their knowledge system. Its holders value their knowledge system and design systems for its distribution, acquisition, use, and dissemination within and beyond the community.[30] Constraint arises when the dominant system (intellectual property law) of protection is imposed on the subordinated system (customary law) of protection. Customary law is marginalised because it is not given recognition beyond traditional communities.

Unless attention is given to the recognition of traditional intellectual property ownership by the modern system, similar rights in preliterate societies will be prejudiced.[31] Negating any impression that technology or a system of protection was lacking in pre-colonial Nigeria and Africa is detrimental to society at large. Creative works and mining activities in West Africa persuaded the colonial administration to introduce intellectual property law to traditional communities in their non-literate state.[32] The transmission of customary law through jurisprudential vectors to jurisdictions beyond its original scope is not beyond international intellectual property law, but it remains a daunting challenge.[33] What is required is an effective framework that sets broad norms and standards in line with core

29 Alex Magaisa, "Knowledge and Power: Law, Politics and Socio-Cultural Perspectives on the Protection of Traditional Medicinal Knowledge Systems in Zimbabwe" (paper presented at AHRB Workshop, Queen Mary Intellectual Property Institute, June 2004).

30 Ibid.; the author quoted Peter Drahos to support his view that "all societies have had to devise norms for regulating the ownership and use of different kinds of information … One can thus identify customary equivalents in [indigenous communities] of intellectual property."

31 Sodipo's *Overview of Intellectual Property Rights Protection* (n 32).

32 Mark C. Suchman, "Invention and Ritual: Notes on the interrelation of magic and intellectual property in preliterate societies." (1989) 89 *Columbia Law Review* 1265. "Intellectual property rights actually pervade preliterate societies and figure prominently in the concept of magical beliefs surrounding numerous aspects of daily life. These rights do not wholly parallel their Western counterparts, however they play an equally central role in the formulation and diffusion of ideas. Although the preliterate society lacks the interventionist administrative apparatus commonly associated with intellectual property protection in the West, preliterate inventors and Western inventors alike experience strong incentives to monopolize new technologies."

33 Anthony Taubman, "Saving the Village: Conserving Jurisprudential Diversity in the International Protection of Traditional Knowledge" in K.E. Maskus and J. Riechman (eds) *International Public Goods and Transfer of Technology Under a Globalized Intellectual Property Regime* (Cambridge University Press, 2005) 564.

IP principles and allows functional vectors of customary law, linked to the subject matter of protection, to pass from the original jurisdiction to foreign jurisdictions.[34]

3.3 Suppressing of traditional knowledge, customs and customary law during the colonial era

The eve of the colonial conquest and occupation, Africa was far from being primitive, static, and asleep or in a Hobbesian state of nature. On all fronts – economic, political, social, and even intellectual.[35]

The arrival of the European colonial powers wrought a fundamental revolution in African Legal arrangements, the results of which are with us to this day.[36]

When the European colonisers arrived, it was wrongly presumed that there were no frameworks for articulating and protecting intellectual property among the colonised peoples of Africa.[37] Traditional knowledge was compared to scientific or Western knowledge, and a conclusion was reached on behalf of traditional peoples that it was inferior.[38] Scientific knowledge was seen from a rigidly Eurocentric perspective as the essence of modernisation, without giving recognition to science in African traditional knowledge systems.

There were claims that African traditional knowledge systems showed a trend of barbarism.[39] Any development based on a traditional knowledge system was condemned as useless, with no value for the modern world.[40] Ignorance was the defence in this situation, and it gradually dispersed with the discovery of medicines and creative works dependent on African traditional knowledge systems. "Early Europeans in Indigenous communities were ignorant of the power and value of Indigenous medical knowledge

34 Ibid.

35 A. Adu Boahen, *African Perspective on Colonialism* (Johns Hopkins University Press 1987) 23.

36 N. Allot, "The Future of African Law" in H. Kuper and L. Kuper, *African Law: Adaptation and Development* (University of California Press 1965) 220.

37 Lakshmi Sarma, "Biopiracy: Twentieth Century Imperialism in the Form of International Agreements." (1999) 13 *Temple International and Comparative Law Journal* 107.

38 Traditional peoples is adopted to reflect African people holistically, so that everyone regardless of present status, is considered a traditional person. However, there is a traditional person, though differing perspective that some remain in their lifestyle prior to colonisation, such as the San Bushmen of South Africa, the Maasai of Kenya, the Koma of Nigeria, and more.

39 Colonisation of Africans was partly justified on the hypothesis of the racial superiority of Europeans and the inferiority of the savages and primitives.

40 B. Easlea, *Witch-Hunting, Magic, and the New Philosophy: An Introduction to Debates of the Scientific Revolution, 1450–1750* (Haverfield Press 1980).

systems; otherwise, they would have taken them seriously and supported them."[41]

The laws applicable in each African colony were dependent on the colonisers.[42] The French system of direct rule left little room for the flourishing of customary law.[43] The British system of indirect rule encouraged the practice as well as the development of customary law through the use of the institutions of chieftaincy, local councils, and traditional tribunals as the organs of local government, so long as it was beneficial to them.[44] The Portuguese and Spanish colonial theory classified their colonies as integral portions of metropolitan Portugal or Spain.[45] Conscious recognition was not given to the existence of the customs and usages of traditional peoples. Laws were introduced into the African territories of Portugal and Spain as if those lands were entirely inhabited by Iberian communities.[46] As described by Shabalala using a storytelling technique:

> Tsandi was once a direct chieftainship, but during colonisation, the chieftainship was abolished. Colonial authorities sought to punish the nation for the chief's participation in anti-colonial resistance by killing any claimants to leadership.[47]

The attempt to eradicate traditional knowledge, especially in sub-Saharan Africa, and the artful ways in which Africans evaded or subverted colonial powers are evident in various literatures.[48] In British colonies such as parts of Cameroon and Nigeria, herbal medicine was suppressed where it offended the morality or seemed contrary to the political interests of the British.[49] Where it furthered British medical purposes or coincided with their cultural views, traditional medicine was supported or claims to

41 Alex Tawanda Magaisa, "Knowledge Protection in Indigenous Communities: The Case of Indigenous Medical Knowledge Systems in Zimbabwe" (PhD Thesis, University of Warwick School of Law, September 2004) 177.
42 A. Endeshaw, *Intellectual Property Policy for Non-Industrial Countries* (Dartmouth 1996) 150.
43 T.O. Elias, "The Evolution of Law and Government in Modern Africa" in H. Kuper and L. Kuper, *African Law: Adaptation and Development* (University of California Press 1965) 184.
44 Ibid.
45 Ibid.
46 Ibid.
47 Dalindyebo Shabalala, "Taking Customary Law Seriously (Part III): The Story of Oko Mmapule Tadesse." (1 November 2024) *Technology, Sustainability and Human Rights* https://dalishabalala.com/2024/10/16/taking-customary-law-seriously-domestic-recognition-of-traditional-knowledge-part-i/ accessed 20 December 2024
48 Kent Maynard, *Making Kedjom Medicine: A History of Public Health and Well Being in Cameroon* (Praeger) 20.
49 Ibid.

believe in traditional medicine were made.[50] There was a lack of understanding of Africa's "ancient and honourable traditions and institution of state craft."[51] Traditional institutions that evolved through Africa's Indigenous traditions were discarded on the basis that they were of savage origin, crushing the value of African traditional knowledge systems.

Customary law was no longer based on traditional authority but on colonial administrative authority.[52] The traditional way of ensuring appropriate conduct in traditional societies was reduced to nothing. In Southern Rhodesia (Zimbabwe), elders or chiefs were no longer allowed to settle disputes.[53] Their wisdom and experience were seen as incompatible with what is regarded as the principles of civilisation.[54] Traditional medicine knowledge continued to exist and thrive during colonisation because traditional medicine institutions went unnoticed in some parts, and groups resorted to secretive or non-obstructive practices in certain circumstances.[55] "The British colonialist seldom enforced ordinances regulating healing methods, this attitude reflects persistent developmentalist assumptions about 'superiority' of European practices."[56] In order to make a success of the indirect rule in British colonies and the native administration system, no harsh steps were taken to eliminate traditional medicine.[57] Missionaries also had an impact on traditional medicine by taking concerted steps toward Indigenous medicine and religion.[58]

There were attempts to undermine local authorities and cosmology.[59] A distinction was not made between herbal remedies, witchcraft, and magic; everything was grouped as backward or evil. However, the shortage of

50 Ibid.
51 B. Davidson, *West Africa before the Colonial Era: A History to 1850* (Longman 1998) 235.
52 N. A. Ollennu, "The Structure of African Judicial Authority and Problems of Evidence and Proof in Traditional Courts" in M. Gluckman, *Ideas and Procedures in African Customary Law* (International African Institute for Oxford University Press 1969) 110.
53 E. V. Mittlebeeler, *African Custom and Western Law: The Development of the Rhodesian Criminal Laws for Africans* (Africana Publishing Company 1976) 19.
54 Ibid.
55 Kent Maynard, *Making Kedjom medicine: A History of Public Health and Well Being in Cameroon* (Praeger) 21.
56 Ibid., 22.
57 Ibid.
58 Kojo A. Senah, Joseph Kofi Adusei, Samuel A. Akor, "A Baseline Study into Traditional Medicine Practice in Ghana" (MOH/DANIDA Project 2001). Missionaries joined in the campaign of enforcing the acceptance of colonial administrators' medical regime by threatening ex-communication of converts who participated in many cultural practices.
59 Maynard's *Making Kedjom Medicine: A History of Public Health and Well Being in Cameroon* (n 25), the shortage of missionaries could be seen as a blessing in disguise because traditional practices that are still useful in our times were preserved. Otherwise, they were eroding very quickly due to external influence and the imposition of Western views.

missionaries kept in place many traditional medicinal and religious practices. Traditional medicine refused to wither away and flourished in luxuriant new ways, but it was also effectively subordinated to allopathic practice due to the political and economic dominance of the colonisers. Customary law continued to respect this knowledge system, but common law and statutes relating to the use or development of traditional medicine prohibited its existence.

There were so many conflicting issues about African traditional knowledge systems generally and traditional medicine in particular that no provision was made for its protection.[60] There was no precision as to whether to inculcate such practices or stamp them out. Imported colonial laws at this time were not seen as a means of protection for African traditional knowledge systems. Documentation of customary law changed to suit the Western concept that erodes the essence and value of this system to traditional peoples in Africa. This erosion can easily be achieved by reducing it to writing and embodying it into legislation for reasons other than to benefit traditional peoples. However, if it is documented as it is, a customary system of protection serves as storage for tradition and should not be static if daily occurrences within these tribes are documented and serve as an upgrade, amendment, or abrogation as in Sharia law. Its existence for a long period can also be proven. Will customary law be lost if not documented? Will it die with those who know it, leaving only remnants or nothing for the coming generation? These are questions that cannot be easily answered, considering the number of years customary law has been in existence. The challenge in this era is eroding traditions.

3.4 Living and codified customary laws: protecting traditional knowledge systems saga

Communities, as well as customary laws, experience changes and development in a similar manner to other societies and laws. Some norms remain the same, but some change over the years based on the needs of the communities, and the same applies to the knowledge system which these norms protect. Without doubt, the intangible aspect of customary law and traditional knowledge is difficult to grasp, proving that they are birds of a feather and belong together.[61] The British were under the perception that it

60 Indigenous people were made to consume modern products for their new modern bodies at one moment, and at the next, they were told to revive their traditional knowledge of creativity and innovation.

61 Douglas Brown and A. P. J. Allen, *An Introduction to the Law of Uganda* (Sweet and Maxwell, African University Press 1968) 31.

was more convenient to permit the application of customary law alongside their own laws, particularly in the area of tangible properties. Recognition was not given to intangible properties, which they continued to appropriate.[62] It should not be forgotten that the concept of intellectual property arose from tangible property.

"New efforts to create property rights for information are the continuation of a trend that began in the earliest periods of human societies, with the development of rules governing property rights in intangible things."[63] Customary law guided these properties for the social and economic benefits of traditional communities. In reality, traditional communities were not so different from Western societies in placing rules on what can be owned, how it can be owned and the benefits and obligations of ownership. Nonetheless, the colonisers made sure customary law was controlled within their limits.

Colonial provisions were made for the application of customary law under various legislations, and definitions were given to customary law under various statutes with slight differences in the wordings, but the interpretations were the same.[64] In areas with a large population of Muslims, native law and custom were defined to include "Moslem law."[65] The statutory definitions of customary law have been few and far between since it was considered difficult to define, but it could nevertheless be instantly recognised when seen.[66]

The official version of customary law in Africa was applied in customary courts, and their jurisdiction was not exclusive. General courts could determine and apply the official customary law when it was raised in legal

62 Ibid.

63 Renee Marlin-Bennett, *Knowledge Power: Intellectual Property, Information and Privacy* (Lynne Rienner Publishers 2004) 11.

64 In Nigeria (former Eastern Region) under the High Court Law (cap. 104, 1963 Revision) s 2, customary law was defined as 'local custom includes a rule which in a particular district or among the members of a tribe or clan or class of persons, has, from long usage, obtained the force of law and also local customary law'. In Tanzania under the Interpretation and General Clauses Ordinance (cap. 1, as inserted by the Magistrates' Courts Act 1963, sixth Schedule) s 2 (1): "Customary law means any rule or body of rules whereby rights and duties are acquired or imposed, established by usage in any Tanganyika African community and accepted by such community in general as having the force of law made under the Local Government Ordinance, but does not include any rule or practice which is abolished, prohibited, punishable, declared unlawful or expressly or impliedly misapplied or superseded by written law; and references to native law and custom shall similarly be construed."

65 Northern Nigeria Native Courts Law of 1956, s 2.

66 Ibid.

proceedings.[67] From various jurisprudential perspectives, there is no doubt that in the contemplation of English law with respect to Anglophone-speaking countries, custom is law.[68] It is important to note that a custom, as a rule of law, becomes customary law when it attains a binding or obligatory character.[69] Customary law, as a proposed rule, is fortified by established usage. Satisfactory evidence of usage has to be adduced, and the courts must still decide whether such usage has obtained the force of law or governs legal relationships.[70] What people do and what the court wants them to do or say they do has created unresolved problems as to how far courts may depart from previous precedents on customary law.[71] The flexibility of customary law overrides any precedent in its application, and courts were advised to avoid rigidity by avoiding any laid-down format. If rigidity is not avoided, the essence of the application of customary law will be lost.

In determining customary law, members of statutory customary courts are presumed to know the norms and practices of traditional peoples, and they can apply such knowledge to disputes.[72] Judges in general courts are not presumed to be familiar with customary law and are prevented from relying on such personal knowledge as their prior experience might provide.[73] It is noteworthy that intellectual property statutes are part of the general laws in Africa, and provisions in such statutes referring to traditional knowledge will therefore fall within the jurisdiction of general courts. The reason for importing laws was to protect the political strength

67 P. Kuruk, "African Customary Law and the Protection of Folklore." (2002) XXXVI *Copyright Bulletin* 10.

68 C.K. Allen, *Law in the Making* (7th edn, Clarendon Press, 1964) 67–70.

69 Ibid.

70 A.N. Allot, *New Essays in African Law* (Butterworths 1970) 154.

71 Ibid.

72 N.A. Ollennu, "The Structure of African Judicial Authority and Problems of Evidence and Proof in Traditional Courts" in M. Gluckman, *Ideas and Procedures in African Customary Law* (International African Institute and Oxford University Press 1969) 110–119. W.B. Harvey, "The Evolution of Ghana Law Since Independence" in H. W. Baade and R. O. Everett (eds) *African Law* 1963; A. Allot, *Essays in African Law* (Butterworths 1970) 99–116. Customary law was administered in Ghana mainly through the native courts, created by the colonial governor. The appointment of members of a native court was not based on status; mostly, elders and chiefs were selected. It was generally assumed they were conversant with the customary law of their respective areas. See also B. Wanda, "The Role of Traditional Courts in Malawi" in P. Takirambudde (eds) *The Individual under African Law* (KUniversity of Swaziland Department of Law 1982) 76. In Malawi, cases involving customary law and simple criminal cases were left to be determined by the traditional courts. M. Ndulo, "Customary Law and the Zambian Legal System" in P. Takirambudde, *The Individual under African Law* (University of Swaziland Department of Law, 1982) 121.

73 Ibid.

and economic market of the colonialists, especially relating to the importation of their drugs. Intellectual property law at this time was for the industrialised countries to protect their rights in their colonies and beyond. Intellectual property was not considered for traditional medicine or traditional knowledge. The only laws that were made in recognition of native medicine were those against the administration of poison.

In Nigeria the Drugs and Poison Ordinance of 1915 banned the production or use of poison except by registered biomedical practitioners. The ordinance explicitly stated that native preparations were not necessarily poisonous:

> Nothing in … this ordinance shall apply to the sale of any of the following articles … (5) Any herbal or native preparation not being a poison which is supplied by any person dealing only with herbal or other native preparation used as medicine in Nigeria.[74]

There was no clarification as to what or who determines poisonous substances. The 1878 Native Customs Regulation Ordinance prohibited customary practices by depleting traditional healers as "insincere juju men living in neurosis of the illiterate folk."[75] In Uganda traditional medicine was legislated under the Witchcraft Act of 1957 prior to independence.[76] Colonialist equated traditional medicine with witchcraft in many African countries, further suppressing the practice of traditional medicine.[77] In addition, after independence, traditional medicine practitioners were allowed to practice if they did not claim to be registered practitioners according to the 1968 Medical and Dental Practitioners Act.[78]

74 Kent Maynard, *Making Kedjom medicine: A History of Public Health and Well Being in Cameroon* (Praeger) 182.

75 Kodjo A. Senah, Joseph Kofi Adusei and Samuel A. Akor, *A Baseline Study into Traditional Medicine Practice in Ghana* (MOH/DANIDA Project August 2001) 6.

76 *Traditional Medicine in Uganda: Historical Perspective, Challenges and Advances (English).* Indigenous Knowledge (IK) Notes, no. 67 (World Bank Group). http://documents.worldbank.org/curated/en/208041468121755812/Traditional-medicine-in-Uganda-historical-perspective-challenges-and-advances accessed 12 December 2024.

77 N. K. Mubiru, "Current Policies of Traditional Medicine in Uganda" in Kolawole Adeniji, *2001–2010: OAU Decade For African Traditional Medicine* (Organisation of African Unity/Scientific, Technical and Research Commission 2002) 98; in Zambia, chiefs and headmen were made to punish traditional healers and the Witchcraft Act was enacted to restrict the practice of traditional medicine; see Richard Haamachila, "Promotion of African Traditional Medicine and Medicinal Plants" in Robert N. Mshana and Mbaye Ndoye, *African Traditional Medicine and Medicinal Plants* (OAU/STRCH 1999) 184.

78 Ibid.; the partial recognition given to traditional knowledge resulted from the after independence trend of strengthening national and cultural identities by the Ugandan government.

Medicinal plants, as important biological resources, were not given much attention at the initial stage. There were no laws protecting medicinal plant species from cultivation or trade. The concern then was more for biological resources classified as cash crops, which were more important to the colonisers. Consequently, laws were enacted to ensure that the production of cash crops was limited to the colonial plantations. Human activities and access to natural resources were generally restricted through the enactment of laws. Such laws affected the use and harvesting of medicinal plants. Norms regarding sacred ecological areas were disregarded, and social norms that formed the foundations of African resources and use patterns were ignored. Rules and policies on special or protected areas of biological resources were established; however, traditional peoples, their resources, and pharmacopoeia were not considered.[79] African communities were alienated from their traditional sources of medicine. Their values, knowledge, and conservation practices were not reflected in colonial government policies, legal frameworks, and institutional frameworks.[80]

3.5 Limiting the status of customary law protection

Customary law became applicable in traditional African communities subject to these conditions: the customary law rule is not repugnant to natural justice, equity, and good conscience, and that it is not incompatible, directly or by implication, with any law in force at that time.[81]

3.5.1 The repugnancy test

The repugnancy test serves as a "cleansing and modernising provision, originally entrenched by the colonial government to divest customary law of its ostensibly 'barbaric' relics."[82] Stripping customary law of its barbarism was confirmed by Lord Wright in the case of *Laoye & ors.* v *Oyetunde*.[83] The former British African territories only applied customary

79 For instance, the Colonial Tea Ordinance Cap. 200 1948 (Laws of Kenya) s 3 restricted the planting of tea on any land in Kenya unless such a person was in possession of a licence.

80 Joy K. Asiema and Francis D.P. Situma, "Indigenous Peoples and the Environment: The Case of the Pastoral Maasai of Kenya." (1994) 5(1) *Colorado Journal of International Environmental Law and Policy* 149.

81 Adegoke A. Olanrewaju, *Indigenous African Law: A Comparative Study in Epiphany Azinge and Animi Awah, Legal Pluralism in Africa: A Compendium on African Customary Law* (Nigerian Institute of Advanced Legal Studies 2012) 52.

82 Reginus N. Nwabueze, "The Dynamics and Genius of Nigeria's Indigenous Legal Order." 1(2002) *Indigenous Law Journal* 175.

83 [1944] A.C. 170 "The courts which have been established by the British Government have the duty of enforcing these native laws and customs, so far as they are not barbarous, as part of the land'; 'The policy of the British Government in this and other respects is to use

law so far as it was not repugnant.[84] The repugnancy test was deemed to give flexibility to the administration of justice by putting the extent of the operation of customary law ultimately into the hands of judges, mainly foreign, who were confronted with the application of the repugnancy doctrine.[85] There are various reasons attributed to the repugnancy clause, but it is primarily to strike out what is deemed to be below a minimum standard of civilised values.[86] Moreover, the courts have found it difficult to provide a meaning for the clause.[87]

This doctrine applied to living and official customary law. Where native laws and customs are applied "(example, through an unofficial tribunal or through the customary court) to a given case, an official appellate court may declare the native laws and customs repugnant to natural justice, equity, and good conscience, and therefore void.'.[88] It is within the discretion of the judge (and previously was within the discretion of the administrative officer-magistrate) whether to allow a certain rule of customary law to operate or not. This discretion is expected to be a judicial one, which could be exercised, as much as possible, on clear and satisfactory principle.[89] Therefore, the application of customary law relating to the use of traditional knowledge can be controlled if found to be repugnant to intellectual property law in African countries.

The suggestion that African countries have to abolish the repugnancy clause as a vehicle to condemn and reject customary African norms should be seriously considered.[90] Maintaining such a clause reinforces the view that the values of Western culture should be used as a yardstick to indicate the standards African people should follow. In addition, the legal

---

for purposes of the administration of the country the native laws and customs insofar as possible and insofar as they have not been varied or suspended by statutes or ordinances … so far as they are not barbarous."

84 A.N. Allot, *New Essays in African Law* (Butterworths 1970) 158.

85 "The official courts adhere strongly to the colonially imposed, locally sustained repugnancy test. This remains the situation despite the fact that the native, traditional case management avenues play important roles."

86 Leon Sheleff, *The Future of Tradition: Customary Law, Common Law and Legal Pluralism* (Frank Cass 2000) 122; quoting T.O. Elias, *British Colonial Law: A Comparative Study of the Interaction between English and Local Laws in British Dependencies* (Stevens 1962) 104; Akintunde Olusegun Obilade, *The Nigerian Legal System* (Sweet and Maxwell 1979); the two Privy Council cases are *Laoye v Oyetunde* (1944) A.C. 170 and *Eshugbayi Eleko v Officer Administering the Government of Nigeria* [1931] A.C. 662.

87 Ibid.

88 Ibid.

89 Ibid.

90 William Burnett Harvey, *Introduction to the Legal System in East Africa* (East Africa Literature Bureau 1975) 524.

framework of British control established and developed during colonisation will remain in use in independent African countries. Customs deemed to be uncivilised because they do not conform to British ways are restricted, though they may be beneficial to traditional communities. Nevertheless, a rule of customary law that sentences a community to perpetual penury and servitude and does not permit socio-economic growth should not be permitted. The rules of customary law are not often against the development of a community. It should not be repugnancy leading to rejection but respect leading to rejuvenation that is required.[91]

3.5.2 The incompatibility test

A rule of customary law protecting traditional medicine practitioners can be perceived as incompatible with a local statute if the said statute is intended to govern a subject matter to the exclusion of customary law.[92] It was not made clear whether incompatibility with imperial statutes of general application or other applied extraneous laws, common law and equity is caught by legislative provisions.[93] Some scholars have come to the conclusion that a "statute should be construed as not affecting a transaction governed by customary law unless it expressly or by necessary implication provides to the contrary. The main argument in favour of this conclusion is the manifest absurdity which would otherwise result."[94] Reliance is on the good sense of the judges to deal with the situation with the hope that the whole matter will be cleared up by the enactment of express rules governing the point.

Whether intellectual property law is expected to govern traditional knowledge to the exclusion of customary law is not certain. What is certain is that customary law has protected traditional knowledge, and protection has been missing under intellectual property statutes, except in recent times when the protection of folklore has been included under copyright law in some African countries. One can simply assume that customary law recognises traditional knowledge and presides over it. Intellectual property, on the other hand, has limited control over customary law relating to traditional knowledge protection. Moreover, African copyright laws refer

91 Leon Sheleff, *The Future of Tradition: Customary Law, Common Law and Legal Pluralism* (Frank Cass 2000).

92 A.N. Allot, *New Essays in African Law* (Butterworths 1970), 177.

93 Ibid.

94 I bid quoting L.C.B. Gower, "Nigerian Statutes and Customary Law' (1964) 1 *Nigerian Law Journal* 73. A discussion by the author mainly centring on the provision of the old Nigerian Native Courts Ordinance s. 10(1), which uses the phrase 'inconsistent with any provisions of any other ordinance."

to the protection of folklore without stating whether such protection is limited to the guidelines of the statute to the exclusion of customary law.

> It is palpably wrong to use intellectual property criteria to invalidate customary law rules ... prescribing an incompatibility test by reference to intellectual property statutes means the virtual abolition of rights in folklore. Such a destructive effect could not have been the intent of the legislature, especially as African governments have historically recognised customary law and have accommodated it under their legal system.[95]

Customary law is applicable to persons who subject themselves to its rule, including traditional peoples and all Africans who subject themselves to it as a personal law. In situations where a party decides to resort to imported laws, such person is bound by that law and cannot find solace under customary law. Where parties to a dispute are Nigerians, it is acceptable to apply customary law, but where one of the parties is not Nigerian, it will be seen as unfair to apply customary law.[96] The same criteria apply in other African countries. In addition, if the parties have agreed that a transaction should be governed by English law (intellectual property law), or where a transaction is unknown to local law and custom, then customary law will not be applicable.[97]

Customary courts apply the customary law prevailing in the area of their jurisdiction and no other customary law.[98] These courts often take account of, and apply, the personal law of the parties, if they are not local dwellers but their law can be ascertained.[99] Problems relating to jurisdiction

95 P. Kuruk, "African Customary Law and the Protection of Folklore." (2002) Vol. *XXXX1 Copyright Bulletin* 20.

96 T. O. Elias, *The British Commonwealth: Nigeria The Development of its Laws and Constitutions* (Stevens and Sons 1967).

97 In *Griffin v Talabi* [1948] 12 W.A.C.A. 371; the West African Court of Appeal was of the view that the transaction is unknown to native law and custom. In addition, it was stated that the documents and conduct of the parties show an intention that customary law should not govern the transaction. English law was therefore held to govern the case. Similarly, in *Okolie v Ibo* [1958] N.R.N.L.R 89, it was held that the nature of their respective occupations, the transaction between them, and the commodity in which they dealt indicated that neither Islamic law, applicable in Jos, nor Ibo customary law should apply. The parties were therefore held to have intended the application of English law.

98 In a Nigerian case, the word prevailing was explained in order to reduce its ambiguity since it could mean the various bodies of law existing in the area or the body of law dominant in the area. In *R. v Ilorin Native Court ex p. Aremu* (1953) 20 N.L.R. 144, it was held that "prevailing" meant "dominant".

99 H. F. Morris, *The British Common wealth: Uganda The Development of its Laws and Constitutions* (Steven and Sons 1966) 402.

rarely arise since the jurisdiction of territorial courts is well defined in legislation governing the courts.[100] The question usually is whether a customary court has jurisdiction over the subject matter of the litigation concerned.[101] General courts lack jurisdiction over defendants that ordinarily are subject to a non-statutory adjudication process where such defendants moved across borders to join their kinsmen in a neighbouring country. Nevertheless, such jurisdictional problems are not likely to occur under the non-statutory adjudication systems since the authority of elders or chiefs transcends nationality and would extend to the whole social unit, including portions of it located in another country.

3.6 The coming of intellectual property law into African traditional communities: destabilising the status of customary law

How and why intellectual property law was introduced to Africa highlights some of the reasons why it has not protected African knowledge systems. The evolution of laws in Africa, as well as the vast majority of developing countries, was interrupted during colonisation.[102] Laws were transferred to African countries on the assumption that the imperial powers ought to civilise their subjects.[103] Since the Europeans were the major colonisers of African societies, it is appropriate to look at the origin of intellectual property in England and how it was made applicable to traditional African communities. The focus will be on copyright and patents, since they are the two forms of protection presently being considered by African countries for the protection of folklore and traditional knowledge, respectively.

Rulers in Europe were known to acknowledge individuals with exclusive rights to trade or sell a product. Later privileges were associated with inventions. While patents arose from a systematic use of monopoly privileges to encourage inventions,[104] copyright was the result of book privileges. The Statute of Anne Copyright Act 1709 (8 Anne C. 19) was the first

100 Ibid., 403.

101 Usually, where the parties are Africans, they could be tried in a native or territorial court, provided that these courts have jurisdiction over the subject matter concerned. Where both have concurrent jurisdiction, the case shall be tried in the court in which in the proceedings were commenced; African Court Act (1957) Uganda s 10.

102 Deborah Wassel, "From Mbube to Wimoweh: African Folk Music in Dual Systems of Law." (2009) 20 *Fordham Intellectual Property Media and Entertainment Law Journal* 297.

103 A. Endeshaw, Intellectual *Property Policy for Non-Industrial Countries* (Dartmouth, 1996) 150.

104 Edith Tilton Penrose, *The Economics of the International Patent System* (Johns Hopkins University Press 1951) 2.

copyright Act to be passed to outlaw piracy of books, thereby preventing a practice detrimental to authors.[105] This statute created exclusive rights by vesting them in the author not the publisher. However, authors could contract with publishers. The extension of copyright continued to areas such areas as engravings, sound recordings, films, broadcasts, and foreign works. Copyright protection continued to develop as the need arose in order to protect many Indigenous industries.[106] "The 1911 Act established a single code which conferred copyright protection on a number of works (whether published or not, and including many previously unprotectable works such as works of architecture, sound recordings, and films)."[107]

Patents were first granted to persons who introduced new and useful skills in the form of letters giving privileges and monopolies.[108] Parliament passed England's Statute of Monopolies 1623 (21 Jac. 1, c.3) declaring monopolies to be void except those granted for patents to inventors.[109] The patent term was limited to 14 years in contrast to the Venetian patent statute of 1474, which offered protection for a period of ten years. Some scholars have claimed that patent law and procedure originated in Venice in the 15th Century.[110] Florence in 1421 yielded to Brunelleschi's unprecedented demand for a limited right to sole commercial exploitation of his invention by granting him a public letter.[111] Patent law in England continued to develop according to industrial needs. In 1883 the Crown was relieved of its duties to grant patents and the patent office was set up to grant patents following the 1852 Act.

The English legal regime was introduced to African territories with minimal regard to existing local conditions. However, it was apparent that there was a fundamental philosophical divergence between the African legal system and Anglo-Saxon jurisprudence generally, particularly with

105 J. Holyoak and P. Torremans, *Intellectual Property Law* (Butterworths, 1995) 9; Statute of Anne Copyright Act 1709, 8 Anne C. 19.
106 J. Davis, *Intellectual Property Law* (Butterworths 2001) 3.
107 Lionel Bentley and Brad Sherman, Intellectual Property Law (Oxford University Press, 2004) 31.
108 D. Vaver, *Intellectual Property Law: Copyright, Patents, Trademarks* (Irwin Law 1997); the author gives a brief introduction to the development of intellectual property in England.
109 It is noteworthy that Parliament's reaction was against existing practice and the trading monopolies to which this practice gave rise, but it may have also been influenced by the idea that, in certain circumstances, a market monopoly would be necessary as an incentive to innovate.
110 Ikechi Mgbeoji, *Global Biopiracy: Patents, Plants and Indigenous Knowledge* (Cornell University Press 2006) 16.
111 Ibid.

particular reference to intellectual property protection.[112] Industrialisation resulted in the development of intellectual property rights and the scramble by African countries for natural resources and commodities.

Common law copyright was introduced into African countries through ordinances from England. The English Copyright Act of 1911 was the first major copyright act to be extended to Anglophone African countries (former British colonies). The Copyright Act of 1911 has been revised and extended over the years in different African countries due to pressure from developed countries and industries. Local piracy apparently was not an issue during this period since local commercial publishers and local music recording companies were absent.[113] There was no urgent need to make laws protecting local creators.[114] The appropriation of traditional knowledge started as far back as the colonisation period; recognition was not given to such theft because the appropriators were the persons making the rules.

The rights of the locals were not the paramount aim of the extension of the Act.[115] The extension of the 1911 Act was primarily to protect British books, art, music, films, and broadcasts.[116] Prior to the 1911 Copyright Act, consideration was given to British colonies. The colonies that adopted the terms of British copyright legislation were allowed to import cheap reprints of copyright materials.[117] There is no evidence to show Africa benefited from the Foreign Reprints Act. Patents gained recognition in African countries in the late nineteenth and early twentieth centuries. The patent system in Nigeria, Ghana, and most of the British colonies was a re-registration system governed by patent registration ordinances. Patent law was based on the registration system of the United Kingdom Patent Act, which provided that an invention registered in the UK may be registered through an authorised agent in these colonies.

The majority of the populace not being literate was taken into consideration in the application of intellectual property rights. This consideration was reflected in the case of *Otegbeye v Little*, where it was held that printed conditions limiting liability are only effective if drawn to the

112 Adebambo Adewopo, "The Global Intellectual Property System and Sub-Saharan Africa: A Prognostic Reflection" in Alexandra George (ed) *Globalization and Intellectual Property* (Ashgate Publishing Ltd 2006) 752.

113 B. Sodipo, *Piracy and Counterfeiting: GATT TRIPS and Developing Countries* (Kluwer Law International 1997).

114 Ibid.

115 Ibid.

116 Ibid.

117 B. Zorina Khan, "Intellectual Property and Economic Development: Lessons from American and European History" (A report commissioned by the Commission on Intellectual Property Commission) http://www.iprcommission.org/papers/word/study_papers/sp1a_khan_study.doc accessed 28 May 2008.

illiterate's notice.[118] There is no evidence to show the administration of a fully fledged patent system before the turn of the twentieth century. Patents were not granted; rather, they were extended from foreign countries. The rate of scientific inventions in African countries was seen as very low, and traditional inventions were ignored. The low level of patenting inventions is not only attributed to the low level of inventiveness but also to the lack of local patent agents with a scientific background. Solicitors were rarely trained to write patent specifications and apply for patents, and the high cost of first obtaining a UK patent and the administrative hurdles to procure foreign exchange to pay for the services of a foreign patent agent, contributed to this issue.

The patent system in Africa has not been successful because of the reasons stated above. In Nigeria the Patents and Designs Decree of 1970 provides for the original registration of a patent in Nigeria if the invention is new, results from inventive activity, and is capable of industrial application. The patent confers upon the patentee the right to preclude any other person from making, importing, selling, or using a patented product or using a patented process. A patentee may grant a licence to anyone to exploit a patent, or the court may grant a compulsory licence to any person to do so. Notwithstanding the provisions in existence for granting a patent, the number of patents in Nigeria and Africa generally is relatively low.

The Nigerian Patents Decree of 1970 allows a government department or agency or any person if so authorised by a Federal or State Commissioner, to make, use, exercise or vend any patented article or invention for the services of the Federal Republic. The ministry concerned shall furnish the patentee with information as to the extent of the use of such patented article, unless it appears to the commissioner to be contrary to the public interest to do so. The authority of the commission may be given retrospectively; it exempts any person, government department, or agency from liability to make any payment by way of royalty or otherwise to the patentee or any person deriving title from him by licence, assignment or agreement. The articles affected by this Decree are defined to include drugs, pharmaceutical preparations, substances or materials, and any plant, machinery or apparatus whether fixed to land or not after importation[119]

118 (1907) 1 N.L.R. 70; see also T.O. Elias, *The British Commonwealth: Nigeria the Development of its Laws and Constitutions* (Stevens & Sons Ltd 1967) 412.

119 A. V. Nylander, "Recent Commercial Legislation" in T. O. Elias, *Law and Social Changes in Nigeria* (University of Lagos and Evans Brothers Limited 1972) 75

3.7 Post-colonisation: two knowledge systems and pluralistic legal system: seeking a balance

Colonisation did not completely eliminate traditional knowledge systems, customs, and customary law.[120] Conversely, European influence cannot be eradicated from Africa. The practicality of reinstating traditional legal systems of the pre-colonial past remains challenging.[121] Traditional communities continue to change. African countries are now part of the modern, industrialised world, and their legal systems must recognise that fact.[122] Even if it is impossible to restore African legal institutions to their pristine state, it has been suggested that there is a need to recapture the essence of tradition in new laws which should be consciously constructed for Africa.[123] The fundamental structure of the legal systems in Africa and the relationship between the Europeans and Africa remains the same. Colonial government and laws were merely replaced by national institutions and statutes containing similar dispositions.[124] National constitutions and statutes authorise customary law as a major source of law to be determined and applied in legal proceedings when it is raised by the parties.

The codification of customary law did not stop after the departure of the colonisers.[125] Different methods have been adopted in African civil law countries to create a unified systematic law.[126] In Ethiopia codification has gone ahead without prior study of the local and very diverse customary laws. In common law African countries there has been little attempt to add to the initial deposit of codes. Attempts have been made to investigate the breach of the law with a view to producing a new law that would largely unify or integrate the previously diverse systems of written, customary, and religious laws. These attempts have not been successful. More successful

120 Deborah Wassel, "From Mbube to Wimoweh: African Folk Music in Dual Systems of Law." (2009) 20 *Fordham Intellectual Property Media and Entertainment Law Journal* 293.

121 A. N. Allot, "The Codification of the Law of Civil Wrongs" in *Common Law African Countries in Integration of Customary and Modern Legal Systems in Africa* (African Publishing Corporation and University of Ile-Ife Press 1964) 172.

122 Ibid.

123 Ibid.

124 A. N. Allot, "The Future of African Law" in Kuper and Kuper, *African Law: Adaptation and Development* (1965) 222.

125 John Adebisi Arewa, "Post-Colonial Africa and the Imperative of Fusion of Laws and Courts" in Epiphany Azinge and Animi Awah, *Legal Pluralism in Africa: A Compendium on African Customary Law* (Nigerian Institute of Advanced Legal Studies 2012) 155,

126 A.N. Allot, A.L. Epstein, and M. Gluckman, "Procedures" in M. Gluckman, *Ideas and Procedures in African Customary Law* (International African Institute for Oxford University Press 1969), 32. Ethiopia is included in this category of countries. In Madagascar, codification has been preceded by a long search and investigation of the local customary laws, while others have not taken the same steps.

were the attempts to restate in an authoritative form the customary laws of a given country.[127]

The Ghanaian constitution includes common law and the rules of customary law.[128] In this constitution, customary law is referred to as rules of law that by custom are applicable to particular communities in Ghana.[129] As a result, customary law is enforceable in judicial proceedings since it is part of the national law. In South Africa, customary law encompasses the domains of public and private law. In the field of public law, customary law with regard to traditional government and administration, certain traditional crimes, and the law with regard to traditional courts, procedures, and evidence are still applicable, although amended and significantly limited by various statute.[130]

In some African countries, traditional law stands on an equal footing with common law. In no sense is customary law fundamentally inferior or subsidiary.[131] The practicality of this statement can, however, be queried. More often than not, common law has a dominating position. The Lesotho Independence Order of 1966 defines existing law as including the customary law of the country,[132] and the constitution defines law as including the customary law of Lesotho.[133] The rule of customary law is usually ascertained through the use of assessors, who are regarded by the court as having expert knowledge of the particular local law and custom.[134] Presiding judges are not bound by the opinion of assessors.[135] In addition, evidence by an assessor can be dispensed with where an alleged rule of customary

127 Countries like Kenya, Malawi, Zambia and Swaziland have tried to restate authoritative forms of customary law, rather than an attempt unification.

128 Constitution of the Fourth Republic of Ghana (Promulgation Law), P.N.D.C.L. 282 (1992) art 11(2).

129 Ibid., art 11(3).

130 L.P. Vorster, "Indigenous Knowledge and Customary Law in South Africa." 24 (2) *Southern African Journal Ethnology* 52.

131 V.V. Palmer and S.M. Poulter, *The Legal System of Lesotho*, Legal Systems of Africa Series, Lesotho (The Michie Company 1972) 99–100.

132 s 4(5).

133 s 139(1) of the Constitution.

134 H. F. Morris, *The British Common wealth: Uganda The Development of its Laws and Constitutions* (Steven and Sons 1966); the author quoted a statement made in *Joel Motsoene v Sir Richard Harding* [1954] H.C.T.L.R. (reporting a decision given in 1940): "It is true that in the phrase Basotho law and custom the word custom is used, but in fact what we are dealing with here is a law. And that Law being an unwritten law, the best evidence one can obtain regarding it is the evidence of those who by virtue of their experience may be expected to be familiar with it."

135 Ibid.

law has been so frequently been used before the courts that judicial notice should be taken of it.[136]

African countries retained traditional legal systems. They have also retained the colonial system of government, laws, and culture.[137] Legal pluralism, as well as cultural pluralism, exists. The philosophical divergence between Africa and the West is visible in contemporary Africa. There were attempts by African leaders to avoid the Western dominance by pledging themselves to the elaboration of a genuine national and African body of law, which would require the retention, in varying degrees, of customary law. Ghana, under Nkrumah tried to control the post-colonial legal order with no success by calling for the "Africanisation" of the laws of Ghana.[138]

Traditional medicine knowledge in the 1960s under Nkrumah's policy was promoted as the "African Personality." There was a quest for an authentic African way of life, such as the Ghana Psychic and Traditional Healing Association (GPTHA).[139] There were, however, squabbles between psychics (diviners) and non-psychics (herbalists), Western and traditional medicine practitioners, and those who wanted to maintain tradition and the elites. The lack of success was due to elites under the colonial administration resenting limitations on the colonial legal order. This resentment finally led to the overthrow of Nkrumah and philosophies known to Africa.

African countries now associate modernisation with reliance on extended Western legislation without taking into consideration the types of law that will favour development. However, the intended modernisation of Africa to which Western legal infrastructures were transplanted has not been realised. It is worth mentioning that the United States has also tried to influence the intellectual property laws of African countries.[140] Africans are adhering to the American international relations and unilateral trade measures. The

136 Thierry Verhelst, "Safeguarding African Customary Law: Judicial and Legislative Processes for its Adaptation and Integration" (Occasional Paper No 7, Africa Studies Centre University of California, Los Angeles, addressed at the opening of Ghana Law School, 4 January 4 1962) (1962) 6 *Journal of African Law* 103.

137 Tanzania attempted to Indigenise the judicial process by developing alternative mechanisms of dispute settlement outside regular courts; see Dias L.J. et al., *Lawyers in the Third World: Comparative and Developmental Perspective* (1981) 295.

138 D. Brokensha, "Chieftaincy in Larteh" in Crowder and Ikimi *West African Chiefs: the Changing Status under Colonial Rule and Independence* (Caxton Press West Africa) 402. There was a sentimental regard for traditional customs. This was reflected by Nkrumah when he allowed himself to be enstooled as chief of his home area in Nzima in 1960.

139 Kodjo A. Senah, Joseph Kofi Adusei, and Samuel A. Akor, *A Baseline Study into Traditional Medicine Practice in Ghana* (MOH/DANIDA Project 2001) 7.

140 A. Endeshaw, *Intellectual Property Policy for Non-Industrial Countries* (Dartmouth) 157.

concern of the United States about the level of intellectual property protection in African countries is increasing. Their major concern has been the level of software piracy in African countries.[141] "The intriguing silence with which the relevance of western legal development to non-industrial countries of Africa is upheld as positive and sacrosanct has not helped the cause of change in Africa, whether economic, technological or even legal."[142]

The intellectual property system, which was incorporated in the borrowed colonial laws, is still applicable after independence. It was the starting point for future laws in African countries. Ghana and Nigeria gradually made adaptations to colonial legislation in this area.[143] The former French colonies had to create their own legislative systems with regard to industrial property. They were faced with a complete legal void apart from the French laws. The colonies did not develop independent provisions or administrative bodies capable of handling intellectual property applications. They took the opportunity to integrate by drawing up a set of common laws and a common office for registration and the grant of industrial property titles in collaboration with France's National Institute of Industrial Property (INPI).[144] The renunciation of national sovereignty by this integration resulted in a single title of protection valid in each former colony and one law that each of them applied. The African Intellectual Property Organization (OAPI) arose from this integration in 1962 with a supposedly new set of laws, assisted by France, the former colonial power.[145]

The usage of traditional medicinal knowledge after colonisation has become more prominent. As much as 80 per cent of the African population use traditional medicine for primary health care.[146] In Ghana, Mali, Nigeria, and Zambia, the first line of treatment for 60 per cent of children with high fever resulting from malaria is herbal medicine at home.[147] WHO estimates that in several African countries, traditional birth attendants assist in the majority of births, and 75 per cent of people living with HIV/

141 See the Fourth Annual BSA and IDC Global Software Piracy Study http://www.ifap.ru/library/book184.pdf accessed 28 May 2008.

142 A. Endeshaw, *Intellectual Property Policy for Non-Industrial Countries* (Dartmouth) 157.

143 Ibid.

144 Ibid.

145 Ibid.

146 Message from the WHO Regional Director for Africa, Dr Matshidiso, on African Traditional Medicine (31 August 2022) https://www.afro.who.int/regional-director/speeches-messages/african-traditional-medicine-day-2022 accessed 20 December 2024.

147 Yusuf Ghazali, Ibrahim Bello, Adeola Kola-Mustapha, "The Use of Herbal Medicines among Outpatients at the University of Ilorin Teaching Hospital (UITH), Ilorin, Kwara State." (2019) *Complementary Therapies in Medicine* https://doi.org/10.1016/j.ctim.2018.11.016.
https://www.sciencedirect.com/science/article/pii/S0965229918306794

AIDS use traditional medicine in South Africa.[148] The global market for herbal medicine is growing. Medicinal plants are a major asset to African countries and an immeasurable resource for the pharmaceutical industry.

> There is an increasing interest in the use of herbal medicines due to the everyday consumer's preference of products of natural origin resulting in a growing number of national traditional medicine research institutes in developing countries such as Nigeria, China, Ghana, India, Madagascar and Vietnam.[149]

Traditional knowledge of medicinal plants, such as the use of natural insecticides and repellents, fertility-regulating drugs, edible plants, animal behaviour, and skin and body treatments, is used across countries in Africa.[150] Useful plant materials for the cure of malaria, a leading cause of mortality in Africa, include roots, root bark, leaves, seeds, or plants.[151] These materials could be used in their original form, or powdered or the necessary active ingredients could be extracted. It is claimed that three-quarters of traditional medicine based on plants is known to traditional communities.[152] In many instances, as earlier stated in the introductory chapter, unauthorised users are granted patent rights over products or processes based on traditional knowledge without acknowledging traditional communities.

Traditional medicine, though it qualifies for protection, might not be easily inculcated into the modern legal system, particularly if it has become common knowledge. Traditional medicine in recent times may easily fit into the modern legal system of protection. However, Africans are very concerned about the continued expansion of intellectual property rights to living organisms. As much as intellectual property rights are being contemplated, they frown at the manner in which the Western world uses this instrument to covet all things. One such ways is declaring that traditional knowledge is seen at best as pieces of historical and often incremental information that reside in the public domain.[153]

African countries are now confronted with what strategies to maintain in protecting traditional knowledge. They have both the traditional

148 Ibid.
149 Ibid.
150 D. Posey, "Ethnoentomological survey of Brazilian Kayapo Indians" in Kristina Plenderleith (ed) *Indigenous Knowledge and Ethics: A Darrell Posey Reader* (Routledge 2004) 29.
151 Jasper Ogwal-Okeng, "Traditional Herbal Treatment of Malaria in Uganda – Is there any scientific basis?" in Robert N. Mshana and Mbaye Ndoye, *African Traditional Medicine and Medicinal Plants* (OAU/STRC 1999) 96
152 Ibid.
153 Chidi Oguamanam, *International Law and Indigenous Knowledge: Intellectual Property, Plant Biodiversity, and Traditional Medicine* (University of Toronto Press 2006) 160.

and modern systems of legal protection at their disposal. These challenges have transcended to the international community, where there are still difficulties in drafting an international instrument for traditional knowledge systems. Since 2001, the World Intellectual Property Organisation (WIPO) has been at the negotiations table for twenty years for a treaty providing protection for genetic resources and associated traditional knowledge, due to its importance to traditional peoples and communities.[154] On 24 May 2024, the Diplomatic Conference on Genetic Resources and Associated Traditional Knowledge adopted the Treaty on Intellectual Property, Genetic Resources and Traditional Knowledge.[155] However, this new treaty does not bring the journey of seeking an appropriate protection mechanism to an end because other areas of traditional knowledge systems are still awaiting protection.[156]

3.8 African jurisprudence: the dilemma of the public domain concept on customary law and traditional peoples

Whether traditional knowledge is in the public domain or not is an issue that has to be examined since the public domain renders some information unprotectable in aspects of intellectual property law. Some scholars have described traditional knowledge as property of the public domain. However, other scholars perceive the public domain as foreign and inappropriate because it contains traditional cultural forms that were appropriated in violation of customary laws without their prior informed consent.

A general overview of the public domain concept shows it has not been given much attention in the statutes establishing and regulating intellectual property.[157] It is implicit in most statutes.[158] No statutory definition has been provided for this term.[159] The requirements for original works

154 Ayla do Vale Alves, "WIPO's New Treaty on Intellectual Property, Genetic Resources and Traditional Knowledge – A Turning Point for Indigenous Heritage." (19 September 2024) 13(11) *ESIL Reflections* 2.

155 Ibid.

156 Ibid.

157 A. S. Oddi, "The Tragic Comedy of the Public Domain in Intellectual Property Law." (2002) 25 *Hastings Commercial and Entertainment Law Journal* 1.

158 The concept of public domain is implicit in the requirement of originality by an author or inventor. The term public domain has not appeared in various patent statutes and has only recently appeared in the US copyright statute (17 U.S.C.A. s. 101) by the addition of s. 104A (Copyright in Restored Works) to comply with WTO Agreements as implemented by the Uruguay Round Agreement Act.

159 Ruth L. Okediji, "Traditional Knowledge and the Public Domain." June 2018 176 *Center for International Governance Innovation (CIGI)* Papers 2 https://www.cigionline.org/sites/default/files/documents/Paper%20no.176web.pdf accessed 10 October

of authorship and novelty in innovations are arrows that point towards uniqueness, implicitly stating that works in the public domain are no longer original or new. Simply put, the public domain is a space where intellectual property rights do not exist, a 'commons that includes those aspects of copyrighted works which copyright does not protect'.[160] This domain consists of knowledge and information that have no individual owner or owners, and it is available to all members of society for use, development, or experimentation.

Permission is not necessary to use information (when their duration has expired) in the public domain in some countries. Traditional knowledge is often claimed to belong in the public domain without the initial intellectual property protection and in the absence of the expiration of a duration. Much of this information was not transferred with the consent of traditional peoples, nor were the applicable customary laws examined to determine the status of this knowledge system. Scholarly research has shown that for centuries, collected data have been published, and some are available on the internet, thus feeding information into the public domain. Once information is passed into the public domain, the originators lose the option to seek intellectual property protection.[161] The view that traditional knowledge is in the public domain is further reinforced by the assumption that properties of traditional peoples are free, based on the concept of "*intellectual terra nullius.*"[162] The public domain is seen as conveniently obscuring inequalities, "particularly those of Indigenous groups, and their lack of ability to equally access, use and benefit from a commons constructed without consideration for their interests."[163] This claim contrasts with the view that the public domain is an ideal that assumes equal access to the goods within it.[164]

2024. "More pointedly, the claim that protection for traditional knowledge is largely pre-empted by 'the' public domain lacks support in international IP law. There is no widely accepted view of the public domain and competing views of the public domain exist at national levels. The public domain is not a legal construct in any of the leading international IP conventions. Finally, the fundamental principle that IP rights are territorial leaves delimitation of the public domain to national laws."

160 Jessica Litman, "The Public Domain." (1990) 39 *Emory L.J.* 965–968.

161 AAAS Project on Traditional Ecological Knowledge: Traditional Knowledge and the Public Domain, http://shr.aaas.org/tek/publicdomain.htm accessed 24 October 2005.

162 D. Posey, "Ethnoentomological survey of Brazilian Kayapo Indians" in Kristina Plenderleith (ed) *Indigenous Knowledge and Ethics: A Darrell Posey Reader* (Routledge 2004), 203.

163 A.S. Oddi, "The Tragic Comedy of the Public Domain in Intellectual Property Law" (2002) 25 *Hastings Commercial and Entertainment Law Journal* 1.

164 Ibid.

> We stress that there are striking similarities between seizing our territories and the taking of our knowledge by defining it as part of the public domain. Both are based on the notion that they constitute *res nullius*, the property of no one, and can be treated as such. Placing our knowledge into the public domain turns it into a freely available resource for commercial utilisation.[165]

It is detrimental to traditional peoples for their knowledge systems to be in the public domain. Placing traditional knowledge in the public domain creates the possibility of patenting inventions derived from traditional knowledge by third parties. The criteria for novelty, the necessary inventive step, or the level of creativity which are prerequisites for protection under patent law are seen as unachievable by traditional knowledge holders.[166] The resources and associated knowledge of traditional peoples are susceptible to privatisation as intellectual property, even though the public domain is seen as protecting an intellectual commons against the encroachment of private property.[167] This view is usually reached by claiming that traditional knowledge lacks those requirements stated above. It can be argued that traditional knowledge of the past, although common to traditional communities, is relatively novel to the western world and its use should be authorised.[168] Traditional knowledge of the present is often novel because it consists of new innovations and creations which are expected to be passed on to future generations. Using the same criteria as those used under intellectual property to determine properties in the public domain, the following conclusions will arise:

A. Traditional knowledge is not in the public domain because it is protected by traditional legal systems such as customary law.

165 Indigenous Peoples and the International and Domestic Protection of traditional Knowledge – A Review of Developments Pertaining to the Promotion and Protection of Indigenous Peoples, Including Their Human Rights and Fundamental Freedoms (Joint statement from the Indigenous World Association and Indigenous Media Network, Working Group on Indigenous Populations twenty-third session 18–22 July 2005, Item 4 of the Provisional Agenda) Document: E/CN.4/Sub.2/AC.4/2005/CRP.3.

166 S. Biber-Klemm, "Incentives to Bring about Conservation and Sustainable Use of Genetic Resources in the Framework of the World Trade Order" in T. Cottier and P.C. Mavroidis (eds.) *Intellectual Property: Trade, Competition, and Sustainable Development*, World Trade Forum Volume 3 (University of Michigan Press 2002) 494.

167 Anupam Chander and Madhavi Sunder, "The Romance of the Public Domain." (2004) 92 *California Law Review* 1333.

168 A.K. Gupta, "Conserving Biodiversity and Rewarding Associated Knowledge and Innovation Systems: Honey Bee Perspective" in T. Cottier and P. C. Mavroidis (eds.) *Intellectual Property: Trade, Competition, and Sustainable Development* World Trade Forum, Volume 3 (University of Michigan Press 2002) 372.

B. The absence of aspects of intellectual property law protection for traditional knowledge systems does not place them in public domain.
C. Where aspects of intellectual property protection are sought, the public domain criteria become applicable on the expiration of protection.
D. Traditional knowledge in this era may not fail to satisfy formal or substantive requirements of aspects of intellectual property law.
E. Traditional knowledge in customary law is protected in perpetuity; there is no limitation as to time; therefore, protection does not terminate or become invalidated.
F. Secrecy is a mode of protecting traditional medicine knowledge, making it private property and out of the realm of the public domain.

Traditional knowledge has been communally used for generations because traditional peoples believe in communal sharing of produce. Its continued use without intellectual property protection reflects the fact that communal sharing does not infringe nor is it disrespectful to the originators of traditional knowledge, whether of an animate or inanimate nature. The public domain is expected to be in the interest of the public because it increases the stock of free public knowledge. Denying traditional peoples the capacity to be part of the labour market through the dominance of the public domain concept, in which their knowledge is made easily appropriable, takes away their freedom to development and eradication of poverty.[169] Some scholars see a viable and vigorous public domain as indispensable to inventiveness.[170] However, it is presumable that a vigorous public domain, as it is perceived by some (a sanctuary for unprotectable or unprotected intellectual properties), is dispensable to inventiveness within traditional communities. Nature, on the other hand, is indispensable to inventiveness because knowledge can be continually drawn from it by traditional peoples. Traditional communities in Africa made the commons of both tangible and intangible resources available to all members of their communities. They guarded against the overuse of the commons; elders or heads of a community or family determined who is allowed to use resources and the length of time for which such resources can be used.[171]

In an attempt to develop protection mechanisms for traditional knowledge systems, the public domain concept, as it affects the status of traditional

169 Amartya Kumar Sen, *Development as Freedom* (Oxford University Press 2001) 87–112.

170 J. Otieno-Odek, "Public Domain in Patentability after the Uruguay Round: A Developing Country's Perspective with Specific Reference to Kenya." (1996) 4 *Tulane Journal of International and Comparative Law* 15

171 George Monbiot, "Tragedy of Enclosure." (January 1994) *The Scientific American Journal* https://www.monbiot.com/1994/01/01/the-tragedy-of-enclosure/ 30 September 2024.

knowledge systems and customary law, should be given adequate consideration. Unless traditional knowledge holders seek intellectual property protection apart from their customary law protection, they should not be bound by concepts associated with intellectual property rights, such as the public domain concept. Traditional legal systems in Africa protecting intangible properties remain tenacious, and due accord should be given to them. If recognition is given to traditional norms, the transfer of communal intellectual properties into the public domain can only be achieved by communal consent and not by unauthorised exposure.

3.9. Developments in literatures on the status of African traditional knowledge systems and customary law

A system of protection for African traditional knowledge should be consistent with customary law.[172] A system of protection that is not useful to traditional peoples or of which they are unaware, or that they do not know how to benefit from regarding their knowledge system, should be avoided. To date, the intellectual property system of protection is unknown in many communities in Africa. In addition, there is limited knowledge among the elites, including legislators, the legislators, judiciary, legal professionals, stakeholders, and more, about this protection mechanism. The difference between customary law and state law lies mainly in the limitations of the former. In this regard, local governance systems should ideally be addressed by improving them rather than creating parallel ones, as if these will automatically function better.

Literatures reflect the various views of scholars on protection mechanisms and property rights as they relate to traditional peoples at the communal level in Africa and beyond. It is noteworthy that two major issues continue to surface while reviewing these literatures: the lack of recognition of traditional norms within the formal structure and the failure of the formal structure to recognise the intellectual property rights of traditional peoples in Africa.

Traditional knowledge should be viewed from a bottom-up approach in order to accommodate traditional legal systems in existence within the intellectual property framework in most African countries. Viewing the protection of traditional knowledge systems from a top-down approach, though a common practice, relegates traditional peoples and their legal

172 Graham Dutfield, "Protecting Traditional Knowledge and Folklore" in Grosheide F. W. and Brinkhof J. J. *Intellectual Property Law Articles on Cultural Expressions and Indigenous Knowledge* (Intersentia 2002).

systems.[173] Eurocentric perspectives are dismissive of other non-Western jurisprudence. A pluralistic jurisprudential approach would include the use of provisions within classical intellectual property rights whilst also exploring communal intellectual property provisions.[174] Sole reliance on the Western perspective of ways to protect the traditional knowledge systems of Africans will be detrimental to the holders of such knowledge systems and the continent as a whole. Customary law protection of traditional knowledge systems in Africa is, without a doubt, a pre-colonisation system of protection. There should be a detailed review of what exists in traditional African communities prior to creating appropriate national and international laws.

The claim that African traditional knowledge is located primarily among traditional or local peoples who are often socially and economically marginalised is debatable. The dependence on this system of knowledge, particularly traditional medicine knowledge, is relatively high within both the rural and urban settlement areas of Africa. Every African, elite or otherwise, belongs to a tribe, and all tribes have their knowledge systems. It is therefore not viable to assume traditional peoples are relegated to a stipulated area. There are traditional peoples that fit into the Indigenous peoples' category and those that do not. Indigenous peoples are predominantly found in Australia, Canada, South Africa (an African country with white settlers after independence), and the United States. In these countries, the marginalisation of Indigenous groups is prominent. Their physical and intangible resources are constantly being appropriated. The majorities (original settlers) have become the minorities. The minorities (white settlers) have become the majorities. In contrast, traditional peoples remain the majority in most African countries and continue to be the poor people of Africa.[175]

Often ignored is the fact that traditional communities profited from their knowledge systems in the past and continue to do so in the present and future. Traditional knowledge that symbolises religious and spiritual beliefs, practices or customs is sacred and offensive if commercialised. Nevertheless, sacred objects and knowledge have been exploited alongside other forms of traditional knowledge for commercial purposes. Traditional

173 S. von Lewinski (ed) *Indigenous Heritage and Intellectual Property: Genetic Resources, Traditional Knowledge and Folklore* (Kluwer Law International 2004).

174 Ibid.

175 Josue Dione, "Science and Technology Policies for Sustainable Development and Africa's Global Inclusion" (address at the ATPS Conference, Abuja, Nigeria, 11 November 2002) 2. "Twenty-five of the world's 30 poorest countries are found in Africa ... Fifty per cent of the population in this part of Africa live in extreme poverty, i.e. on less than US$1 a day, and are unable to have access to the minimum basic needs of food, shelter, education and health care."

communities can differentiate between forms of traditional knowledge that are sacred or not. All forms of traditional knowledge require adequate protection and reverence. The objects and knowledge identified as sacred have been respected and protected within traditional communities for centuries. Those that have not been declared as sacred have no economic restrictions if holders of such knowledge give authorisation to use.[176] African societies are not oblivious to the economic gains from traditional knowledge at the communal level. Despite their awareness, it remains difficult to control, protect and develop this sector in Africa.[177] Nevertheless, the market-oriented aspect of intellectual property ensuring a share of economic benefits goes to the innovator cannot be avoided.[178]

The interests of traditional peoples are dictated by the political contexts in which they operate.[179] "In one context, traditional knowledge is more an aspect of self-determination and survival. In another, it may be a question of economic empowerment."[180] On the platform of self-determination, traditional peoples are more concerned about reaffirming their reaffirming rights as they relate to the environment and the management of their resources. These rights are reinforced in certain situations in legal and policy contexts at national and international levels.[181] The capacity of traditional communities to become economically empowered is low. Even though traditional knowledge is often exploited, traditional communities derive little or no benefits from the exploiters. Conversely, benefiting from the use of their knowledge should enhance their development

176 There are opposing views as to whether economic or commercial benefit from traditional knowledge is the push for protection rather than the need for holders of such knowledge to protect the holistic nature or sacredness of such knowledge from distortion or misappropriation by external users. However, available evidence shows that African countries are aware of the need for competition and profit-making due to years of poverty and hardship. The interest in growing economically has increased, and the possibilities have been made available by globalisation. Even though they want to keep what is holy and sacred, there is still an interest in benefiting from goods that are commercially viable.

177 Paulo P. Mhame, "The Role of Traditional Knowledge (TK) in the National Economy: The Importance and Scope of TK, Particularly Traditional Medicine in Tanzania" UNCTAD Expert Meeting on Systems and National Experiences for Protecting Traditional Knowledge, Innovations and Practices Geneva 30 October–1 November 2000.

178 David R. Downes, "How Intellectual Property Could be a Tool to Protect Traditional Knowledge." (2000) 25 *Columbia Journal of Environmental Law* 259.

179 Chidi Oguamanam, *International Law and Indigenous Knowledge: Intellectual Property, Plant Biodiversity and Traditional Medicine* (University of Toronto Press 2006), 77.

180 Ibid.

181 Tyler D. Jessen et al. "Contribution of Indigenous Knowledge to Ecological and Evolutionary Understanding." (2022) 20(2) *Front Ecol Environ* 93–101, 94 DOI:10.1002/fee.2435. See also Petosky, John, "International Traditional Knowledge Protection and Indigenous Self-Determination." (2020) 6(1) *The Indigenous Peoples' Journal of Law, Culture & Resistance* DOI: 10.5070/P661051241.

economically.[182] Economists remain optimistic that the integration of liberal trading policies into the global economy will encourage growth and raise poor countries out of poverty.[183] Traditional knowledge is indispensable to Africans. It contributes to the present-day survival of a large part of humanity and is an asset to trade.[184]

The uniqueness of culture can generate income and be socially beneficial to the holders of such knowledge.[185] Knowledge systems of Africans cannot readily be found in their original state in western countries but can be seen in the everyday activities of African traditional communities. The need to enjoy life, notwithstanding the current political, medical, social, and economic upheaval, has not hindered the innovative or creative ability of Africans, either in the area of science or arts.[186] Happiness is generated from cultural activities. Traditional knowledge has a symbiotic relationship with culture. The intellectual activity that creates traditional knowledge stems from the habits and customs of the society.[187] These activities are

182 A.K. Gupta, "Conserving Biodiversity and Rewarding Associated Knowledge and Innovation Systems: Honeybee Perspective" in T. Cottier and P.C. Mavroidis (eds) *Intellectual Property: Trade, Competition and Sustainable Development* (The University of Michigan Press, 2003) 373.

183 K.E. Maskus and J.H. Reichman, "The Globalisation of Private Knowledge Goods and the Globalisation of Global Public Goods" in K.E. Maskus and J. Reichman (eds) *International Public Goods and Transfer of Technology Under a Globalised Intellectual Property Regime* (Cambridge University Press 2005) 3, see also note 1 Nicholas Stern, "International Action for Fighting Poverty: An Historic Opportunity," lecture presented at Duke University on September 2, 2003; J. H. Reichman, "Managing the Challenge of a Globalized Intellectual Property Regime" paper presented to the second Bellagio Meeting on Intellectual Property and Development, UNCTAD/ICTSD, 17–20 September 2003.

184 S. Biber-Klemm, "The Protection of Traditional Knowledge at the International Level – Reflections in Connection with World Trade" United Nations Conference on Trade and Development (UNCTAD) Expert Meeting on Systems and National Experiences for Protecting Traditional Knowledge, Innovations and Practices Geneva 30 October–1 November 2000.

185 T. Fenta, "Biodiversity Conservation and Utilisation on the Basis of Farmers' Traditional Knowledge: Ethiopian Experience" United Nations Conference on Trade and Development (UNCTAD) Expert Meetings on Systems, National Experience for Protecting Traditional Knowledge Innovations and Practices, Geneva, 30 October–1 November 1 2000.

186 http://www.worldbank.org/research/Poor_Peoples_Knowledge.pdf accessed 10 April 2005.

187 S. Scadifi, "Intellectual Property and Cultural Products." (2001) 81 *Boston University Law Review* 810.

money-generating for the communities,[188] and the cultural value attached to them is always visible.[189]

Protecting the economic rights of traditional knowledge holders is crucial, even though some scholars focus more on the moral rights of knowledge holders.[190] They seem to be of the view that traditional knowledge holders, as opposed to Western knowledge holders, do not require or seek economic compensation for their knowledge because of its tie to the earth. However, Finger and Schuler focused on promoting the invention of knowledge and creative skills of poor people in poor countries and the economic interests of traditional peoples.[191] African music and craft are presented as having great economic value.[192] The promotion of traditional commodities and better training for the creators of these works is emphasised.[193]

3.10. The multidisciplinary nature of traditional knowledge systems: customary law versus *sui generis* system

A *sui generis* means "of its own kind,"[194] an alternative to intellectual property rights which should accommodate the concerns of traditional communities to protect their knowledge systems and resources and to prevent others from privatising them.[195] However, in protecting the intellectual property rights of traditional peoples, this system is not completely free of intellectual property rights. Intellectual property rights and *sui generis* systems are contenders in protecting traditional knowledge systems; hardly is customary law considered. There is a perspective that the protection

188 A.K. Gupta, "Conserving Biodiversity and Rewarding Associated Knowledge and Innovation Systems: Honeybee Perspective" in T. Cottier and P.C. Mavroidis (eds) *Intellectual Property: Trade, Competition and Sustainable Development* (The University of Michigan Press 2003) 373.

189 S. Subbiah, "Reaping What They Sow: The Basmati Rice Controversy and Strategies for Protecting Traditional Knowledge." (2004) *Boston College International and Comparative Law Review* 530

190 Ayoyemi Lawal-Arowolo, "Economic Significance of Protecting Expressions of Folklore in Nigeria" in Isaac O. Agbede and Ayoyemi Lawal-Arowolo (Eds), *Babcock University Essays on Contemporary Legal Issues* (Princeton 2017) 136.

191 J.M. Finger and P. Schuler, *Poor People's Knowledge: Promoting Intellectual Property in Developing Countries* (Oxford Press and World Bank 2004).

192 Ibid.

193 Ayoyemi Lawal-Arowolo, "Economic Significance of Protecting Expressions of Folklore in Nigeria" in Isaac O. Agbede and Ayoyemi Lawal-Arowolo (eds), *Babcock University Essays on Contemporary Legal Issues* (Princeton 2017) 137.

194 Patricia Lucia and Cantuaria Marin, *Providing Protection for Plant Genetic Resources, Patents, Sui Generis Systems and Biopatnership* (Kluwer Law International 2002) 68.

195 Darrell A. Posey and Graham Dutfield, *Beyond Intellectual Property: Towards Traditional Resource Rights for Indigenous Peoples and Local Communities* (IDRC 1996) Chapter 9.

of traditional knowledge should not be limited to aspects of intellectual property law or a flexible but similar concept in the form of a *sui generis*.[196] Traditional peoples should be able to use a suitable system of protection, the same way western countries have been able to.[197] According to William Hennessy, "what is sauce for the goose is sauce for the gander."[198] In view of the fact that developed countries have demanded compensation through their government trade officials for the use of their intellectual properties in developing countries, the latter should be able to do the same with their tradition-based intellectual properties in developed countries.[199]

A complex interaction between various disciplines of a Western nature, such as human rights law, land law, environmental law, and intellectual property protection, is visible. There are customary laws that cut across the same disciplines. Darrell Posey examined the bundle of rights that can be used for protection, compensation, and conservation of knowledge and resources under traditional resource rights (TRR). TRR is an "integrated concept that recognises the inextricable link between cultural and biological diversity" and "sees no contradiction between the human rights of Indigenous and local communities, including the right to development and environmental conservation."[200] Nevertheless, it is the aspects of intellectual

196 William O. Hennessy, "Toward A Conceptual Framework for Recognition of Rights for Holders of Traditional Knowledge and Folklore" http://www.faculty.piercelaw.edu/hennessey/RghtsfrHldrs.pdf accessed 20 March 2006. The rights of traditional peoples may be extended to include (but are perhaps not limited to) (1) the right to identification, which is in consonance with the fundamental principle of self-determination of peoples enshrined in Article 1.2 of the United Nations Charter (2) the right to information (3) the right to participation, which is inherent in the principle of mutual benefit, formalised in Article 9.2(c) of the International Treaty of Genetic Resources for Food and Agriculture adopted by the FAO conference on 3 November 2001; the right to participate is also found in Article 15(4) of the CBD and the principle of mutual benefit in Common Article 1(2) of the International Convention on Civil and Political Rights (ICCPR) and the International Convention on Economic, Social and Cultural Rights (ICESCR). "Traditional Knowledge holders need to be treated equally before the law." (4) the right to sharing of risk and benefit, which is one of the principles of the CBD, Article 8(j) and 15(7) and Article 9.2(b) of the International Treaty on Genetic Resources for Food and Agriculture adopted by the FAO available at ftp://ext-ftp.fao.org/waicent/pub/cgrfa8/iu/ITPGRe.pdf (5) the right to conservation of the natural environment, which is intimately implicated in the right of peoples to the preservation of their culture, and (6) the right to preservation, giving traditional peoples the right to freely pursue their economic, social, and cultural development, and its prohibition against depriving a people of their own means of subsistence; customary law is viewed as providing protection with a price.

197 Ibid.

198 Ibid.

199 Ibid.

200 Darrell A. Posey and Graham Dutfield, *Beyond Intellectual Property: Toward Traditional Resource Rights for Indigenous Peoples and Local Communities* (IDRC 1996) Chapter 9.

property law, including copyright and other related rights, patents, trademarks, industrial designs, and geographical indications, in contrast to the other laws mentioned above, that protect the rights based on the produce of the mind.[201]

Aspects of intellectual property law have their differences, but "one factor that they share in common is that they establish property protection over intangible things such as ideas, inventions, signs, and information."[202] Intellectual property law assigns exclusive rights to creative works, inventions, commercial symbols, etc., and to the use of information for economic gain in order to solve problems of appropriation and to avoid market failure.[203] Aspects of intellectual property law are important to persons who wish to exploit their intellectual produce. A monopoly over intellectual produce is dependent on the holder. Traditional knowledge systems are protectable by intellectual property law, including but not limited to traditional music, technology, symbols, designs, medicine, foods, and cosmetics. Some aspects of intellectual property law are more suitable for protecting some aspects of traditional knowledge systems.

Aside from the economic aspect, intellectual property law fulfils functions that are based on purely moral rights.[204] It is a body of law intended to achieve a particular set of ends, economic or otherwise in nature. With this perspective of intellectual property law, some still find it an inappropriate system of protection for traditional knowledge found in Africa and various developing countries;[205] even though there are similarities in the creative and inventive process.[206] These difficulties arise due to the superiority and inferiority dichotomy, and industrialised economies have often exploited the tangible and now the intangible resources of developing economies in

201 J. Phillips and A. Firth, *Introduction to Intellectual Property Law* (Butterworth and Lexis Nexis 2001) 4.

202 Lionel Bentley and Brad Sherman, *Intellectual Property Law* (2nd edn Oxford University Press 2004) 1

203 Susette Biber-Klemm, "Rights to Plant Genetic Resources and Traditional Knowledge: Basic Issues and Perspectives on Law and Policy" SDC/WTI First Expert Workshop, 24–26 November 2002, Bern, Switzerland.

204 Ibid.

205 The protection of traditional knowledge is not seen as intrinsically inconsistent with intellectual property systems that support private ownership of information, even as they respect national sovereignty.

206 T. Cottier, "The Protection of Genetic Resources and Traditional Knowledge: Towards More Specific Rights and Obligations in World Trade Law." 4 *Journal of International Environmental Law* 561, 569–573 (1998), see also T. Cottier and M. Pazzon, "Legal Perspectives on Traditional Knowledge: The Case for Intellectual Property Protection" in K. E. Maskus and J. Reichman, *International Public Goods and Transfer of Technology Under a Globalized Intellectual Property Regime* (Cambridge University Press 2005) 510.

the trading arena.[207] The development goals that are, in theory hindered by strong intellectual property rights have become the fodder of the larger conflict between developed and developing countries over global protection of intellectual property rights,[208] and the controversies and problems that come with the institutionalisation of the intellectual property system in non-western societies.[209] Intellectual property rights remain new to African countries in comparison to the developed world and developing countries with emerging economies. African countries should seek a better understanding of intellectual property rights in order to protect their knowledge systems, their local industries, and for economic development.[210]

3.11. Advocacy for a *sui generis* system: customary law losing its status

A *sui generis* system should at least provide for an intellectual property right to be compatible with international instruments such as the Trade-Related Aspects of Intellectual Property Rights (TRIPs).[211] The TRR, Traditional Intellectual Property Rights (TIP-Rights), and Community Intellectual Property Rights (CIPR) are forms of *sui generis* systems advocating for a bundle of rights including intellectual property rights. Therefore, the advocacy for a *sui generis* system may result in the creation of another

207 V. Shiva, *Biopiracy: The Plunder of Nature and Knowledge* (Green Books in Association with The Gaia Foundation 1998) 15. "IPRs are a prescription for a monoculture of knowledge."

208 C.A. Primo Braga and C. Fink, "Reforming Intellectual Property Rights Regime Challenges for Developing Countries." (1998) 1 *Journal of International Environmental Law* 545. The TRIPS intellectual property system disfavour developing countries and it has often been often criticized. See also David R. Downes, How Intellectual Property Could Be a Tool to Protect Traditional Knowledge (2000) 25 *Columbia Journal of Environmental Law* 253, 255. The TRIPS Agreement in its present form and scope primarily responds to the needs of industrialised countries.

209 Ikechi Mgbeoji, "Patents and Traditional Knowledge of the Uses of Plants: Is a Communal Patent Regime Part of the Solution to the Scourge of Bio-Piracy?" (2001–2002) 9 *Indiana Journal of Global Legal Studies* 163. "Given the European cultural milieu in which the patent system originated, the institutionalisation of the patent law system in non-western societies has been both controversial and problematic."

210 African countries did not have the opportunity to properly develop their intellectual property law until recently. See K.E. Maskus, *Intellectual Property Rights in the Global Economy* (Institute for International Economics 2000) 15. A major reason for this is their classification as users and importers of technology. Over the years, countries with weak intellectual property law have been responsible for tens of billions of dollars in lost sales annually, according to surveys conducted by the United States International Trade Commission (1984, 1988).

211 *Patricia Lucia and Cantuaria Marin's Providing Protection for Plant Genetic Resources* (n 89).

dominant system secondary to intellectual property rights, further emphasising inequality in knowledge systems and underrating the sophistication of traditional knowledge.[212]

The intellectual property system remains superior even though a *sui generis* system is feasible and a forceful rival in the protection of traditional peoples knowledge.[213] Some of the reasons justifying an alternative system have been identified by scholars as the difficulties in identifying owners or authors and the definite term of protection or the originality and novelty requirements of copyright and patent law.[214] These reasons are seen as disadvantageous to the interests of traditional peoples. The irreconcilable nature of traditional knowledge and intellectual property rights has been highlighted from the onset of discussions regarding the protection of traditional knowledge systems.[215] The difficulty in classifying traditional knowledge innovations and practices into categories of intellectual property was raised. The lines between Indigenous religion, culture, business, and intellectual and physical property are not as distinct or mutually exclusive; therefore, they cannot be owned as private rights under intellectual property law.

As earlier mentioned, TRR is intended to reflect the utilisation of the concepts of protection and reward,[216] "recognising that traditional resources both tangible and intangible are covered under a number of international agreements and these can be used to form the basis for a *sui generis* right."[217] It is proposed that a TRR framework will take account

212 "It can easily be assumed that traditional knowledge fails to exhibit the defining eligibility criteria while western/scientific knowledge easily qualifies and is eligible for protection. Also, traditional knowledge holders 'find it difficult to conceptualise intellectual ownership of these resources and their encapsulation in private rights." T. Cottier and M. Pazzon, "Legal Perspectives on Traditional Knowledge: The Case for Intellectual Property Protection" in K.E. Maskus and J. Reichman, *International Public Goods and Transfer of Technology Under a Globalized Intellectual Property Regime* (Cambridge University Press 2005).

213 Padmashree Gehl Sampath, *Regulating Bioprospecting: Institute for Drug Research, Access and Benefit Sharing* (United Nations University Press: 2005) 121. A system of *sui generis* community intellectual property rights is classified as one of the most effective options to protect traditional medicinal knowledge/ethnobotanical knowledge.

214 S. Sand, "*Sui Generis* Laws for the Protection of Indigenous Expressions of Culture and Traditional Knowledge." 22 (2003) *University of Queensland Law Journal* 188–198.

215 F. Yamin and D.A. Posey, 'Indigenous Peoples, Biotechnology and Intellectual Property Rights' (1993) 2 *Review of European Community & International Environmental Law.*

216 Darrell Posey and Graham Dutfield, *Beyond Intellectual Property: Toward Traditional Resource Rights for Indigenous Peoples and Local Communities* (International Development Research Centre 1996).

217 M. Llewelyn, "Which Rules in World Trade Law – Patents or Plant Variety Protection" in T. Cottier and P.C. Mavroidis, *Intellectual Property: Trade, Competition, and Sustainable Development* (United States of America: The University of Michigan Press 2002) 352.

of rights arising out of moral and ethical considerations; soft law, which emanates from customary practice and non-legally binding international instruments; legally binding instruments; and the need to provide an equitable basis for all participants, enabling full participation in the establishment of policy and practice.[218]

The *sui generis* system is popular among scholars because an intellectual property right in its present form is deemed prejudicial to the rights of traditional peoples. Intellectual property rights are perceived as rigid, while communal rights are subject to change; they are fluid concepts, and as such should not be confined or constrained by restrictive legal definitions.[219] As much as customary law is the known system of protection in traditional communities, and it has some similarities in some instances with aspects of intellectual property law, it is hardly considered. Western notions of intellectual property law are not incompatible with traditional knowledge and its products based on a legally pluralistic perspective. Regardless of the fact that traditional knowledge does not fit into all the areas of intellectual property norms perfectly, it can nevertheless be applied to the areas where it is suitable, if the parties desire. Customary law, on the other hand, can continue to apply to the areas it has existed over the years from generation to generation, most especially those areas where aspects of intellectual property law are not suitable.

> Whereas there is no doubt that some TK holders and indigenous peoples have used the IP system to protect their cultural creations like songs, arts and handicrafts, the IP regime has some deficiencies in protecting TK. First, the IP regime fails to acknowledge and recognize TK and the customary laws and systems developed and used by TK holders to protect, safeguard and perpetuate their heritage and knowledge. Thus, the IP regime fails significantly to offer robust protection to tradition-based knowledge systems with their holistic nature while 'ensuring cultural preservation and access to knowledge. For instance, whereas the territories, lands and resources of TK holders are vital to the continued generation, use and transmission of TK, the scope of the IP regime does not extend to those aspects.[220]

As much as a *sui generis* system appears attractive, the politically inclined inequalities that come with intellectual property rights will remain. The

218 Ibid.
219 Ibid.
220 Kariuki, Francis, "Protecting Traditional Knowledge in Kenya: Traditional Justice Systems As Appropriate Sui Generis Systems" (October 1, 2020). SSRN: https://ssrn.com/abstract=3705175 or http://dx.doi.org/10.2139/ssrn.3705175

sui generis option has its problems and has proven ineffective in some situations.[221]

> Critics charge, justifiably, that *sui generis* laws are limited because they are typically unenforceable outside of the communities in which they develop. Critics argue that, in the absence of corresponding state sanctioned enforcement mechanisms, focusing on tribal law systems is futile.[222]

The search for an alternative protection mechanism to intellectual property rights continues in many African countries and at the international level. There are specific laws on traditional law in some African countries.[223] The is an urgent call for Nigeria to embark on a similar journey. [224]

3.12 Conclusion

This chapter reveals the beginning of Western dominance and neglect of African knowledge systems and customary laws. Traditional knowledge

221 Margaret Llewelyn, "Which rules in World Trade Law – Patents or Plant Variety Protection?" in T. Cottier and P. C. Mavroids, *Intellectual Property: Trade, Competition and Sustainable Development, The World Trade Forum Volume III* (The University of Michigan Press 2003) 329.

222 Angela Rilley, "'Straight Stealing': Towards an Indigenous System of Cultural Property Protection." (2005) 80(1) *Washington Law Review* 74. See also Rashwet Shrinkhal, "Protection of Traditional Knowledge and Traditional Cultural Expression (TCEs): Some Reflections" Sampratyaya, September 2024 1 (3), DOI: https://doi.org/10.21276/smprt.202409.1s3.a3, 30. "In spite of the … positive aspects of developing *sui generis* mechanism based upon customary practices there is a flip side to it which represents the challenges and practical difficulties in implementing bottom-upward approach towards the protection of TK. First, customary laws of tribes and indigenous peoples are uncodified principles and in order to develop any indigenous code for the protection of TK it needs to be codified. The very idea of codifying the customary laws may be intimidating to many indigenous peoples who chose to enjoy the flexibility of oral traditions. Second, indigenous peoples are a heterogeneous group with divergent customary laws. There is all likelihood of concurrence of sui generis laws within a particular region."

223 "There are also policies that have specific provisions on TK protection. In addition, the 2010 Constitution and the Protection of Traditional Knowledge and Cultural Expressions Act 2016" Kariuki, Francis, Protecting Traditional Knowledge in Kenya: Traditional Justice Systems As Appropriate Sui Generis Systems (1 October 2020). https://ssrn.com/abstract=3705175 or http://dx.doi.org/10.2139/ssrn.3705175

224 Byron, I.P. "The Protection of Traditional Knowledge Under the *Sui Generis* Regime in Nigeria". (2021) 36(1) *International Review of Law, Computers & Technology* 17–27. https://doi.org/10.1080/13600869.2021. 1997086, see also Uwadineke Charles Kalu and Ezeama Chidiebele Kene, "Protecting Traditional Knowledge/Secrets under Intellectual Property Law: A Comparative Analysis of the Adequacy of Protections Using Nigeria as a Case Study." (2019) 6(1) *Nnamdi Azikiwe University Journal of Commercial and Property Law* 109.

during the colonial era faced suppression but survived largely because Africans continued to depend on these knowledge systems and the colonisers, in adopting the indirect rule, permitted some customs to remain as law as long as they were not repugnant to natural justice, equity, and good conscience; neither were they incompatible. Traditional peoples in Africa have a better understanding of knowledge systems embedded in their cultural and biological diversity. Customary laws are the people's laws, springing directly from the African consciousness and moulded to their own desires and practices by those subjected to them.

Though intellectual property law, like other foreign laws, was imposed on traditional peoples in Africa, over the years these laws have become part of the African system through unification, dualism, or pluralism of laws. Based on this acceptance, the distinction between African legal systems ceases to have relevance, but the differences in origin, principles, and methods of European and traditional legal systems continue to exist. In this regard, the survival of cultural pluralism is dependent on the continued existence of legal pluralism. It is imperative to emphasise everything that is traditional and everything that is valuable and to maintain traditional African institutions and values as expressed in their legal system. Concepts relating to aspects of intellectual property law, such as the public domain, do not fit perfectly into African society due to their occidental nature. Such concepts are constructed without consideration for the interests of African cultures.

4 Technology, intellectual property rights protection, and Nigerian development

Ikechukwu Chime

4.1 Introduction

The aphorism "the world is a global village" receives validation in today's world, an interconnected world that has been made possible with the coming of technologies, which presents a lot of opportunities and challenges to how the old traditional-based system operates. Chief among these issues is the protection of intellectual property rights (IPRs), which have become threatened by the limitless boundaries of the digital age.[1] Notwithstanding, intellectual property (IP) and technology share certain distinct qualities that are a catalyst for growth and development, especially in Africa, where the development and technology ratio is the lowest among all the continents. The intersection of IP and technology refers to the interaction between the legal protection of intellectual works, such as patents, copyrights, and trademarks, and the continually changing technical world. This intersection relates to the preservation and enforcement of IPRs in the digital age, as technology has made it simpler to duplicate, distribute, and share creative works.[2] The rise of new technologies, such as artificial intelligence, blockchain, biotechnology, etc., has created new difficulties and opportunities for IP protection and creativity. The field of IP and technology continues to grow and change, as laws and policies must keep up with technological advancements to ensure that creators and innovators are appropriately motivated and protected.

IP plays a very important role in technological innovation and development, especially for individual creators, entrepreneurs, start-ups, and small and medium-sized enterprises (SMEs).[3] IP serves an industrial agenda by

1 Georgitte Losper, "Copyright: Challenges of the Digital Age" (Doctoral Dissertation, University of Namibia 2011) http://digital.unam.na/bitstream/handle/11070.1/879/losper_copyright_2011.pdf?sequence=1 accessed 27 August 2024.

2 Ibid.

3 Beverley Agbakoba-Onyejianya and Uchechi Ofoegbu, "Technology and Intellectual Property – IP as a Tool for Promoting Innovation and Sustainability" (Mondaq 2022) https://www.mondaq.com/nigeria/new-technology/ accessed 17 August 2024.

DOI: 10.4324/9781003602989-5

ensuring that creators and innovators are incentivised for their creations by giving them the legal right to exclusively use their creations for a limited period, the moral right to be recognised as creators, and the economic right that is associated with their creation. Through this tripartite incentive structure, creators and innovators are encouraged to create more and join the innovation bandwagon because they are assured that if they are infringed upon, they have legal remedies. Additionally, the protection of IPRs gives consumers a guarantee of the product's safety and reliability because of the product's association with a recognised brand.

The global economy is transitioning from resource-based to knowledge-based, where economic growth and development are inspired and stimulated by knowledge, innovation, and technology, with IPRs playing a very important and necessary role in this economic rejuvenation.[4] Africa is witnessing the transformative effects of technology within the e-commerce sector, health and pharmaceuticals, research and development in artificial intelligence, blockchain, renewable energy, and biotechnology, which have been recognised as key drivers of development. Within the public and private sectors, the protection and enforcement of IPRs create an avenue to put African countries at the forefront of the global economy.[5] For instance, Dr Samuel Achilefu, a Nigerian scientist, devised a pair of high-tech goggles that can assist surgeons in identifying cancerous tissues during surgery. His efforts were recognised with a prestigious award for African entrepreneurs, the Africa Prize for Engineering Innovation.[6] Another example is seen in South Africa, where a firm named Lumkani created a low-cost fire detection system that employs heat sensing rather than smoke detection to reduce loss of life and property in informal settlements. The corporation was able to obtain patents for its creation, which gave it exclusive rights to the technology.[7]

Nigeria's development is tied to the constant creation of innovation, a trend which can be seen in thriving countries and continents. In 2022, a study by the Nigerian Bureau of Statistics showed that the Nigerian tech sector has been on the rise due to significant investment pouring into the sector. It revealed a tremendous $1.3 billion worth of funds raised for startups, while indicating a 20.32% contribution to the country's GDP

4 Aggrey Ambali and others, "Strengthening Africa's Intellectual Property Capacity to Enhance Innovation and Commercialisation" (NEPAD 2023) https://www.nepad.org/blog/ accessed 17 August 2024.

5 Ibid

6 Ben Ezeamalu, "Nigerian-born Scientist Wins Award for his Cancer-seeing Glasses" (*Premium Times* 2015) https://www.premiumtimesng.com/featuresand-interviews/ accessed 19 August 2024.

7 LM Palmer, "Balancing Intellectual Property Rights with Public Obligations in Developing Nations: Lessons from Africa." (2006) 20(1) *Critical Arts*, 62–82.

in the third quarter of 2022.[8] This was the highest contribution the sector has ever made to the Nigerian economy in over half a decade. However, Nigeria's poor performance in the 2023 innovation input is further reflected in the continent's poor performance generally when it comes to technology and innovation.[9] In 2022, Africa accounted for only 0.5 per cent of patent applications, while Asia had an enormous 66.6%, North America 19 per cent, and Europe 10.9 per cent.[10] This trend is deeply upsetting since technology creation and development are closely connected to economic growth. Nigeria remains a nation heavily blessed with natural and intellectual resources; hence, it must leverage the protection of IPRs to develop speedily. In the past, the main focus of IP in Nigeria has been to develop and establish IP rules, infrastructure, and regulatory frameworks; with this being achieved, the focus of IP in Nigeria tilts towards the effective utilisation of IP frameworks to achieve the nation's economic objectives.[11]

This chapter will analyse the existing IP framework in Nigeria, focusing on unravelling its effectiveness in the technological landscape and how it can be leveraged for the economic growth and development of Nigeria. This chapter is divided into eight parts: Section 4.1 has introduced the topic and drawn a nexus between IP, technology, and development, in the Nigerian context. Section 4.2 will provide a conceptual analysis of the term "development" in line with the Sustainable Development Goals (SDGs) and its relation to IP. Section 4.3 will examine the intersection of IP and emerging technologies such as AI, blockchain, NFTs, etc. Section 4.4 will examine the legal frameworks under Nigerian laws and their impact on technological innovations in the country. Section 4.5 will reveal how IPRs and technology can be leveraged for Nigeria's development, while Section 4.6 reveals the gap between the protection of IPRs and technology and the opportunities that exist. Section 4.8 will highlight the recommendations and policy initiatives that can be undertaken by Nigerian stakeholders, while Section 4.8 will conclude the chapter after providing a prospective outlook for the protection of IPRs in the technological sector for Nigerian development.

8 Templars, "Nigeria 2023 Tech Outlook: Sailing through the Headwinds" (25 January 2023) https://www.templars-law.com/knowledge-centre/ accessed 17 August 2024.

9 WIPO, "Nigeria Ranking in the Global Innovation Index 2024" (2024) https://www.wipo.int/gii-ranking accessed 17 August 2024.

10 Kei Tagawa, "Towards Effective Intellectual Property Ecosystems for Sustainable Development" https://www.un.org/osaa/news/ accessed 19 August 2024.

11 Francis Gurry, "Intellectual property for an emerging Africa" (WIPO 2015) https://www.wipo.int/wipo_magazil accessed 17 August 2024.

4.2 Defining the concept of development

Development has frequently been seen as an economic concept, but it should in fact be seen as multidimensional, extending into social growth too. This is because development extends beyond maximising money or wealth and goes further to the improvement of people's lives and freedoms. Development is also recognised as a right under international human rights law,[12] and specifically under the African Charter on Human and Peoples' Rights (ACHPR)[13] which states in Article 22 that

> [a] peoples shall have the right to economic, social, and cultural development while respecting their freedom and identity, as well as the equal enjoyment of humanity's common heritage. States must have the responsibility, either individually or jointly, to make sure that there is the exercise of the right to development.[14]

It should be noted that Nigeria is a signatory to the African Charter and in fact played a major role in the drafting of this Charter.[15]

Equally important, development must be sustainable and inclusive of vulnerable, marginalised, disadvantaged, or socially excluded groups, such as women, youth, indigenous, and local communities, as well as the informal sector. "Development that meets the needs of the present generation without compromising those of future generations" is the definition and essence of sustainable development. It requires a change from an economic-based norm to one that includes environmental and social issues, as well as meeting everyone's fundamental necessities and providing them with opportunities to live better lives. The United Nations 2030 Agenda for Sustainable Development, as well as its Sustainable Development Goals (SDGs), is built on the principles of sustainable development. The African Union Agenda 2063 aims to attain a prosperous Africa through the means of inclusive growth and sustainable development.[16] Nigeria has followed suit, having recently approved its National Development Plan, which

12 Declaration on the Right to Development, 1986; Vienna Declaration and Program of Action, 1993 (para 10); and Millennium Declaration, 2000 (para 11)

13 The African Charter on Human and Peoples' Rights, 1981 (ACHPR). The ACHPR is an international human rights instrument that is intended to promote and protect human rights and basic freedoms on the African continent.

14 African Charter on Human and Peoples' Rights, art. 22(1)(2)

15 TO Elias, "The Charter of the Organization of African Unity." (1965) 59(2) *American Journal of International Law* 243–267.

16 Agenda 2063, Aspiration 1.

defines the country's sustainable development goals and principles for the years 2021–2025.[17]

In light of the above discussion, the concept of development must, in all necessity, be widened to include not only economic, but also environmental and social advancement. According to Ncube, economic progress "includes a more comprehensive and systematic reckoning of how people live" rather than simply measuring GDP growth.[18] She goes on to say that environmental aspects of development include concerns about proper management of the earth and natural resources, as well as social factors such as equity, empowerment, participation, and cultural identity, all with the primary goal of reducing poverty.[19] This chapter discusses IP as a driving force behind this type of development. The implementation of sustainable development in Nigeria is especially necessary in light of the United Nations (UN) Agenda 2030 for Sustainable Development and its Sustainable Development Goals (SDGs).[20] The notion of sustainable development is widely recognised as a principle of international law[21] and is incorporated into various international agreements that Nigeria is a part of. Today, sustainable development is wholly recognised as a guiding factor for Nigerian economic policy. Thus, every economic policy, including intellectual property policy, should strive for long-term development.[22]

The link between IP and the SDGs is well established. The World Intellectual Property Organization expressly and comprehensively explains the link between intellectual property and the SDGs, specifically SDG 2 (zero hunger), SDG 3 (good health and well-being), SDG 6 (clean water and sanitation), SDG 7 (affordable and clean energy), SDG 8 (decent work and economic growth), SDG 9 (industry, innovation, and infrastructure), SDG 11 (sustainable cities and communities), and SDG 13 (climate action). The 4th WIPO Director-General, Francis Gurry, believes that:

> Intellectual property as a policy exists to establish an enabling environment for – and to drive investment in – innovation; to build a framework

17 BE Anam and others, "Economic Recovery and Growth Plan, Economic Sustainability Plan and National Development Plan (2021–2025): The Nigerian Experience under President Muhammadu Buhari." (2024) 10(1) *Cogent Social Sciences*, 2289600.

18 CB Ncube, "Harnessing Intellectual Property for Development: Some Thoughts on an Appropriate Theoretical Framework." (2013) *Potchefstroom Electronic Law Journal* 15–16.

19 Ibid.

20 Editorial, "The Sustainable Development Agenda" (United Nations 2024) https://www.un.org/ accessed 19 August 2024.

21 Tladi (2007) at 65

22 R Meléndez-Ortiz and P Roffe (eds), "Intellectual Property and Sustainable Development: Development Agendas in a Changing World." (2009) *Cheltenham*.

> in which innovative technologies can be exchanged and shared globally. The economic motivation that drives innovation is critical to the societal transformation that the Sustainable Development Goals seek to achieve.

On the other hand, the SDGs, as an international development framework, can be used to create development-oriented state intellectual property policies and legislation.[23]

4.3 The intersection between intellectual property and emerging technologies

The phrase "innovate or die" has become the mantra for innovation and development as the world evolves from the days of mechanical and traditional approaches to the present time marked by technological breakthroughs made possible with the advent of emerging technologies such as Artificial intelligence (AI), blockchain technology, non-fungible tokens (NFTs) 3d printing, etc.[24]

4.3.1 IP and AI

The pivotal role of IP in AI machine learning systems, models, and technology is based on the conceptual framework of IP protection residing in human authorship and inventorship. All cases that have been decided by courts around the world since the advent of AI have focused on the authorship and inventorship of machines and on trying to balance that alongside the IP laws placing protection on humans.[25] In Nigeria, while there is not yet any case on AI in front of our superior courts, there have been convincing arguments being made both in the affirmative and negative on the issue of AI authorship and inventorship, particularly the controversy that has surged regarding the issue of human input as a criterion for protection. Since the disruption of AI, countries are still finding it hard to shape IP laws and policies to flow with the tides, especially with the courts emphasising human authorship as a major criterion for IP protection.[26]

For example, in 2016, a group of academics released *The Next Rembrandt*, an AI-generated portrait that examined thousands of works by the 17th-century Dutch artist Rembrandt van Rijn and used that data to

23 M Cadogan, "Using SDGs to Leverage National Intellectual Property Strategies." *Centre for International Governance Innovation Policy Brief* (2019) 2

24 Blessing Nwankwo, "The Intersection between AI and IP" (Mondaq, 2023) <https://www.mondaq.com/> accessed 18 August 2024.

25 DJ Gervais, "The Machine as Author." (2019) 105 *Iowa L. Rev.* 2053.

26 Blessing (n 24).

recreate a modern-day reproduction of his work. Another painting made by an AI algorithm sold at auction in 2018 for more than $400,000.. In 2018, an AI connectionist machine was able to create two devices for use in households. Also, with the creation of ChatGPT, an AI language model with the capacity to create texts, images, and code, the debate on human authorship has extended to the issues of AI copying works protected by copyright. Due to this, numerous cases have been instituted against OpenAI, the creators of ChatGPT, for the infringing content of the AI. The issue of human authorship is hinged on two elements of IP: the work must be original and novel, and the work must emanate from the intellectual and creative capacity of the creator.

Furthermore, AI technologies frequently rely on complicated algorithms, datasets, and software, all of which may be protected by intellectual property laws such as patents, copyrights, and trade secrets.[27] Identifying which sorts of intellectual property protection apply to a certain type of AI technology, as well as obtaining the most robust legal protection, is frequently ambiguous and necessitates a thorough study of the quickly growing law on the subject.[28] IP infringement occurs when AI models, training data, or algorithms are not properly licensed or unwittingly breach third-party IP rights. Determining ownership rights may also pose challenges, particularly in collaborative AI development initiatives involving various stakeholders or outsourcing AI-related services to third-party providers.[29]

4.3.2 IP and blockchain

Blockchain can be defined as a ledger that is unchangeable and that now acts as a digital information storage system. Data is scattered among the nodes of a computer network. Blockchains are very important in cryptocurrency systems such as Bitcoin because they keep a secure and decentralised record of transactions. Unlike traditional databases, which have stored information in a tabular style, blockchains put information into groups or blocks with predetermined storage space. When a block has been filled, it gets closed and is then linked to the next available block, resulting in the blockchain. Blockchain data is irreversible and is also

27 Katarina Foss-Solbrekk, "Three Routes to Protecting AI Systems and Their Algorithms Under IP Law: The Good, the Bad and the Ugly." (2021) 16(3) *Journal of Intellectual Property Law & Practice* 247–258.

28 Lidia Mowad, Daniel Marks, and Mark Avsec, "Navigating the Intersection of Intellectual Property and Artificial Intelligence" (Lexology 2024) https://www.lexology.com/library/detail accessed 19 August 2024.

29 Ibid.

timestamp-protected.[30] Blockchain is one of the most recent technological revolutions, with the ability to change companies and industries. Blockchain technology is now in its early stages, with rather few uses; however, this has been projected to change in the future. Many industries, which include banking, healthcare, finance, and automotive, are likely to see it become a major disruptor, causing heavy changes.

One of the most important components of intellectual property is determining whether or not the owner or inventor is legitimate. While the issue is less common with patents because the creator can register a patent with the patent office, copyrights are imperilled in that the owner must prove ownership of the work. In today's internet age, anyone can easily plagiarise or steal any content and use it as they see fit.

Blockchain can help in three ways:[31]

1. Creation of digital credentials for artistic works and time stamping them:[32] Once data has been saved on the blockchain, it is almost impossible to hack or access without permission; when a certificate is created with blockchain, it gives incontrovertible evidence of ownership by accessing original data on blockchain ledgers, which can help in the prevention of piracy.
2. By acting as an authentication method, it establishes and proves lawful ownership.[33]
3. Blockchains can also help to authenticate the integrity of intellectual assets because duplicate data cannot be stored on them.

As a result, blockchain time-stamping and validation capabilities can be an effective means to safeguard intellectual property.

4.3.3 IP and NFTs

The introduction of NFTs has transformed the world of digital art and collectables. One-of-a-kind digital assets, which are authenticated on the blockchain, have brought about a global craze and have changed our perception of ownership in the digital age. However, as the popularity of

30 Eugenia Politou et al., "Blockchain Mutability: Challenges and Proposed Solutions." (2019) 9(4) *IEEE Transactions on Emerging Topics in Computing* 1972–1986.

31 Editorial, "Intellectual Property Rights and Blockchain Technology" (19 July 2024) https://medium.com/@cryptow929 accessed 19 August 2024.

32 YC Wang, CL Chen and YY Deng, "Authorisation Mechanism based on Blockchain Technology for Protecting Museum-digital Property Rights." (2021) 11(3) *Applied Sciences* 1085.

33 Ibid.

NFTs grows, concerns about intellectual property rights and their junction with this technology have come to the fore.[34] Non-fungible tokens are digital assets that use blockchain technology to ensure their uniqueness and ownership. Unlike transferable cryptocurrencies like Bitcoin or Ethereum, NFTs are unique and cannot be traded for one another. They can represent a variety of digital assets, including artwork, music, films, virtual real estate, and more.[35]

NFTs offer a novel answer to the long-standing problem of verifying ownership and authenticity in the digital world. NFTs provide a verifiable record of ownership by making use of blockchain technology, making it easier for artists and producers to enforce their rights. NFTs also allow producers to integrate metadata, such as the artist's name and copyright information, directly into the token, simplifying correct attribution.[36] NFTs have therefore provided new ways for artists, musicians, and content providers to commercialise their work. They give creators the power to sell their digital works directly to collectors, without the need for intermediaries. This democratisation of the art industry empowers artists and may boost their financial streams.[37] However, it raises concerns about appropriate pay and the effects on established art market dynamics. NFTs give authors the power to insert licensing terms and royalty mechanisms within their digital content. Smart contracts built into the NFT can automatically issue royalties to artists when their works are sold or traded on secondary markets. This technology has the potential to transform the monetisation of creative works by ensuring that artists continue to receive their pay even if their creations change hands.[38]

4.4 Nigerian legal framework

Nigeria boasts several IP laws, some of which will be discussed seriatim in relation to technology, particularly how the various laws have adapted to the technological landscape.

34 Runhua Wang, Jyh-An Lee and Jingwen Liu, "Unwinding NFTs in the Shadow of IP Law." (2024) 61(1) *American Business Law Journal* 31–55.

35 Ibid.

36 Ibid.

37 Richard Florida, "The Rise of the Creator Economy." (2022) *The Creative Class Group* https://creativeclass.com/reports/The_Rise_of_the_Creator_Economy.pdf accessed 19 August 2024.

38 Dan Ankenman, "Money for Nothing?: Can NFTs Solve Musicians' Monetization Problem?." (2023) 26 *Int'l JL Ethics Tech.* https://heinonline.org/hol-cgi-bin/get_pdf.cgi?handle=hein.journals/ijlet2023&section=6 accessed 24 August 2024.

4.4.1 Copyright Act 2022

The Copyright Act was signed into law on the 17th of March 2022, repealing the overdue and long-standing Copyright Act Cap C28 Laws of the Federation of Nigeria 2004 (i.e. the 1988 Copyright Act), which contained provisions that no longer reflected the dynamics of the changing technological world in which we live in. The Act was enacted to fill the gaps in the old law that had existed for 34 years and was not in tune with technological realities.[39] The Act is a major improvement on the old Act and features innovative revisions and fresh provisions that address some of the limitations of the old Act.

It contains certain provisions relating to technology. First, the Act provides that the author of a work now has an extra right to regulate the availability and accessibility of his work by wire or wireless means, allowing members of the public to access it from a location and time of their choosing. This means that an author can now choose whether his or her work is made available electronically or in print. Notably, the Act prohibits the circumvention of technological protection measures.[40] Technological protection measures are those measures attached to a streaming platform to prevent screenshots and direct copying of the work; it also includes software solutions on websites preventing copy and paste; these are infringing acts that have affected copyright protection in the digital age but have now been remedied by the Act.

Also, the Act introduced novel provisions relating to the posting of copyrighted materials on the internet. A copyright owner has the right to issue a written notice to a service provider to remove or disable access to infringing material hosted on its network.[41] When a service provider receives a notification to remove infringing material, they are bound to do so,[42] but they may reinstate it if the subscriber sends a counter notice and the copyright owner does not react within one week.[43] If any party is dissatisfied with the service provider's decision, they may appeal to the Commission.[44] A service provider is also legally required to suspend an account for which multiple notices of infringement have been received. Also, a service provider cannot be held financially liable for copyright infringement if they just offer a conduit for users to access infringing items or store infringing

39 Sandra Eke and others, "A Review of the Nigerian Copyright Act 2022" (SPA Ajibade & Co, 2023) https://spaajibade.com//> accessed 19 August 2024.

40 Copyright Act 2022, 50.

41 Copyright Act 2022, s 54(1).

42 Copyright Act 2022, s 55(1).

43 Copyright Act 2022, s 55(2)(b).

44 Copyright Act 2022, s 55(4).

materials on their system at a user's request.[45] This is only the case if the service provider did not obtain monetary profit from the infringement and took proper action, such as removing the infringing material or blocking access to it after receiving notification.

Furthermore, the Commission has the authority, either directly or with the assistance of another person, to restrict or prohibit access to any content, link, or website maintained on a system or network that it reasonably believes infringes an author's copyright under the Act.[46] However, the Act did not consider the implications of AI-generated content, especially since the Act was enacted when AI-generated content became a hot-button issue; the failure of the Act to provide for this is fatal. It is recommended that the Nigeria Copyright Commission exercise its powers to make regulations concerning the issue of AI-generated content.

4.4.2 Trademark Act

The Trademark Act has no major provisions for protecting brands in the digital age. However, its provisions have some effects in the digital marketplace. The redundancy of the Act is seen in the modern business environment that has witnessed drastic changes as technology advances. New challenges have come to the fore which have affected the online marketplace, such as trademark infringement in online promotions and advertising, cybersquatting, trademark dilution on social media platforms, counterfeiting in online marketplaces, and website domain names.[47]

Trademark infringement in online advertising and marketing can be defined as the unlawful use of trademarked names, logos, slogans, or other protected components in online advertisements, promoted links, keyword targeting, affiliate marketing, and social media advertising.[48] In the same vein, the act of registering or using domain names that are identical or confusingly similar to registered trademarks to profit from their goodwill is known as "cybersquatting." It is the illicit use of another person's trademark in a domain name, typically to sell the domain to the legitimate trademark owner or profit from the brand's reputation.[49] In the fight against trademark infringement, internet platforms and markets have become very important functions. As e-commerce increases, businesses face threats

45 Samuel Eke and others (n 32).

46 Copyright Act 2022, s 61.

47 Anna Pokrovskaya, "Protection of Trademark Rights on E-commerce Platforms: An Updated Outlook." (2024) *Journal of Comprehensive Business Administration Research* http://ojs.bonviewpress.com/index.php/JCBAR/article/view/2153 accessed 19 August 2024.

48 Ibid.

49 Ibid.

such as unlicensed vendors, counterfeit merchandise, and brand dilution. Firms have been forced to adopt strategies such as monitoring and enforcing restrictions inside online marketplaces using automated infringement detection tools such as TESS (Trademark Electronic Search System), Google Ads, Keyword Planner, etc.

4.4.3 Patent and Design Act 1970

The Act is the longest-standing law on intellectual property. While this may appear good, it is quite embarrassing for a statute in an area of law that prides itself on innovation and being in alignment with the shifting tides of development. A patent is a country's grant to an inventor of an exclusive monopoly right to prevent another person from exploiting, creating, using, importing, or selling their invention without their consent for a set term of 20 years.[50] The monopoly is provided in exchange for the creator publicly disclosing their innovation to those who will be able to use it 20 years after filing a complete patent application. It is assumed that during the era of such a monopoly, the inventor would have earned the most financial benefit from the commercialisation of the invention. The regulatory authority also makes sure that technologies that have the potential to improve citizens' quality of life are used to benefit the greatest number of people.

Notwithstanding that patent has the strongest leanings towards technological realities because of its protection of inventions and inventive processes, the Act provides no succour for technology, least of all for development. The Act's only allurement to technology is contained in the requirements for an invention to be patentable; these requirements are set out in section 1(1) of the Patent and Design Act:

1. It must be a new invention.
2. It must have an inventive step that is not obvious to someone with knowledge and experience in the subject.
3. It must be capable of being made or used in some kind of industry and not be a scientific or mathematical discovery, theory or method, a literary, dramatic, musical or artistic work, a way of performing a mental act, playing a game or doing business, the presentation of information, or some computer programs, an animal or plant variety, a method of medical treatment or diagnosis.
4. The invention must not be against public policy or morality.

50 Editorial, "Patent Law and Right of a Patent in Nigeria" (Resolution Law Firm 2020) https://www.resolutionlawng.com/patents-law-in-nigeria/ accessed 18 August 2024.

5. An invention results from inventive activity if it does not follow from the state of the art, either as to the method, the application, the combination of methods, or the product which it concerns or as to the industrial result it produces.
6. An invention is capable of industrial application if it can be manufactured or used in any kind of industry, including agriculture.

Furthermore, the Act also caters for patent licensing, an important aspect of technology transfer that is incidental to economic growth and development.

4.4.4 National Office for Technology Acquisition and Promotion (NOTAP) Act

Up until 1992, NOTAP was formerly known as the National Office of Industrial Property (NOIP), which was a parastatal under the Federal Ministry of Science and Technology. NOTAP was established under Decree No. 82 of 1992, with the name change intended to come into alignment with the agency's expanded functions.[51] NOTAP is in charge of monitoring, regulating, and making the influx of foreign technology in Nigeria more possible. NOTAP's mandate is mainly centred on the review and registration of technology transfer agreements, which must be filed with NOTAP within 30 days after their effective date.[52]

NOTAP, as a corporate body, is responsible for carrying out the acquisition, promotion and development of technology, as well as rectifying any flaws in foreign technology acquisition. NOTAP's emphasis has upgraded from regulatory and control to promotional and developmental activities in response to globalisation and economic liberalisation. The new area of focus aims to attract international technologies and investment while also developing indigenous technology. NOTAP was established as one of the primary vehicles for carrying out the National Policy on Technology Development. This policy includes encouraging the flow of technology into the country to guarantee industrial development and encouraging domestic firms to buy foreign technologies that are appropriate for the local environment.[53]

A main aspect of NOTAP's work is the registration of Technology Transfer Agreements and contracts entered into for the transfer of technology to Nigerian parties. These agreements are legally binding documents

51 CC Ajibo et al., "Technology Transfer for Development in Nigeria: Patterns, Problems and Prospects." (2019) 45(1) *Commonwealth Law Bulletin*, 70–91.
52 Ibid.
53 Ibid.

that contain the terms and conditions under which technical skills, specialised knowledge, technical know-how, and other proprietary rights for the manufacture of goods and services are transferred from one individual, enterprise or organisation to another through licensing and other contractual arrangements that benefit both parties.[54] Agreements that are subject to NOTAP regulation in Nigeria include those relating to hotel management, trademark licensing, software licensing, value-added services, shared services, management services, technical know-how and franchising. Before registration, NOTAP makes an assessment of these agreements for their legal, economic and technical benefits to the Nigerian economy.

Technology transfer may include the following:

1. The use of trademarks.
2. The right to exploit patented inventions.
3. The provision of technical expertise such as blueprints, diagrams, and operating instructions.
4. The supply of fundamental and detailed engineering.
5. The services include supplying machinery and plant, providing operating staff or managerial support and training individuals.

Such contracts must be registered, such that any profit or advantage that is owed to foreign partners under the contract cannot be repatriated or transferred to them through the Central Bank of Nigeria.[55] However, certain technology transfer agreements cannot be registered with NOTAP, such as when the technology is obsolete or freely available in Nigeria, when the price is not commensurate with the technology acquired, or when the contract requires the transferee to submit to a foreign jurisdiction in the event of a dispute.

However, in *Stanbic IBTC v FRCN & NOTAP*,[56] the Nigerian Court of Appeal (Lagos Division) overturned the decision of the (trial) Federal High Court, ruling that the non-registration of a technology transfer agreement under the National Office for Technology Acquisition and Promotion (NOTAP) Act does not make it invalid or unenforceable. In reaching its decision, the Court focused on the literal meaning of relevant parts of the NOTAP Act. The Court ruled that nothing in the Act indicates that the legislature intended that non-registration of a technology transfer agreement render it defective, null and unenforceable. The Court reached

54 Uche Matthew and Olukolade Ehinmosan, "An Overview of the Role of Nigeria's NOTAP in the Promotion of Technology Transfer and Intellectual Property" (2019) https://www.mondaq.com/nigeria/contracts-an accessed 18 August 2024.

55 NOTAP Act, s 7

56 (2018) LPELR-46507(CA)

this judgment while quietly criticising the trial Court for demonstrating "purposeful judicial inventiveness" at the expense of literally applying the NOTAP Act's obvious and unmistakable terms.

4.5 How intellectual property rights and technology can be leveraged for Nigeria's development

The intersection of IP and development in Nigeria offers a unique opportunity to promote social and economic prosperity. Exploring the consequences of IP on crucial Sustainable Development Goals such as no poverty, quality education, and clean water and sanitation reveals that the strategic use of IP rights can expedite development across the continent.[57]

4.5.1 IP and poverty reduction: SDG 1

Patent systems and IPRs can help in stimulating of local innovation that directly tackles poverty. Patents on agricultural innovations, for example, can help Nigerian farmers to raise crop yields, better manage pests and improve food security, all of which contribute directly to SDG 1: No Poverty. However, in order for this promise to be realised, these advances must be accessible and cheap to those who require them the most. Local and federal government must enter into collaboration to guarantee that IP regulations do not impede but rather assist the spread of life-changing innovations.

4.5.2 Education through IP: SDG 4

Quality education (SDG 4) is another area where IP shows great promise. Educational technology, including e-learning platforms and educational software, frequently relies on copyright protection. These tools have the potential to improve educational access in Nigeria's remote locations by delivering scalable solutions that can be monetised through intellectual property. Furthermore, establishing knowledge of intellectual property rights among young Nigerian entrepreneurs might inspire students to pursue creative solutions, thereby encouraging an innovation culture from the bottom up. An IP Hackathon held in Cape Verde is a wonderful illustration for Nigeria of how innovative initiatives may propel IP education forward. Young Cape Verdeans were encouraged to develop solutions based on intellectual property, with an emphasis on real-world difficulties

57 Diogo Antunes, "World IP Day 2024: Intellectual Property as a Catalyst for Achieving Sustainable Development Goals in Africa" (Inventa 2024) https://inventa.com/en/news/article/986/ accessed 19 August 2024.

in energy and tourism.[58] This seminar not only educated participants on IP strategies but also demonstrated practical implementations, generating a deeper understanding and appreciation for IP's role in the development of local ideas.

4.5.3 Clean water and sanitation innovations: SDG 6

In terms of clean water and sanitation (SDG 6), IPRs can play a transformative role by protecting innovations that address water management concerns in Nigeria. Patented technology in water purification, efficient plumbing systems, and sustainable water management can bring about improvements in the continent's standard of living. The problem is to ensure that patentable solutions are not impeded by excessive costs or intellectual property challenges, which could make them unavailable to the populations that most need them. A striking case in South Africa provides Nigeria an example of how IP has the potential to transform agricultural waste into lucrative resources. Researchers at Stellenbosch University have created a method for converting waste pulp into a new feedstock for the chemicals industry.[59] This innovation not only meets SDG 12 (responsible consumption and production), but it also helps to guarantee economic sustainability by generating new goods from waste materials.

4.5.4 Climate action: SDG 13

SDG 13, which focuses on climate action, recognises IP's heavy contributions to environmental sustainability. The intellectual property industry actively supports climate action by encouraging the development of green technologies and nurturing environmentally beneficial innovations. This business promotes the seamless transfer and widespread adoption of sustainable practices through strong intellectual property rights, and this heavily contributes to the worldwide effort to battle climate change. Intellectual property-compliant countries provide legal safeguards that not only encourage the development of environmentally friendly solutions but also speed the global diffusion of these important technologies.

58 WIPO, "From Gaming Apps to Nation Branding in Cabo Verde: Youthful Cabo Verdeans Propose Innovative Ideas at WIPO-Organized IP Hack" https://www.wipo.int/pressroom/en/stories/hackathon-caboverde.html accessed 19 August 2024.

59 WIPO, "Transforming Waste Pulp into a New Feedstock for the Chemical Industry" https://www.wipo.int/wipo_magazine/en/ip-at-work/2021/transforming_pulp.html accessed 19 August 2024.

4.5.5 *Renewable energy and clean technology: SDG 7*

The link between IP and renewable energy developments is becoming stronger. Patents, in particular, play a very important role in inspiring advancements in solar energy innovation, such as technology that improves the efficiency of solar panels or solar windows, wind energy innovation, including the various patented technologies used with wind turbines, and new sustainable technologies such as grid integration or tidal energy. The protection of these innovations and their patents is necessary if achieving the objective of providing inexpensive, reliable, sustainable, and contemporary energy to everybody is going to be possible.

4.5.6 *Healthcare and well-being: SDG 3*

In the context of healthcare and well-being (SDG 3), IP appears as an important engine of progress. Patents and intellectual property rights facilitate the development of medical technologies and medications, resulting in dramatic improvements to world health. These safeguards not only promote medical research and development but also make it easier to share life-saving technologies. As a result, they can help to attain the ultimate goal of increasing global health and well-being.

4.5.7 *Agriculture and sustainable food production: SDG 2 and SDG 12*

In sustainable food production, IP is becoming increasingly important in addressing SDGs such as hunger and responsible consumption. Patents and intellectual property rights, for example, stimulate researchers and inventors to develop better crop-growing techniques, invent new farming tools, and practise sustainable farming. These new technologies and techniques will aid in the production of more food, resulting in improved food distribution (SDGs 2 and 12). Protecting these technologies ensures that we can fulfil rising food demand while at the same time reducing environmental impact, resulting in a more sustainable and resilient food system.

4.6 Challenges and opportunities for leveraging intellectual property and technology in achieving development

One of the most important issues is guaranteeing the accessibility and equitable distribution of technologies. While intellectual property protection is very necessary to encourage innovation, it frequently poses accessibility difficulties, particularly in the case of technologies and pharmaceuticals that are critical. Striking a balance between protecting intellectual property rights and ensuring that breakthroughs reach those in greatest need is a difficult task on the path to sustainable development.

Besides these challenges, businesses and innovators have great opportunities to leverage IP for sustainable development. They can increase the impact of their ideas by committing to SDG 17, developing global collaborations, entering into licensing agreements, and collaborating on initiatives. Businesses that prioritise ethical and sustainable practices not only contribute to the achievement of the Sustainable Development Goals but also establish themselves as industry leaders. The importance of providing supportive policies and legal frameworks is crucial and necessary, allowing politicians to encourage entrepreneurs and innovators to bring their efforts into alignment with sustainable development ideals.

4.7 Moving forward with strategic intellectual property management

To fully realise IP's potential to help sustainable development in Nigeria, policymakers, corporate leaders, and all concerned stakeholders must take a balanced approach. The following recommendations are useful to create a path that Nigerian policymakers, business leaders, and stakeholders can take in order to strategically manage IP for national development.

Firstly, there has to be a creation of IP policies that support national development goals and are accessible to local entrepreneurs. While the country has IP laws, virtually all of these laws lack provisions that are specific to the promotion of targeted sectors that are necessary for national development. For example, the patent system could be strengthened by making expedited processing available for inventions that relate to do with renewable energy, sustainable agriculture, or medicinal investments. Furthermore, existing IP policies are rather costly for local entrepreneurs, especially SMEs, to take advantage of. It would then follow that procedures should be simplified; fees should be reduced, and there should be increased access to legal assistance, which would give local innovators the power to protect and commercialise their creations.

Furthermore, the government should actively promote technology transfer and collaboration between research institutions, universities, and local businesses. Many individuals are unaware of their IP rights or the importance of protecting their creations. This lack of awareness makes innovation difficult and limits the potential for economic growth. This could involve creating incentives for joint research projects, establishing technology transfer offices within universities, and facilitating licensing agreements that benefit both the technology provider and the recipient. IP education should be integrated into school curricula at all levels, and this will help to inject life into a culture of creativity and innovation from a young age. Targeted IP awareness programmes should be developed for entrepreneurs and creators, with these programmes focusing on practical aspects of IP protection, commercialisation, and enforcement. Public awareness campaigns making use of various media platforms can further promote IP knowledge and its role in bringing about economic and social development.

There has to be an investment in intellectual property education and awareness efforts to promote an innovative and creative culture: Public-private partnerships (PPPs) can be powerful vehicles for making use of IP to achieve development goals. However, due to a lack of trust in governmental organisations, misaligned incentives, and bureaucratic complications, existing PPPs in Nigeria are faced with many challenges. Nevertheless, to make sure that PPPs are successful, there has to be a clear and transparent legal and regulatory framework. This framework should clearly define the roles and responsibilities of each partner, provide mechanisms for dispute resolution, and ensure that the IP rights of each (especially the weaker parties) are protected. Incentives, such as tax breaks or grants, can encourage both public and private sector entities to engage in collaborative projects that make use of IP for social and economic benefits. Furthermore, creating knowledge-sharing platforms and open innovation ecosystems can help to foster collaboration and maximise the impact of PPPs in the IP and technology sector.

4.8 Conclusion

As Nigeria faces increasingly complicated developmental difficulties, intellectual property can be an effective tool for long-term progress. The country can make use of innovation and creativity to meet fundamental needs like poverty, education, and water sanitation by bringing its intellectual property strategy into alignment with the SDGs. This chapter has looked into the relationship that exists between technology, intellectual property rights (IPR), and development in Nigeria. It has pointed out the enormous potential of emerging technologies like AI, blockchain, and NFTs to inject economic growth and social progress into the country. However, it has also shown that there are some challenges that the inadequacy of an IP framework and a lack of awareness regarding the importance of IP protection pose to economic and social development in any country. This analysis has shown that while Nigeria has made progress in technological innovation in areas such as app development and fintech, overall, the country's contribution to global innovation is actually limited. This is partly due to a lack of awareness and a lack of understanding of IP rights among entrepreneurs, creators, SMEs, and the general public. It is also partly because the IP laws and enforcement mechanisms that are already in existence in Nigeria have not been fully equipped to resolve the complexities of some emerging technologies, potentially putting up obstacles to innovation and investment.

In order to take advantage of the full potential of IP and technology for Nigeria's development, a multi-faceted approach is required. This includes ensuring that the IP framework is strengthened, promoting IP education and awareness, and establishing public-private partnerships in such a way that they become successful. All of this will guarantee that there is access to patented technologies. This approach not only expands economic prospects but also secures a long-term and bright future for all.

5 Apprenticeship system (*Igba Boyi*) of preserving Indigenous knowledge in Igbo Land, Southeast Nigeria and technology transfer in patent law

A necessary linkage

Nneka Chioma Ezedum

5.1 Introduction

Technology transfer is the process utilised by research institutions, universities, and production companies to transfer technology to industries or companies where the inventions can be developed into commercial products or services.[1] The World Intellectual Property Organisation (WIPO) defines it as "a collaborative process that allows scientific findings, knowledge and intellectual property to flow from creators, such as universities and research institutions, to public and private users."[2] This form of knowledge transfer has been effectively used within the patent system to reap a rich harvest of know-how and human capital development, which has resulted in a boom in economies over the last century.[3] The apprenticeship system, otherwise referred to as *Igba boyi* by the Igbo Tribe in South East Nigeria, is a method of human development where know-how and skills are passed from a "master" to his apprentices. "The Igbo apprenticeship system (IAS), a communal enterprising framework where successful businesses develop others, and over time provide capital and give away their customers to the new businesses."[4] The *Igba boyi* system has also guaranteed that Indigenous knowledge is preserved and sustained, ensuring that the skills and practices of Indigenous peoples are passed from

1 "Technology Transfer" https://www,uspto.gov/ip-policy/patent-policy/technology-transfer Accessed 2 June 2024.

2 WIPO, "Intellectual Property and Technology Transfer" https://www.wipo.int/web/technology-transfer# Accessed 1 June 2024.

3 Kamil Idris, *Intellectual Property A Power Tool for Economic Growth* (World Intellectual Property Organisation (WIPO) Publication No. 888) 84.

4 Ndubuisi Ekekwe, "A Nigerian Model for Stakeholder Capitalism" *Harvard Business Review*, https://hbr.org/2021/05/a-nigerian-model-for-stakeholder-capitalism. Accessed 1 June 2024.

DOI: 10.4324/9781003602989-6

generation to generation, empowering the new generation and improving the economy of society.

The agitation for the protection of Indigenous knowledge as a form of intellectual property right can be argued on the basis that strategies that work within the current intellectual property systems were hitherto used by Indigenous communities to sustain and preserve their Indigenous knowledge. Recognition of this mode of sustaining knowledge transfer in Indigenous communities is relevant in arguing for the protection of Indigenous knowledge, acknowledging the similarities between technology transfer in patents and the apprenticeship system of Indigenous knowledge.

5.2 *Igba boyi* – a model for knowledge transfer and strategic business growth

The Igbo Apprenticeship System (IAS), popularly referred to as *Igba boi* or *Igba boyi*, was in existence before Nigeria was colonised by Britain. It experienced spontaneous growth after the Nigerian Civil War, following the effect of the government seizing the savings of Igbos from their bank accounts and issuing them with only £20. This resulted in Igbo young men taking the initiative to scout for a means of livelihood and a way to boost and grow the economy and wealth of the Igbos. As the elders blessed them, they dropped a message: "*Onye aghala nwanne ya*," which is interpreted to mean "do not leave your brother behind." "As people made progress, they came back home to pick up their relatives to share opportunities in the cities with them. That concept propelled a region that should be considered the poorest in Nigeria and is currently regarded by the United Nations as the most secure in human development."[5] The system thrived on the spirit of kinship and brotherhood.

The *Igba boyi* system is a means whereby young people (mostly boys) served their master (*Oga*) for some years. The boys were unpaid but basically spent the service period learning the rudiments of the trade, business, practice, or whatever it was that they were interested in. At the end of the apprenticeship period, they were rewarded by the master with a reasonable amount to start their own business; some masters could also go the extra mile of allowing the *nwa boyi* (the apprentice boy) to take some of his clients or customers as a show of goodwill. The *Igba boyi* system also had some formalities, though not written; both parties brought people who witnessed the agreement, but there was really no fixed amount that the

5 African Business, "Igbo Apprenticeship System Fuels Nigeria's Entrepreneurs." Sourced from the interview granted by Ndubisi Ekekwe to BBC's Igbo Service. https://Africa.business/2021/06/energy-resources/igbo-apprenticeship-system-fuels-nigerias-entrepreneurs Accessed 1 June 2024.

master was mandated to give the apprentice at the end of the apprenticeship period. Some masters rewarded their apprentices based on how faithfully they served and how industrious they were.

Acknowledging that the *Igba boyi* system was a method of knowledge transfer and a means of learning a lifelong skill hands-on, it was equally a model that developed and sustained businesses and skills, ensuring that there was a continuous cycle of transfer of knowledge. The system creates opportunities in society for people to utilise, and it is a means to eradicate poverty because businesses grow out of it for the benefit of the participants.[6] Currently, it is known as the largest business incubator system globally, grooming young people to become established business owners.[7] One of the benefactors of the *Igba boyi* system, Cosmas Maduka of the Coscharis Group, has utilised his apprenticeship skills and currently has a multimillion-naira business empire.[8] Innocent Chukwuma of Innoson Motors, Cletus Madubugwu Ibeto of the Ibeto Group, and Chief Alexander Chika Okafor of the Chikason Group, who are Igbo multi-billionaires, are also products of the scheme.[9] Chief Innocent Chukwuma, who founded Innoson Vehicle Manufacturing (a subsidiary of the Innoson Group), Nigeria's first Indigenous automobile manufacturing company, was an apprentice to Chief Romanus Eze Onwuka, who was the biggest motorcycle parts seller in the Nnewi market in Anambra State. Chief Innocent Chukwuma was also an apprentice to Pius Maduka, elder brother of Cosmas Maduka, for about seven months, learning the trade of spare parts.[10] Chukwuma's knowledge of motorcycle spare parts helped him venture into producing complete motorcycles at cheaper prices. His company currently manufactures cars, motorcycles, tricycles, spare parts, etc., and is estimated to be

6 Rudolf Ogoo Okonkwo "Igba Boi, Ekekwe & BBC's Distortion of Igbo Apprentice Scheme" https://www.thecable.ng/igba-boi-ekekwe-bbcs-distortion-of-igbo-apprentice-scheme/amp/ Accessed 15 June 2024.

7 Adekunle Sulaimon, "Why Igbo Apprenticeship is World's Largest Business Incubator System" https://www.google.com/amp/s/punchng.com/why-igbo-apprenticeship-is-worlds-largest-business-incubator-system-don/%3famp Accessed 15 June 2024.

8 "How a Nigerian Scheme Forged in War Creates Billionaires" https://www.google.com/amp/s/www.bbc.com/news/world-africa-56985304.amp Accessed 3 January 2025.

9 Titus Eleweke, "Declining Glory of Igbo Apprenticeship System that Bred Billionaire Bizmen" https://www.igbojournalreview.com/2022/03/declining-glory-of-igbo-apprenticeship.html?m=1 Accessed 3 January 2025.

10 Ayo Onikoyi, "Documentary: Freeman on Igbo Apprenticeship System, Nnewi Businessmen Lights Up Showmax" https://www.google.com/amp/s/www.vanguardngr.com/2024/04/documentary-freeman-on-igbo-apprenticeship-system-nnewi-businessmen-lights-up-showmax/amp/ Accessed 3 January 2025.

worth about $1.5 billion, which is a result of values and skills acquired via the Igbo Apprenticeship System.[11]

Apprenticeship is a model for skill and technology transfer. In it, one gains knowledge of a particular business and uses that knowledge to set up one's own business. The mentor of this traditional business school aids the apprentice financially and otherwise in setting up his or her own business.[12] The Igbo Apprenticeship System, a unique way of knowledge transfer now studied at Harvard, is also suggested to be implemented as a platform for young lawyers to perfect the skill of legal practice.[13] The system also mentored Ifeanyi Ubah, who owns Capital Oil & Gas, one of the biggest private fuel depots in Africa.[14]

This practice was strategic, an extension of the Igbo people's enterprising and industrious spirit and an informal means of an unstructured training program.[15] This can be likened to a scholarship awarded to a student wherein the student pays no tuition but is offered free and full tutorials that equip him and strategically place him in a position to compete effectively in the global market. The apprenticeship system exposes the apprentice to various skills by simply watching and learning from the master. Apart from the focal skill the apprentice aims to acquire, the apprentice also learns relationship management, analytical skills, leadership skills, managerial skills, accounting, innovative skills, etc.

Traditional local apprenticeship is one of the forms by which traditional knowledge was preserved, a system of teaching by the learner watching or doing. This system was utilised in trade learning, in traditional knowledge, and in various forms of traditional tutelage, and it was very effective. Knowledge passed down via this means is not forgotten because the learner has the advantage of patiently watching the process or procedure repeatedly. The apprentice practices the process or knowledge under the supervision of the master until the apprentice is certified, well-trained, and fit to be released. Apart from the preservation of Indigenous knowledge,

11 Ayo Onikoyi, "Documentary "Freeman on Igbo Apprenticeship System, Nnewi Businessmen Lights Up Showmax," ibid.

12 George-Franklin Umeh and Chisom Vianney Nnakwe, "Igbo Mentorship (Igba boi): A Philosophical Appraisal." (2024) Volume 4(1) *Nnadiebube Journal of Religion, Culture and Society (NJRCS)*.

13 Emma Ogbuehi, "Igba Boyi: Otti, Maikau, Amadi, others Back Igbo Apprenticeship Model for Young Lawyers" https://www.google.com/amp/s/thenicheng.com/igba-boyi-otti-maikyau-amadi-others-back-igbo-apprenticeship-model-for-young-lawyers/amp/ Accessed 3 January 2025.

14 Ndubisi Ekekwe, "A Nigerian Model for Stakeholder Capitalism" (n 4).

15 Nnamdi Madichie, "Igba Boyi and the Igbo Apprenticeship Scheme in Nigeria: Indigenous Entrepreneurship in Africa" https://www.academia.edu/110652088/igba-boyi-and-the-igbo-apprenticeship-scheme-in-nigeria-indigenous-entrepreneurship-in-africa?uc-sb-sw=97095545 Accessed 15 June 2024.

other advantages of the Indigenous transfer of skill include the apprentice growing the skill and depending on it for daily sustenance.[16]

5.3 Sustenance of Indigenous knowledge through apprenticeship

Indigenous knowledge forms part of the cultural heritage of Indigenous people, ranging from textile designs, traditional songs, medicinal plant knowledge, and environmental conservation.[17] The Igbo Apprenticeship System is a vital mechanism for safeguarding techniques, practices, and customs. It is the system of skill transmission; it involves a master or skilled craftsman training an apprentice in a particular trade or craft. This intergenerational transfer of knowledge ensures the survival of various aspects of cultural heritage and protects it from dilution, loss, and extinction. Indigenous knowledge, otherwise referred to as traditional knowledge, is primarily of a practical nature and is referred to by the World Intellectual Property Organization (WIPO) as knowledge, know-how, skills, and practices of a community.[18] WIPO Intergovernmental Committee on Intellectual Property and Genetic Resources, Traditional Knowledge and Folklore (IGC), which is a platform to discuss issues pertaining to Indigenous people's traditional knowledge, refers to traditional knowledge as knowledge originating from Indigenous, local communities that is dynamic and evolving and is the result of intellectual activity, experiences, spiritual means, or insights in or from a traditional context, which may be connected to land and environment, including know-how, skills, innovations, practices, teaching, or learning.[19] Indigenous knowledge bears its origin to a particular Indigenous community and is therefore communally owned.[20] Indigenous knowledge is intangible, which is referred to as incorporeal, and, when applied to property, would include intellectual property.[21] Its communal nature does

16 Patience Mofolasade Ojo, '"Indigenous Technology: An Anchor for Skill Development in Nigeria." https://ibadanadulteducationjournals.com.ng Accessed 20 June 2024.

17 "The Indigenous World 2023: World Intellectual Property Organization" https://www.iwgia.org/en/world-intellectual-property-organization-wipo/5161-iw-2023-wipo.html Accessed 20 June 2024.

18 WIPO, "Traditional Knowledge" https://www.wipo.int/tk/en/tk/ Accessed 29 July 2024.

19 Intergovernmental Committee on Intellectual Property and Genetic Resources, Traditional Knowledge and Folklore, "The Protection of Traditional Knowledge: Draft Articles." WIPO/GRTKF/IC/47/14 (Document Prepared by the Secretariat at the Forty-Seventh Session of the WIPO-IGC, Geneva, held from 5–9 June, 2023) https://www.wipo.int/meetings/en/doc-details.jsp?doc_id=611455 Accessed 3 September 2024.

20 D Oriakhogba and I Olubiyi, *Intellectual Property law in Nigeria: Emerging Trends, Theories and Practice* (1st edn Paclerd Press Limited, 2021) 30

21 D J Gervais, "Spiritual but not Intellectual? The Protection of Sacred Intangible Traditional Knowledge." (2003) Volume 11 *Cardozo J. of Int'l & Comp. Law* 467.

not refute the fact that Indigenous knowledge has the intellectual ingenuity that is involved in creating it.

Though traditional knowledge has been recognised and acknowledged as important to the global community, its inadequate protection under the extant intellectual property system has had devastating effects on its custodians. Traditional knowledge is often exploited, and traditional communities derive little or no benefits in comparison to the feasible profits made by exploiters.[22] Traditional knowledge is a great asset[23] but inadequately protected, which leads to its exploitation by third parties. The protection of Indigenous rights is recognised in the United Nations Declaration on the Rights of Indigenous Peoples (UNDRIP). The UNDRIP provides that Indigenous people have a right to maintain, protect, and develop their cultural heritage, traditional knowledge, and traditional cultural expressions and also the intellectual property over their rights, which manifests in medicines, designs, etc.[24] Indigenous rights of communities are important to their survival and development; it is indispensable for any community.[25] Though traditional knowledge was ineffectually protected as an intellectual property right, Indigenous communities apply hands-on experience, such as apprenticeship in sustaining their knowledge systems.[26] Apprenticeship is replayed in various aspects of Indigenous knowledge and guarantees the transmission and sustenance of our culture. Various forms of Indigenous knowledge are passed down to the younger generation through apprenticeship, which is equal to the quality of time spent with the elders or people knowledgeable in that area. In Igbo land in southern Nigeria, traditional healthcare practitioners inherit the skill of using medicinal knowledge to heal from their forefathers.[27] The skill of making fabrics from traditional fibres, such as bark and bast from trees, raffia from palm trees, wool from

22 Ayoyemi Arowolo, "African Traditional Knowledge Systems Management: The Struggle Between Science and Tradition." (2011) Volume IX(4) *The IUP Journal of Knowledge Management.*

23 K Idris, *Intellectual Property A Power Tool for Economic Growth* (n 4) 238.

24 United Nations Declaration on the Rights of Indigenous Peoples 2007, Article 31. The UNDRIP is not a legally binding document; however, it is the most comprehensive international instrument on the rights of indigenous peoples and has been noted to be the first human rights international document that deals with the rights of indigenous peoples.

25 Ayoyemi Arowolo, "African Traditional Knowledge Systems Management: The Struggle between Science and Tradition" (n 23).

26 T D Mdhlulli, Sekgothe Mokgoatsana, Stewart Lee Kugara, Vuma Lucky "Knowledge Management: Preserving, Managing and Sharing Indigenous Knowledge through Digital Library" https://www.researchgate.net/publication/356153507_Knowledge_Management_Preserving_Managing_and_Sharing_Indigenous_Knowledge_through_Digital_library Accessed 20 June 2024.

27 Emeka Okonkwo, "Traditional Healing Among Nsukka Igbo." (2012) Volume 1(1) *Journal of Tourism and Heritage Studies.*

sheep, etc., is unique to Nigeria's rich heritage.[28] The dye and bonding techniques, which protect the fabric from damage, are skills passed on through apprenticeship. Akwete cloth weaving is Indigenous to the Igbo tribe and is said to be as old as the Igbo nation.[29] It is not in doubt, therefore, that apprenticeship is primarily responsible for transmitting Indigenous values and skills from generation to generation.[30] It is advocated that there should be a return to the Indigenous apprenticeship scheme, where the apprentice could start up a business immediately after he concludes his tutelage, rather than Western education, which has young people seeking nonexistent jobs.[31]

Colonisation, though, has its benefits, but it also tends to strip traditional people of the essence of their heritage and culture. Colonisation played a devastating role in relegating the cultural heritage of Indigenous people and replacing it with the belief system of developed countries that colonised them. The cultural heritage and knowledge of ndigenous people was trivialised, and their belief systems and practices were viewed as unimportant and insignificant. This suppression affected the religious, ethnic, cultural, and linguistic aspects of cultural heritage. In effect, there were no laws formulated to protect the rights of Indigenous people.

Intellectual property rights were introduced to countries currently referred to as developed countries during a period that was considered a phase of technological stagnation and intellectual darkness; at that time, the countries were developing but not developed.[32] The period of the fifteenth and sixteenth centuries in England was when the Queen made aggressive use of intellectual property rights, such as patent monopoly, to

28 The Guardian, 2023 "Ethnographic Relevance of Nigeria's Indigenous Knowledge" https://guardian.ng/ethnographic-relevance-of-nigerias-indigenous-knowledge/ Accessed 20 June 2024.

29 McPhilips Nwachukwu and Appolos Oziogu Ibebabuchi, "Akwete Cloth: An Igbo Textile Art" https://www.vanguardngr.com/2012/07/akwete-cloth-an-igbo-textile-art/ Accessed 20 June 2024.

30 A O Okadi, FC Onah, L U Ekenta, and E I Abeya, "Promoting Apprenticeship as Panacea for Sustaining Skill Acquisition and Industries in Nigeria." (2020) Volume 2(1) *Vocational and Technical Education Journal (VOTEJ).*

31 Essien Ukpe, "Annang Indigenous Apprenticeship Education: An Alternative to Western Education for the Development of Annang Land" https://www.researchgate.net/publication/359364556_Annang_Indigneous_Apprenticeship_Education_An_Alternative_to_Western_Education_for_the_Development_of_Annang_Land Accessed 20 June 2024.

32 Craig Allen Nard, *The Law of Patents* (3rd edn, Wolters Kluwer Law & Business 2014) 8. This led to the enactment of the first known patent statute, the Venetian statute, to protect the works of known men "so that others who may see them could not build them and take the inventors' honor away, more men would then apply their genius, would discover , and would build devices of great utility and benefit to our Commonwealth."

encourage the growth of manufacturing and to lure skilled foreigners.[33] These inventions introduced new technologies and science and, therefore, brought development to the Western world. The protection made available to inventors and creators and the incentives thereof were part of the motivation to do more and also encouraged innovation. The development of intellectual property rights has progressed extensively to what is currently obtainable. However, the intellectual property system was designed to suit private needs, which was obtainable in those countries since property in those countries was privately owned and different from Indigenous rights, which are communally owned.[34]

The laws that were initially enacted to protect intellectual property rights were structured to protect private rights in countries that showed advancement in technology. Those laws did not contemplate communal rights in Indigenous communities. Consequently, there are intellectual property laws such as patents that give temporary protection to technological inventions and copyright that offers longer-lasting rights to literary, artistic, and musical works.[35]

The violation and deprivation of rights associated with Indigenous knowledge resulted in stagnation in the economic growth and development of Indigenous communities. These skills and practices came naturally to them and should have been a means for strategic economic development. For instance, patents granted for inventions are a tool for economic development:

> Patent law can be viewed as an incentive-based system of laws that offers a potential financial reward as an inducement to invent, to disclose technical information, to invent capital in the innovation process, and to facilitate efficient use and manufacturing of invention through licensing.[36]

The patent system was also utilised negatively by third parties in patenting inventions that originate from Indigenous communities. Though in the traditional African context, knowledge and experience are communally owned, the concept of property rights did not exist because that system did not recognise private ownership of such rights.[37] However, Indigenous

33 Craig Allen Nard, *The Law of Patents*, ibid., 12.

34 WIPO, "What is Intellectual Property" https://www.wipo.int/about-ip/en/ Accessed 26 June 2024.

35 P Torremans and J Holyoak, *Holyoak and Torremans Intellectual Property Law* (9th edn, Oxford University Press 2019) 12.

36 C A Nard, *The Law of Patents* (n 34) 59.

37 Archibold Mposhi, Charity Manyeruke, Shakespeare Hamauswa, "The Importance of Patenting Traditional Medicines in Africa: The Case of Zimbabwe." (2013) 3 *International Journal of Humanities and Social Science* 2..

peoples who are custodians of traditional knowledge require protection of that knowledge in the same way intellectual property is protected.

Traditional knowledge is used as an input into modern industries and, therefore, plays an important role in the world economy.[38] Various forms of traditional knowledge are obtained from local communities and Indigenous people; the knowledge is modified and subsequently commercialised by production companies. This provides an economic boost for the companies and little or no benefit for the local communities that are custodians and owners of the knowledge, who have guided the knowledge over the years and passed it down to their descendants. The patent system enables foreign companies to access Indigenous knowledge in various forms and commercialise it without any benefit going to the custodians of the cultural heritage. According to the African Centre for Bio-Safety:

> International businesses, institutions and other players have created profitable private monopolies over African patrimony by staking out patent claims on Africa's genes, plants and related traditional knowledge. The patent claims are not only economically unjust but are a moral affront to the many generations of Africans who have cared for and created the continent's rich genetic and cultural diversity.[39]

In view of the misappropriation of traditional knowledge, some countries like India and South Africa have amended their patent laws as a mechanism to oppose the grant of patents for their Indigenous knowledge. While South Africa mandates an attachment stating whether the invention is derived from a form of traditional knowledge,[40] India has opened an avenue to oppose a patent application on the basis of the invention arising from the existence of traditional knowledge.[41] Currently, India has compiled data on the country's traditional knowledge known as the Traditional Knowledge Digital Library Database (TKDL), which forms part of its defensive approach to protecting traditional knowledge.

Though Indigenous knowledge rights were not adequately protected under the extant intellectual property structure, colonialism, however, developed the entrepreneurial spirit of the Igbo tribe, which was known

38 Graham Dutfield, "TRIPS-Related Aspects of Traditional Knowledge." (2001), Volume 33(2) 233 *Case Western Reserve Journal of International Law.*

39 See African Centre for Biosafety, "Pirating African Heritage: The Pillaging Continues" (Briefing Paper 2009) 3, cited in A Oyewunmi, *Nigerian Law of Intellectual Property* (1st edn, University of Lagos Press and Bookshop Ltd, 2015) 249.

40 South African Patent Act, Sec 30(25)(3a).

41 Indians Patent Act, Sec 25(1)(k).

for trading, craftsmanship, etc., and which has been sustained presently by the apprenticeship system.[42]

Apart from being deprived of their rights, Indigenous people were also labelled as backwards and superstitious, culminating in the suppression of our religious, ethnic, cultural, and linguistic particularities. The protection of cultural heritage fosters a sense of ownership and pride in cultural heritage, a sense of *nke a bu nke anyi* (this is our own) and instils confidence that can propel the maximisation and utilisation of our cultural heritage to optimal use.

Currently, the protection of Indigenous knowledge has been recognised, and the close and traditional dependence of many Indigenous peoples and local communities on biological resources is also duly noted. The contribution that traditional knowledge can make to both the conservation and sustainable use of biological diversity has been duly acknowledged.[43] Global recognition of traditional knowledge has created a deep respect that is currently pushing countries to seek ways to involve Indigenous communities and apply their traditional knowledge in conserving and sustaining their ecosystems. This recognition resulted in the development of the Convention on Biodiversity (CBD), which is an international instrument for the "conservation of biological diversity, sustainable use of its components and the fair and equitable sharing of the benefits arising out of the utilisation of genetic resources."[44] The obligation placed on countries is clearly stated in the CBD, which includes preserving traditional knowledge in their territories, the entitlement of traditional right holders to be involved in the commercialisation of their traditional knowledge, and a system of benefit sharing from the utilisation of such knowledge.[45]

The CBD also requires countries "to protect and encourage customary use of biological resources in accordance with traditional cultural practices that are compatible with conservation or sustainable use requirements."[46] This requirement is necessary to ensure that the use of traditional knowledge by third parties does not violate the belief system of the people and does not conflict with their cultural practices. To that effect, traditional practices must be used by third parties in line with the belief system of the

42 Don C Ohadike, "When Slaves Left, Owners Wept: Entrepreneurs and Emancipation Among the Igbo People" https://www.tandfonline.com/doi/abs/10.1080/0144039980857524 Accessed 20 June 2024.

43 "Traditional Techniques Provide Useful Models for Biodiversity Policies" https://www.cbd.int/article/indigenous%26localcommunitiesforbiodiversity-1 Accessed 8 July 2024.

44 UN, "Convention on Biological Diversity, Key International Instrument for Sustainable Development" https://www.un.org/en/observances/biological-diversity-day/convention Accessed 6 July 2024.

45 The Convention on Biological Diversity, Article 8(j).

46 The CBD, Article 10(c).

people; anything contrary will be a violation of what the community prides itself on.

Prior to the commencement of the Convention on Biological Diversity, the global community could freely access genetic resources and associated traditional knowledge without any legal regulatory inhibition. This resulted in the Nagoya Protocol, which requires all parties to the Convention on Biological Diversity to ratify and domesticate it. The Nagoya Protocol on Access to Genetic Resources and the Fair and Equitable Sharing of Benefits Arising from their Utilization is an international agreement that implements the objectives on access and benefit sharing obligations of the Convention on Biological Diversity (CBD). The primary objective of the protocol is to promote "the fair and equitable sharing of benefits arising from the utilisation of genetic resources," while it further seeks to ensure equitable sharing of the benefits of "genetic resources that are held by Indigenous and local communities and traditional knowledge associated with those resources."

It establishes a framework whereby genetic resources can be accessed provided there is a fair and equitable share of the benefits achieved therein, hence ensuring the conservation and sustainable use of biodiversity. Indigenous and local communities may receive benefits through a legal framework that respects the value of traditional knowledge associated with genetic resources.[47] The Nagoya Protocol also covers traditional knowledge (TK) associated with genetic resources that are covered by the CBD and the benefits arising from its utilisation.[48] The Protocol is the first international instrument of particular relevance to Indigenous and local communities negotiated since the adoption of the UN Declaration on the Rights of Indigenous Peoples.[49] As encoded in Article 31 of UNDRIP, which states that Indigenous rights over their traditional knowledge can only be protected in line with their customary laws, Article 12 of the Nagoya Protocol likewise requires parties to "take into consideration Indigenous and local communities' customary laws, community protocols and procedures, as applicable, with respect to traditional knowledge associated with genetic resources."

Domestically, there has been recognition of some forms of Indigenous knowledge. The Nigerian Copyright Act[50] was expanded to accommodate

47 The Nagoya Protocol – Convention on Biological Diversity https://www.dcceew.gov.au/science-research/australias-biological-resources/nagoya-protocol-convention-biological Accessed 9 September 2024.

48 "About the Nagoya Protocol" https://www.cbd.int/abs/about/#objective Accessed 9 September 2024.

49 Nagoya Protocol on Access and Benefit-sharing and Traditional Knowledge https://www.cbd.int/traditional/Protocol.shtml Accessed 9 September 2024.

50 The Nigerian Copyright Act, 2022.

the protection of expressions of folklore, which form part of the people's tangible and intangible cultural heritage.[51] The Act provides for the protection of expressions of folklore from commercialisation and for use outside its traditional or customary context.[52] The protection of the customary use of this form of Indigenous knowledge is in line with the provisions of the CBD, which states that Indigenous peoples' sensitivity should be accommodated when accessing their cultural heritage. The Copyright Act also empowers the Copyright Commission to authorise the use of expressions of folklore. The Act, however, did not make express provisions for the fact that such usage should be on a prior informed basis, nor did it provide that there should be a system of benefit sharing from the utilisation of such knowledge as recognised by the CBD and the Nagoya Protocol.

The forms of expressions of folklore protected by the Copyright Act are forms of tangible and intangible cultural heritage, and this knowledge can be transferred through the *Igba boyi* system. As provided by the Act, expressions of folklore protected therein include the production of folk arts, in particular, drawings, carvings, sculptures, pottery, terracotta, mosaics, woodwork, metalware, jewellery, handicrafts, costumes, and Indigenous textiles.[53] The know-how involved in this cultural heritage is transferred by a master to his apprentice for the benefit of the *nwa boyi* (the apprentice) and the development of society at large. Access to these forms of Indigenous knowledge through the apprenticeship system is granted with the consent of the knowledge holder and benefits him in one way or another. Therefore, access to any third party, as provided by the Copyright Act, ought to be with the consent of the knowledge holder, with consequential economic benefit. The Copyright Act does not provide for the economic value that should be derived from the commercialisation of Indigenous knowledge; it merely states that usage by third parties should be with authority that can be provided by the Copyright Commission. A further expansion of the Copyright Act to recognise the economic value of Indigenous knowledge would strategically position Indigenous communities better.

There is also further development in protecting Indigenous knowledge under the patent system. The World Intellectual Property Organization (WIPO), along with the Intergovernmental Committee on Intellectual Property and Genetic Resources, Traditional Knowledge and Folklore (WIPO-IGC), has for several years deliberated and negotiated on producing an international legal instrument for the protection of traditional

51 The Nigerian Copyright Act, Sec 74(5).
52 Ibid., Sec 74(1).
53 Ibid., Sec 74(5)(d).

knowledge, traditional cultural expressions, and genetic resources.[54] The mandate of the WIPO-IGC was to address the three new themes that shared certain distinct features: GRs, TK, and TCEs were regarded as the "common heritage of humanity" and as intellectual valuables requiring appropriate forms of IP protection. Recently, WIPO member states released a new treaty on Intellectual Property, Genetic Resources and Associated Traditional Knowledge, adopted by the Diplomatic Conference. This is the first WIPO Treaty that makes provision for Indigenous peoples/communities and creates an interface between intellectual property, genetic resources, and associated traditional knowledge.[55]

The objective of the treaty is to enhance the efficacy, transparency and quality of the patent system with specific reference to genetic resources and traditional knowledge. Part of the aim of the treaty is to prevent patents from being granted erroneously for inventions that are not novel or inventive with regard to genetic resources and traditional knowledge associated with genetic resources.[56] The treaty intends to achieve its objectives by mandating complete disclosure of source. As stated in Article 3 of the New WIPO Treaty, an application for a patent for an invention derived from traditional knowledge must disclose the source of the traditional knowledge.

The treaty serves as a form of protection for Indigenous knowledge, which was hitherto argued to be in the public domain and available for all to access freely.[57] The treaty also ensures that a patent is granted for inventions that have inventive activity as provided by the patent legal framework and not for inventions that form part of the state of the art. However, the treaty does not make provision for any form of benefit sharing when Indigenous knowledge has been used in making an invention, which would enhance the economic advantage of the people. The various forms of protection offered for intellectual property rights generally substantially provide for commensurate commercial benefit for the right owners. This statement also reflects the intent of the general framework for the protection of Indigenous rights, albeit outside the conventional intellectual property framework like the CBD. Equally, under the apprenticeship system, while there is the preservation of the knowledge from extinction, there

54 WIPO, Intergovernmental Committee (IGC), https://www.wipo.int/tk/en/igc/ Accessed 13 September 2024.

55 WIPO "WIPO Member States Adopt Historic New Treaty on Intellectual Property, Genetic Resources and Associated Traditional Knowledge" https://www.wipo.int/pressroom/en/articles/2024/article_0007.html Accessed 25 May 2024.

56 WIPO Treaty on Intellectual Property, Genetic Resources and Associated Traditional Knowledge, Art 1.

57 WIPO, "Traditional Knowledge and Intellectual Property" https://www.wipo.int/edocs/pubdocs/en/wipo.pub_tk_1.pdf. Accessed 4 June 2024.

is also some form of benefit that goes to the custodian of the knowledge from the services of the apprentice.

The WIPO treaty, however, failed to recognise the moral and economic value of traditional knowledge as contemplated by the CBD and its Nagoya Protocol. The economic value of traditional knowledge would be best actualised if the treaty specifically stated that the patent applicant must also disclose evidence of prior informed consent and a benefit-sharing structure for the proceeds of the invention. Therefore, to adequately protect Indigenous knowledge from undue exploitation, the Nigerian Patent Act should be expanded to incorporate the provisions of Article 8(j) of the CBD and its Nagoya Protocol on prior informed consent and mutual benefit sharing of the proceeds of inventions derived from traditional knowledge.

5.4 Technology transfer and patent system

The patent system, as discussed, is utilised in protecting intellectual property rights through modalities such as technology transfer, and it is argued in this work that this system is similar to the *Igba boyi* apprenticeship system. Patents serve two purposes: first, to encourage inventive activity by protecting the rights of inventors and, second, to encourage further inventive activity by requiring complete disclosure of the technical aspects of an invention. Patents are "intended to encourage the making of new inventions and the subsequent innovative work that will put those inventions to practical use"[58] and encourage innovation so that more goods are made available for public use.[59] This is in alignment with the public interest objective of intellectual property protection, which is to make available protected works for the benefit of society.

The grant of a patent offers protection from exploitation provided it satisfies the criteria of being new, has inventive activity, and can be applied industrially.[60] The grant is also subject to complete disclosure of the relevant invention in a manner such that one who has general knowledge in that field would be able to apply it,[61] this is a means of transfer of technology. This ensures that the knowledge, though protected on the one hand, is also made available for further research and improvement in that area of knowledge. The patent system acknowledges that the transfer of

58 William Cornish and David Llewelyn, *Intellectual Property: Patent, Copyright, Trade Marks and Allied Rights* (8thedn, Sweet & Maxwell 2013) 131.

59 Tina Hart, Linda Fazzani and Simon Clark, *Intellectual Property Law* (4th edn, Palgrave Macmillan Law Masters 2006) 4.

60 The Patent & Designs Act, Laws of the Federal Republic of Nigeria, 2004. Sec 1(1).

61 The Patent & Designs Act, Sec 3(2).

knowledge and technology is fundamental to its optimal functioning in society.[62]

The grant of a patent is a medium of protection; however, an invention should be sufficiently exposed for use to enable both the inventor and the public to benefit from the product or process, as the case may be.[63] Avenues for the exploitation of patents have been enabled by provisions of the patent legal structure that accommodate the assignment and licensing of rights for optimal utilisation of the invention. It is argued that mere licensing without transferring the corresponding know-how (technology transfer) will be ineffective.[64] The restriction of patent rights can hinder access to valuable knowledge by developing countries, especially in the area of healthcare.[65]

The purpose of knowledge transfer in patents is to transmit knowledge, skills and competence from those who have generated it to those who will generate economic value from them.[66] This is similar to the *Igba boyi* system of apprenticeship, which enables the transfer of Indigenous skills from the master to the apprentice. This Indigenous skill transfer was well utilised outside the intellectual property structure via the *Igba boyi* system of apprenticeship. There is also the aspect of technology transfer, which is aimed at equipping a developing community to build its capacity to produce.

Technology transfer is the process whereby the owner of a technology transfers its know-how, knowledge, and skill to another in exchange for value such as a royalty, and an important parameter that is considered is whether the technology is protected by patent.[67] Transfer of technology is important and strategic as it forms a catalyst for development in that area of knowledge.

There are different means of activating technology transfer; research institutes and universities can license their patented inventions to businesses

62 WIPO, "Transfer of Technology" https://www.wipo.int/patents/en/topics/technology_transfer.html Accessed 10 July 2024.

63 Adejoke O Oyewunmi, *Nigerian Law of Intellectual Property* (1st edn, University of Lagos Press and Bookshop Ltd 2015).

64 Bart Verspagen, "Intellectual Property Rights in the World Economy" https://www.google.com/search?q=the+use+of+technology+transfer+in+patent&aqs=chrome Accessed 25 June 2024.

65 ""The Importance of Intellectual Property Rights in Technology Transfer" https://aslgate.com/the-importance-of-intellectual-property-rights-in-technology-transfer/ Accessed 25 June 2024.

66 Marta Catarino, "The Role of Patents in Technology Transfer" https://www.wipo.int>pct Accessed 21 June 2024.

67 Bindu Sharma, "The Role of Patents in Technology Transfer" https://www.ciotechoutlook.com Accessed 21 June 2024.

and entrepreneurs who utilise them to create life-saving products.[68] At Ege University, Turkey, a team of four inventors is running their own commercial R&D company, Dermis Pharma, and through the transfer of technology they have been able to strategise and ensure the commercialisation of their invention. The company's skin patch, Dermalix, aids in wound healing and is a source of help to 50 million diabetics.[69]

Technology transfer can also be in the form of the dissemination of complex innovation from developed economies to developing economies, which could enable the commencement of local production of drugs.[70] The Agreement on the Trade-Related Aspects of Intellectual Property Rights (TRIPS Agreement) encourages technology transfer to developing economies: "Promoting and encouraging technology transfer to least developed country members in order to enable them to create a sound and viable technological base."[71] This requires the skills and expertise of firms that are already in that process to be made available to countries that are limited in that area. This mode of technology transfer is highly recommended and can be utilised in emergency situations such as the COVID-19 pandemic. In that case, the production and circulation of vaccines would not be restricted to developing countries to the detriment of growing economies that do not have the requisite technological know-how. If this restriction is implemented, it will defeat the objective of the World Health Organisation, which is to manage emergency situations and ensure the global protection of health and well-being.[72] Technology transfer is core to vaccine development and very essential for innovation. Recognising that there ought to be no constraints in the countries/companies that produce the COVID-19 vaccine in an emergency, there also ought to be no limitation to the transfer of technology.[73] This is basic to sustaining development in any field in every society.

There are different channels through which technology transfer can be achieved in developing countries, which include trade in goods, foreign

68 "What is Technology Transfer" https://patents.princeton.edu/about-us/what-technology-transfer Accessed 21 June 2024.

69 Thomas Bereuter and Ija Rudyk, "'From Research to Lift-Off." Sourced from "Technology Transfer Case Studies" https://www.epo.org/en/learning/ Accessed 21 June 2024.

70 William Fisher, Ruth Okediji, and Padmashree Gehl Sampath, "Fostering Production of Pharmaceutical Products in Developing Countries." (2021), Volume 43, *Michigan Journal of International Law*.

71 The Agreement on Trade-Related Aspects of Intellectual Property Rights (TRIPS) Article 66.2.

72 WHO, "What We Do" https://www.who.int/about/what-we-do Accessed 10 July 2024.

73 Nneka Ezedum "COVID-19 and Access to Vaccines in Nigeria: Balancing Interests between Patent Owners' Rights and Public Interest." Volume 3(2) *Enugu State University of Science and Technology Law Journal*, ESLJ (December 2021) 23–50.

direct investment (FDI), and licensing. Trade in goods involves international trading whereby new and high-quality products are introduced to developing countries. It is the general notion that as goods are transferred, the technology inherent in them is also transferred.[74] This notion can be contested because the transfer of technology involves the methodical transfer of know-how, which is intentionally transferred, and this cannot be discovered from transferring a product. With respect to foreign direct investment, developing countries are provided with more efficient foreign technologies, which translate to technological spillovers.[75] FDI is the process whereby a foreign company sets up business in a host country, and through that means, technology is transferred as part of the FDI process,[76] the local firms can acquire knowledge through imitation or reverse engineering.[77] The local firms can employ former employees of international firms or establish their own firms by physically moving people in the local community. The advantage of this mode of technology transfer is the transfer of managerial and marketing skills to the Indigenes of the developing community.

Licensing, on the other hand, involves authorisation given by the licensor to the licensee to use the patented product for a period,[78] which includes the accompanying technical information and knowledge.[79] Patent law in Nigeria accommodates licensing in various forms; there is the licence of right, contractual licence, and compulsory licence; these rights enable the licensee to have rights in the technology. Apart from the specifications in the patent, the rights include knowledge of how to adapt the invention in particular formats to variations on how to make the most use of it.[80] Using

74 United Nations Conference on Trade and Development (UNCTAD), 'Transfer of Technology and Knowledge Sharing for Development Science: Technology and Innovation Issues for Developing Countries' UNCTAD/DTL/STICT/2013/8, United Nations Publication, 2014.

75 Bernard M Hoekman, Keith E Maskus, and Kamal Saggi, "Transfer of Technology to Developing Countries: Unilateral and Multilateral Policy Options." World Bank Policy Research Working Paper 3332, June 2004 https://documents1.worldbank.org Accessed 11 July 2024.

76 Thomas K Cheng, "Technology Transfers in Developing Countries" https://doi.org/10.1093/oso/9780192857354 Accessed 11 July 2024.

77 United Nations Conference on Trade and Development (UNCTAD), "Transfer of Technology and Knowledge Sharing for Development Science: Technology and Innovation Issues for Developing Countries," ibid., n 42.

78 Desmond Oriakhogba and Ifeoluwa Olubiyi, *Intellectual Property Law in Nigeria: Emerging Trends, Theories and Practice* (n 21) 248.

79 Bernard M Hoekman, Keith E Maskus, and Kamal Saggi, "Transfer of Technology to Developing Countries: Unilateral and Multilateral Policy Options" (n 40).

80 William Cornish and David Llewelyn, *Intellectual Property: Patent, Copyright, Trade Marks and Allied Rights* (n 61) 275.

the patent in ways provided under the patent agreement will not amount to an infringement of the right, but the licensor may try to ensure the licence is exploited adequately and could also charge royalties.[81]

Patenting of rights is a viable means of technology transfer in whatever mode that is desired, as it ensures the parties are bound to the contractual agreement that will arise therefrom. Patents provide the legal framework that ensures strong collaborations are developed from technology transfer synergies and also protect the fruits of such relationships. Technology transfer is utilised for patentable inventions for the benefit of the parties. While this could not be replicated for Indigenous rights because Indigenous rights were not *ipso facto* protectable under the patent regime, Indigenous people have formulated a means of ensuring their skills and knowledge are transferred for further utilisation and economic value to the benefactor; hence, the apprenticeship system of *Igba boyi.*

5.5 The necessary linkage: a factor for advancement in technology

The apprenticeship system of acquiring knowledge and the knowledge transfer mode in international technology transfer are different, as already discussed, but they are similar in some ways. It is established that the two serve the purpose of transferring knowledge and skills for development and the benefit of society at large.

The apprenticeship system arises when an apprentice binds himself to serve and learn a skill from one who is knowledgeable in that area and who is determined to train the apprentice systematically in order to impact that knowledge or skill.[82] The transfer of knowledge in the apprenticeship system is not disputed. However, such transfer of know-how is better equated with developing the individual and society at large. From the analysis of the Igbo apprenticeship system, it can be deduced that the intent was to develop the economic standard of the benefactor/apprentice (the *nwa-boyi*). The apprentice's only mode of payment is to show dedication to learning and to promote the master's trade by being diligent and hardworking. The two parties, though, render some form of service to each other but do not offer any form of monetary payment for the services rendered either way. The master gains from an apprentice whose diligence and hard work enable the master to make a profit from the growth of the master's trade or business.

81 Paul Torremans and Jon Holyoak, *Intellectual Property Law* (n 37) 118.

82 Polycarp Okoro, E Ibu Otor, King James Nkum, and John Omligbe, "Apprenticeship and the Right to Patentable Inventions in Nigeria." (2023) Volume 10(7) *TIJER-International Research Journal.*

The *Igba boyi* system of apprenticeship ensures the preservation of Indigenous knowledge in diverse ways. The skill and know-how attributed to that Indigenous knowledge, by virtue of being transferred to another, would be sustained from generation to generation if such practices were replicated. It is, however, important to note that, due to the recognition of Indigenous knowledge as the heritage of a particular people or community, the transfer of such knowledge would be restricted to people within that community. The maintenance of Indigenous knowledge within a community ensures that third parties do not access the knowledge and thereby commercialise it without recognising or acknowledging the custodians of the traditional knowledge. Such access by third parties should be pre-informed and on terms beneficial to the custodians of the traditional knowledge, such that they would derive economic value from sharing their knowledge.

For the transfer of technology that is recognised under the patent system, the international transfer of technology and know-how promotes development in emerging economies that will increase social and economic stability for the global good.[83] Under the current intellectual property regime, technologies are protected. Patent laws ensure that the technical know-how that results from inventive activity is protected so that in the event of a transfer of technology by whatever means, the rights of the patent owner are protected. This protection is the catalyst for further advancement in that area; when there is an incentive appropriated for development, it encourages further development. This is the channel through which technology and scientific advancement reach societies that are not privileged to such knowledge. The patent system is structured to ensure that the right to access inventions can only be granted by the owner of the invention who holds the patent thereof. This right enables the patentee to work the invention in ways that will give them commercial value for the work put into producing the invention. The right to grant access to inventions, which is determined by the patent owner, should also be applied to Indigenous knowledge whereby the right to access their knowledge should be pre-determined by them, as seen in the apprenticeship system.

5.6 Conclusion

Patents protect technology transfer between countries and companies, as the case may be, and the contract agreement outlines the terms and

83 Edward Harris, WIPO, "Experts: International Tech Transfer Can Benefit All" https://www.wipo.int/pressroom/en/stories/int_tech-transfer.html# Accessed 11 July 2024.

conditions regulating such knowledge development strategies. The transfer of knowledge in the apprenticeship system does not enjoy such regulation as it stands because it is not methodologically structured and regimented and could be orally constructed. However, the non-formal system of the apprenticeship should not deprive Indigenous people of the right to protect and preserve their knowledge and restrict its exploitation. The traditional knowledge of Indigenous people can be protected from exploitation by ensuring that access is on pre-informed consent and on mutually beneficial terms, as provided by international instruments that protect Indigenous knowledge.

Traditional knowledge and its practices are the very existence of Indigenous people. Any attempt to exploit or commercialise such knowledge or practices is equal to the crime of genocide, which amounts to extinguishing a people from the face of the earth.[84] Therefore, every effort to protect and preserve such knowledge should first acknowledge the practice as a human right, which is inherent to them as humans, before adopting any means that allow access to such rights. The Universal Declaration of Human Rights acknowledges the right that everyone has to freely participate in the cultural life of the community.[85] It represents the universal recognition of fundamental human rights, which is equally applicable to everyone with disregard to nationality, gender, ethnicity, colour, religion, status, tribe, etc.[86] and places an obligation on states to refrain from interfering with the enjoyment of human rights. The exploitation and commercialisation of traditional knowledge is an undue interference with the human rights of Indigenous peoples and should not be accommodated under any cloak.

The know-how and skills transferred in traditional practices bear their origin in the particular Indigenous community to which they are linked. They are communally owned by that community, are perpetual in the sense that they are not limited by time, and are passed down from generation to generation.[87] The *Igba boyi* system of apprenticeship is a model for economic development and ensures the preservation of Indigenous knowledge from generation to generation.

84 Charles Kalu Uwadineke and Chidiebele Kene Ezeama, "Protecting Traditional Knowledge/Secrets Under Intellectual Property Law: A Comparative Analysis of the Adequacy of Protection Using Nigeria as a Case Study." (2019) Volume 6(1) *Nnamdi Azikiwe University Journal of Commercial and Property Law.*

85 The Universal Declaration of Human Rights (UDHR), Article 27 (1)

86 UDHR Article 2.

87 D Oriakhogba and I Olubiyi, *Intellectual Property Law in Nigeria: Emerging Trends, Theories and Practice* (n 22) 30.

It is therefore recommended that, as provided by the patent system which protects the right of a patentee to grant third parties access to his inventions, this should be replicated in the protection of Indigenous knowledge. The apprenticeship system shows that access to Indigenous know-how can be on pre-informed consent and on terms that benefit both parties and prioritise the generational preservation of the knowledge.

6 An overview of the patenting scheme

The Nigerian story

Regina Obiechine

6.1 Introduction

> The law does not require of patentees to describe new and old, but merely to distinguish new from old. Otherwise, a patent would be more complex and voluminous than a Welsh pedigree.[1]

Patenting is a process that protects and encourages innovation and invention, which are the dual tools used by progressive economies today for national development. It is important to note that many countries provide financial and other kinds of support to their innovative sector in order to increase, among other things, their productivity threshold. For instance, China provides support for its innovative sector. As part of the wider Made in China 2025 policy to move China's economy from a manufacturing to an innovation base, this has included direct financial incentives to file for patent protection locally and internationally.[2] It was reported by the World Intellectual Property Organisation (WIPO) that in 2018, China filed 53,345 Patent Cooperation Treaty (PCT) applications (second only to the US at 56,142).[3]

In another 2024 WIPO report, China topped the charts, followed by the United States of America, concerning a) which offices received the most patent applications, b) applicants from which countries filed the most patent applications, and c.) the countries that are the biggest users of the PCT

1 *Evans v. Eaton*, 20 U.S. 356 (S.Ct. 1822), cited in Great Patent Quotes, Patent Blurb, https://www.patentblurb.com/great_patent_quotes:start dated 28 December 2024.

2 Tim Jackson, "Patent Incentives in China: A Changing Focus," *The World Financial Review*, 28 May 2019 https://worldfinancialreview.com/patent-incentives-in-china-a-changing-focus/#:~:text=Like%20many%20countries%20China%20provides%20support%20for%20its,to%20file%20for%20patent%20protection%20locally%20and%20internationally Accessed 28 December 2024.

3 Ibid.

DOI: 10.4324/9781003602989-7

System.[4] To put this in a clearer perspective, the number of Chinese patent applicants was 1,642,507, compared with 518,364 for US applicants. The margin is wide enough to indicate that China as a country, the Chinese government and its people have undergone a transformative patent legal regime worth emulating by other economies, especially Nigeria. Patenting comes from the word "patent," which is an exclusive right granted to the patentee to exclude third parties from the use, manufacture, exploitation, selling, marketing, and generally benefiting from the patented invention, by a country or independent government. This chapter will review the patenting scheme in Nigeria in particular and Africa more generally.

6.2 The overview

Many inventors with ground-breaking ideas are creating ice-breaking innovations in Nigeria and across the African continent, which has resulted in increased patent filing worldwide. The WIPO Patents Facts and Figures reported a global increase in patent filing above trademarks and industrial designs in recent years,[5] reporting that while trademark and industrial design filing activity dropped by 14.5 per cent and 2.1 per cent, respectively, patent filings grew by 1.7per cent globally in 2022 globally. It also noted that while trademark filing activity fell to 15.5 million and industrial design filing activity reduced to under 1.5 million, patent filings around the globe reached 3.46 million[6] in the same year.[7] It should also be noted that no African country was listed in the recent global patent filing statistics (though this does not mean that no Africans filed from or through other countries).[8]

The conventional patent system in Nigeria began after Nigerian independence in 1960. Before then, the practice was based on the body of laws introduced and administered by the colonial masters and based largely on the contents of the patent laws of Britain. The question is, prior to the advent of Western schemes, did Africans or Nigerians have any coordinated traditional approaches to identifying and safeguarding Indigenous inventions? Is the African or Nigerian patent system truly "independent"? What was the fate of Indigenous African inventors and creators prior to the Western intrusion into the African economic and intellectual property

4 WIPO, "IP Facts and Figures – Global IP Filing Activity in 2023," *WIPO Statistics Database*, November 2024, https://www.wipo.int/en/ipfactsandfigures/patents Accessed on 28 December 2024.

5 WIPO, "IP Facts & Figures (WIPO Statistics Database)" (2024) www.wipo.int Accessed 10 July, 2024.

6 Ibid.

7 Ibid.

8 Ibid.

landscape? A patent is an exclusive right granted to the patentee to exclude third parties from the use, manufacture, exploitation, selling, marketing, and generally benefiting from the patented invention by a country or independent government. The Nigerian Patents and Industrial Designs landscape is protected under the Patents and Designs Act, 1970, Cap 344, LFN 1990.

This chapter explores traditional patent legal frameworks and practices within the Western and non-Western perspectives in Africa with Nigeria in view, providing an in-depth look at the patent application process, particularly focusing on practices in Nigeria and other African jurisdictions. It highlights the comparison between manual and electronic filing methods, emphasising the efficiency and immediacy of electronic filing while also detailing the complexities of the manual filing process. The chapter outlines essential requirements for a patent application, such as the need for a thorough invention description, claims, and supporting documents. It explains that in Nigeria and most African countries, patents are generally granted based on formal compliance rather than substantive examination, with patents typically valid for 10 to 20 years, subject to annual renewals. The concept of compulsory licensing is also explored, highlighting its significance in addressing public health and affordability issues, with examples from India and Nigeria. Additionally, the chapter briefly discusses international treaties like the Paris Convention and Patent Cooperation Treaty (PCT), which facilitate global patent filings, and the role of regional patent organisations such as the African Regional Intellectual Property Organisation (ARIPO) and the Organisation Africaine de la Propriété Intellectuelle (OAPI). Overall, the chapter serves as a comprehensive guide for navigating the patent application process in Nigeria and Africa while offering insights into key global and regional patent practices.

Patents are granted by the Patents Registrar after an examination by the patent examiners. Examination of patents in Nigeria and most African countries is as to form, and this is one of the significant systemic issues underlying patenting in Nigeria and Africa, namely, the lack of provisions for substantive examination. The implication is that Nigeria and, indeed, Africa can become a dumping ground for non-valuable inventions, and because patent registration in this jurisdiction is by first to register, individuals who are not the inventors, creators, assignors, or persons without any form of permission from the true inventors could register first and then exclude the true inventor from exploiting their intellectual efforts for their benefit. As an extension of the above, information on inventions that are created by locals could become available to foreigners or companies with the financial and other resources, who could either first or also obtain patent grants for the same or similar inventions without recognising, referring, or remunerating the original inventor. This could also lead to massive biopiracy. Biopiracy is a process whereby big corporations, with the assistance of Indigenous peoples, find biological material that has a special healthful use, take it to the lab for research, and thereafter proceed to obtain a patent for it in their name as their own inventions.[9] Biopiracy is therefore "the illegal appropriation of life – micro-organisms, plants, and animals (including humans) – and the traditional cultural knowledge that accompanies it".[10] A patent examination should be meaningfully considered to be granted, and provisions should be made for substantive or semi-substantive examination of the applications, both from locals and foreigners. Furthermore, as stated above, the Patents & Design Act was not primarily made for the Nigerian people; it is archaic and does not address the modern realities of patenting. There is an urgent need for an overhaul of the current laws providing for patent protection in Nigeria and Africa.

However, the Patents & Designs Registry, as a department under the Nigerian Federal Ministry of Trade and Investment, is limited in several aspects, including resources and manpower. There is a need for clarity of purpose, sufficient funding and increased staffing with expert patent officers, including examiners who are experts in different fields. The Nigerian Intellectual Property Commission (NIPCOM) Bill, which is a Bill set to create a Commission for intellectual property practices in Nigeria that has passed through several legislative years without being passed into law, should be reappraised as a reform option for the above challenge.

6.3 In the beginning

Innovative creations and inventions would not have existed as we have them today if it were not for the exceptional intelligence of the inventors, particularly African inventors. Is it at all possible to imagine a life without aeroplanes, medicine, modern buildings, bulbs, computers, or even microphones? Recently, I heard from colleagues about the existence of a remote-controlled life jacket, also known as a lifeguard, which is said to have the capacity to reach people 10 times faster than humans. It could be said that without the brilliant and diligent minds of inventors, innovators, and creators, the world would not have experienced so many changes since the cannibalistic era. Modernisation, industrialisation, and mechanisation depend primarily on the wheels of inventions and inventors. Africans, residing both within and offshore, are noted to be drastically creative, innovative,

9 "Biopiracy: A New Threat to Indigenous Rights and Culture in Mexico" http://www.globalexchange.org/campaigns/mexico/biopiracyReport.html, cited in Marcia Ellen DeGeer, ibid.

10 Ibid.

and inventive, and effectively contributing to local, national, and global developments.

For instance, Thomas L. Jennings was the first Black inventor to receive a patent in the US, paving the way for future inventors of colour to gain exclusive rights to their inventions. Jennings invented an early method of dry cleaning called "dry scouring" and patented it in 1821 – four years before Paris tailor Jean Jolly-Bellin reportedly refined his own chemical technique and established what many people claim was history's first dry cleaning business.[11]

Seyi Oyesola is a Nigerian medical doctor who co-invented the "Hospital in a Box," otherwise known as the CompactOR. The CompactOR is a mini hospital with a solar-powered life-saving operating room that can be transported to remote areas of Africa.[12] Further, Emeka Nelson invented a urine-powered generator. The generator converts urine into hydrogen gas, which is then used to produce electricity. This solves two significant challenges in Nigeria and Africa: waste management and energy scarcity.[13]

Furthermore, after many years of several maternal deaths resulting from internal bleeding during pregnancy, Dr Otu Oviemo Ovadje invented the "Emergency AutoTransfusion" device, also known as the Eatset. The device is used primarily to recover blood from a patient's internally bleeding organs and then re-infuse the blood back into the patient's circulatory system. It works without electricity and prevents blood loss, especially among pregnant women.[14]

There are so many other innovators of Nigerian or African descent who have their inventions patented and utilised largely in developed countries. These inventors have consistently demonstrated their innate abilities to address local, regional, and global needs through their innovative and life-changing inventions. The Nigerian or African inventors are, no doubt faced with many different challenges ranging from the difficulty in protecting their inventions and creativity, betrayal and bullying, difficulty accessing global markets, trust issues, financial setbacks, individualism, etc.[15]

11 Kirstin Fawcett, "10 Black Inventors Who Changed the World," *Mental Floss,* 2024 https://www.mentalfloss.com/article/86923/11-african-american-inventors-who-changed-world Accessed 10 July, 2024.

12 Oghenerume Progress, "Top 5 Inventions by Nigerians," *Pulse.NG*, September 2023, https://www.pulse.ng/lifestyle/food-travel/top-5-inventions-by-nigerians/rrtecwj Accessed 17 August 2024.

13 Ibid.

14 Ibid.

15 The News Express, "How the European Patent Office Stole My Invention – Nigerian Inventor Olusegun Adeleye" (26 August 2024) https://newsexpressngr.com/news/235834/how-european-patent-office-stole-my-invention-nigerian-inventor Accessed 27 August 2024.

Knowledge, innovation, and the patenting system play a critical role in the development pace of African countries. It was noted that national African laws and policymakers should not neglect the patent systems, given the increasingly important role that knowledge plays in national and global economic growth and the fact that the patent system is said to play a crucial role in encouraging commercially relevant innovation from the domestic research capacity of Africa, especially in the public sector.[16] It is apparent that the patent system presents African inventors with opportunities to protect their inventions in both internal and other developing countries such as Nigeria, Ghana, and South Africa, emerging economies such as China, India, Russia, and Saudi Arabia, and developed economies such as the United States of America, Canada, the United Kingdom, France, etc.[17]

It is important to note that the pre-colonial era in most, if not all, African societies was not uniform; there were massive inconsistencies in the societal values, beliefs, behaviours, cultures, and people's way of life. Emeagwali and Shizha opined that during the pre-colonial era, every Indigenous African society possessed its individual scientific body of knowledge, which was put together and utilised primarily for the interest of the masses. The ideas and instruments used by these societies and the ways they organised their labour were both important points of societal, social, and technological development. Diverse reasons were provided to support the arguments, which I believe are correct, that, indeed, the pre-colonial African societies had scientific and technical instruments that were designed and utilised to enhance the quality of life of the Indigenous people in African communities.[18]

There were traditionally Indigenous skills, handwork, ideas, arrangements, and techniques that were used to produce intellectual outputs, arts and crafts, blacksmithing, iron smelting, carding and weaving, and brewing, etc., such as the advanced iron-smelting techniques in Nigeria's Nok

16 Gregory D. Graff and Philip G. Pardey, "Inventions and Patenting in Africa: Empirical Trends from 1970 to 2010." (March 2020) *The Journal of World Intellectual Property* 23(1–2), 40–64 https://doi.org/10.1111/jwip.12139 Accessed 20 August, 2024.

17 Y. Chen and T. Puttitanun, "Intellectual Property Rights and Innovation in Developing Countries." (2005) *Journal of Development Economics* 78(2), 474–493. https://onlinelibrary.wiley.com/servlet/linkout?suffix=null&dbid=128&doi=10.1111%2Fjwip.12139&key=000232325900008&getFTLinkType=true&doiForPubOfPage=10.1111%2Fjwip.12139&refDoi=10.1016%2Fj.jdeveco.2004.11.005&linkType=ISI&linkSource=FULL_TEXT&linkLocation=Reference Accessed 20 July 2024.

18 Mamadou Gaye, "Western Influences and Activities in Africa." *Journal of Third World Studies* 15(1) https://www.jstor.org/stable/45197784 Accessed 21 August 2024.

culture.[19] Igbo-Ukwu bronze is a prominent Nigerian art native to Igbo-Ukwu in the south-eastern state of Anambra. It is widely regarded as the greatest ancient work of art in Nigeria.[20] The terra-cotta artefacts were said to have been discovered as far back as AD 800.[21] Also, mask-wearing is a popular Nigerian art predominantly practised by the Yoruba. It is usually worn by local traditionalists, typically for festivals such as the Gelede festival, which commemorates female elders through the use of large, intricately carved masks symbolising fighting animals and the faces of realistic women. All these and many others were altogether summed up as the African Indigenous patenting and intellectual property system.[22] Notwithstanding, scholars have noted that inventors in the pre-colonial era would usually prefer to keep their new ideas and inventions secret (or within the family line), which is the case in most recent African inventions, except for a few educated and exposed individuals who are well aware of the incidences and benefits associated with the patenting system.[23]

It has been noted that the launching of patent law in the Nigerian colonies and many African countries for the purposes of patenting was not principally organised to promote Indigenous inventiveness, nor was it designed to encourage local research and development; instead, it was to assist in the safeguarding of technologies for the exploitation of minerals and other Indigenous resources and values from the locals, for the benefit of the colonial administration.[24]

At first, the United Kingdom's patent law and system was established as the applicable patent legal system in Nigeria. It brought to the Lagos Colony the Patents Ordinance No. 17 of 1900, which was immediately followed by the Patent Proclamation Ordinance No. 27 of 1900 of Southern

19 James Emeje, "Traditional Iron Working in Parts of the 'NOK Culture' Area: Notes and Posers from Preliminary Investigations." National Commission for Museums and Monuments, Abuja, Nigeria, https://static1.squarespace.com/static/5bd0e66f8d97400eb0099556/t/5bdcea2b21c67c03662981cd/1541204525096/SAFA2008Ameje.pdf Accessed 2 January 2025.

20 Sherif, "List of Nigerian Arts and Crafts," *NaijaQuest Information Hub*, 2024 https://naijaquest.com/nigerian-arts-and-crafts/ Accessed 2 January 2025.

21 Ibid.

22 Emeagwali G. and Shizha E., ibid.

23 B. Hall, C. Helmers, M. Rogers, and V. Sena, "The Choice between Formal and Informal Intellectual Property: A Review." (2014) *Journal of Economic Literature* 52(2), 375–423, cited in Gregory D. Graff, Philip G. Pardey, Inventions and patenting in Africa: Empirical trends from 1970 to 2010." (2019) *The Journal of World Intellectual Property,* https://onlinelibrary.wiley.com/doi/full/10.1111/jwip.12139 Accessed 18 August 2024.

24 G.S. Yankey, "International Patents and Transfer of Technology to Less Developed Countries: The Case of Ghana and Nigeria" (1987), cited in Shafiu Adamu Yauri, "The Patent System in Nigeria," *SCIENCEDIRECT* https://www.sciencedirect.com/science/article/abs/pii/S0172219012000695, Accessed 17 August 2024.

Nigeria. This was followed by the Patents Proclamation Ordinance No. 12 of 1902, which extended the patent system to Northern Nigeria. As a result of the amalgamation in 1914, the different patent ordinances were repealed and replaced by the Patent Ordinance No. 30 of 1916, which was amended in 1925 as the Registration of UK Patents Ordinance No. 6 of 1925.

The law effectively provided for the recognition, registration, and protection in Nigeria of patents already granted in the UK.[25] It was a requirement under the current regime that Nigerian patent applicants first apply and obtain UK patents from the UK Patent Office for their inventions prior to obtaining a patent grant or registration in Nigeria, and this practice continued until the year 1970 when the first Nigerian Indigenous Patent and Designs Act was enacted.[26] It is important to note that the 1970 Act, which was promulgated following the UK patent law, is still the current legal framework for patents and designs in Nigeria. Authors have argued that the introduction of patent law in the Nigerian legal historical antecedent was not based on the need for patent law; it was, instead, based on the basic beneficial interests of our colonialists, and patent law's interests were the sustenance of the raw material needs of the colonialists.[27] It is noted that "this lopsided objective heralded Nigerian independence, leading to inconsistency in policy articulation, formulation and implementation"[28] and the introduction of large biopiracy within Nigeria and the African continent. Therefore, historically, colonial patent laws were ideally designed to protect the interests of colonialists and their partners rather than promote local or Indigenous inventions or innovations. They prioritised the exploitation of local resources over the development of Indigenous innovations or technologies. Before this time, Nigeria had no provisions for

25 Ibid.

26 Judi W. Wakhungu, "IP Protection in Africa, States of Laws, Research and Policy Analysis in Ghana, Kenya, Nigeria, South Africa & Uganda, Acts, Ecopolicy Service No. 16, see CAP 344 Laws of the Federation of Nigeria." (2006) *African Centre for Technology Studies (ACTS)* https://africaportal.org/wp-content/uploads/2023/05/ecopolicy16_1.pdf accessed 16 August 2024.

27 Timothy Okechukwu Umahi, "Access to Medicines: The Colonial Impacts on Patent Law of Nigeria" (December 2011) *ResearchGate Electronic Journal*, DOI: 10.2139/ssrn.1975928 https://www.researchgate.net/publication/228173626_Access_to_Medicines_The_Colonial_Impacts_on_Patent_Law_of_Nigeria Accessed 4 January 2025; Laura A. Foster, "Decolonizing Patent Law: Postcolonial Technoscience and Indigenous Knowledge in South Africa." (2016) *Feminist Formations* 28(3), 148–173. *JSTOR*, https://www.jstor.org/stable/26776840. Accessed 3 January 2025; Marcia Ellen DeGeer, Biopiracy: "The Appropriation of Indigenous Peoples' Cultural Knowledge." https://ipmall.law.unh.edu/sites/default/files/hosted_resources/PLANT_PATENT_ARTICLES/biopiracy_and_indigenous_knowledges.pdf Accessed 3 January 2025.

28 Timothy Umahi, ibid.

patent registrations.[29] South Africa, on the other hand, enacted its patent law over three decades ago with the promulgation of the Patents Act 57 of 1978.[30] It has been noted, albeit unfortunately for Africans, that patent law was and still is inadequate to protect the innovations and creations of Indigenous people as it is written from a colonialist perspective. They may fail to meet the tripartite requirements for patentability and suggest the use of trade secrets for Indigenous inventions; alternatively, to reduce the threshold of patent requirements for locally generated inventions or innovations.[31]

From the foregoing, it is apparent that the current patent laws and systems in Nigeria and most African countries are traceable to the legal systems of their colonial masters. To date, most African countries have yet to amend their laws to conform to their current realities and challenges and recognise the technological needs of the Indigenous peoples.

6.3.1 Patents

Patent awareness amongst peers has been on the increase lately, with many inventors sprouting from Nigeria and Africa. What, then, is a patent? A patent has been defined as:

> An exclusive right granted for an invention, which is a product or a process that provides, in general, a new way of doing something, or offers a new technical solution to a problem[32]. To get a patent, technical information about the invention must be disclosed to the public in a patent application.[33]

It is said that patent rights, unlike the other categories of IP rights, are negative rights, which means that a patent owner has the exclusive right to prevent others from commercially exploiting the invention, i.e. the patented invention cannot be made, distributed, used, sold or imported by third parties, without the prior consent of the patent owner. It is pertinent

29 Boma Geoffrey Toby, "Issuance of Compulsory Licences in Nigeria: Practice and Procedure under the Patents and Designs Act." (2016) *UNIZIK Law Journal* 12, 141 file:///C:/Users/regina.onwumere/Downloads/IssuanceofCompulsoryLicensesinNigeria-PracticeandProcedureunderthePatentsandDesignsAct.pdf

30 James T. Pechacek, "The Past, Present, and Future of South Africa's Patent System." (2012) *MT Mitchell Hamline School of Law* 3(2), 14 https://open.mitchellhamline.edu/cgi/viewcontent.cgi?article=1027&context=cybaris Accessed 22 August, 2024.

31 Marcia Ellen DeGeer, ibid.

32 WIPO, "IP Facts & Figures (WIPO Statistics Database) (2024). www.wipo.int Accessed 10 July, 2024.

33 Ibid.

to note that what is granted is the right to prevent or stop third parties from doing any of the above-highlighted acts without the prior approval of the patentee. A patent is, therefore, summarised as the exclusive right given to protect new inventions from unlawful exploitation of the patented invention within a period of time by an autonomous government like Nigeria, Ghana, South Africa, etc., or a government body like the African Regional Intellectual Property Organization (ARIPO), Organisation Africaine de la Propriété Intellectuelle (OAPI), etc., of a recognised jurisdiction.

Patent right confers on the patentee the right to preclude any other person from doing any of the following acts:

- Where the patent has been granted for a product, the act of making, importing, selling, or using the product or stocking it for the purpose of sale or use;[34]

and

- Where the patent is in respect of a process, the act of applying the process or performing any of the acts above with respect to the process.[35]

Patents, like all other IP rights, are territorial in nature. This means that the exclusive rights granted by a patent are only applicable in the jurisdiction, country, nation, area, or region in which a patent has been granted. Therefore, there are no global patent grants; however, there are geographically specific patent grants.

From the foregoing, it is apparent that the following should be visible in every valid patent grant, they are:

- an invention that satisfied the tripartite requirements for patentability;
- an application to the patents registrar, a document of grant;
- an exclusive right is granted to preclude others from the exploitation of the invention;
- the grant of the right is by an independent government,
- territoriality; and
- creation of a legal situation.

6.3.2 *An invention?*

It is important that every inventor understands the concept of patenting and how to obtain a patent for their inventions. Inventors are known to

34 Section 6 (1)(a) of the Patents & Designs Act.
35 Section 6 (1)(b) of the Patents & Designs Act.

create new things or improvements on existing inventions. If A, who is an electrical engineer, creates a process that results in an alternative to the popular electric bulb, that process is an inventive step. The by-product is a result of an invention, and the grant certificate issued by the patent office upon application by the inventor or an assignee is the patent.

A patent is about inventions, innovation, creativity, and inventing; impliedly, there cannot be a patent without an invention. Inventors are trailblazers in their chosen areas of inventorship, and today, we have inventpreneurs; Steve Jobs and Bill Gates are examples of modern innovative entrepreneurs, also referred to as inventprenuers.[36] Invention and patent are like creative works and copyright; both are the outcome of creative efforts. A patent is a legal term that describes a right granted to protect an inventor of an invention from third-party exploitation in a particular country.

In Nigeria, an invention is patentable if it is new, results from inventive activity, and is capable of industrial application; this is the tripartite patentability requirement. It can also be patentable if it constitutes an improvement upon a patented invention and is also new, results from inventive activity, and is capable of industrial application.[37]

6.3.3 Criteria for patentability

An invention to be patentable must satisfy the following conditions:

6.3.3.1 Newness

It must be new or novel; that is, it must show some new characteristic which is not known in the body of existing knowledge (called "prior art") in its technical field. For the purpose of patenting an invention and meeting the newness requirement, it is important to understand what the law means by "new." Simply put, an invention is new if it does not form part of the "state of the art."[38] The "art" means the art or field of knowledge to which an invention relates, and "state of the art" means everything concerning that art or field of knowledge which has been made available to the public at any time and anywhere (by means of a written or oral description, by

36 Patrick McKenna, "The 9 Different Types of Entrepreneurship" (2023) https://www.indeed.com/career-advice/career-development/types-of-entrepreneurship#:~:text=Innovators%20tend%20to%20be%20very%20motivated%20and%20passionate,and%20Bill%20Gates%20are%20examples%20of%20innovative%20entrepreneurs Accessed 16 July 2024.
37 Section 1 of the Act.
38 Section 1(2)(a) of the Act.

use or in any other way) before the date of filing of the patent application for the invention or the foreign priority date validly claimed.

Put differently, "state of the art" comprises all matter, whether a product, a process, or information, which has been made available to the public in the country or elsewhere by written or oral description, by use or in any other way, immediately prior to the priority date of the invention.[39] It is understood that an invention is not to be deemed to have been made available to the public merely by reason of the fact that, within the period of six months preceding the filing of a patent application for the invention, the inventor or his successor in title has exhibited it in an official or officially recognised international exhibition.[40] Furthermore, in deciding whether there has been a publication of an invention, the universal standard is generally the accepted standard for prior art publication obligations.[41]

6.3.3.2 Non-obviousness or inventive step

It must be non-obvious or involve an inventive step; that is, it could not be deduced by a person with average knowledge in the technical field. An invention results from inventive activity if it does not obviously follow from the state of the art, either as to the method, the application, the combination of methods, or the product to which it pertains, or as to the industrial result it produces.[42] Simply put, non-obviousness implies that even a professor in the field of knowledge or art should not be able to ordinarily know what the invention is all about; they should be able to wonder how the inventor came about the idea and invention. The UK Supreme Court held in *Graham v. John Deere*,[43] that four basic inquiries should be made when addressing non-obviousness, as stated below:

1. The scope and content of the prior art should be ascertained.
2. The level of ordinary skill in the particular field should be assessed.
3. The difference between the prior art and the claims at issue is examined.
4. A determination is made as to whether these differences would have been obvious to a layperson in the applicable field at the time the invention was made.[44]

39 MOORE Patents, "Patents in South Africa: General Information" www.moorepatent.co.za Accessed 20 July 2024.
40 Section 1(3) of the Act.
41 Section 1(2)(a) of the Act.
42 Section 1(2)(b) of the Act.
43 383 U.S. 1 (1966), cited in Marcia Ellen DeGeer, ibid.
44 Ibid.

6.3.3.3 Usefulness and capable of industrial application

The invention must be useful and capable of industrial application. An invention is capable of industrial application if it can be manufactured or used in any kind of industry, including in the field of agriculture.[45] Anyone requiring a patent grant over an invention needs to first undergo investigations and experiments to confirm that the invention has some direct usefulness or utility and will have to describe the usefulness of the invention; if not, the patent office will most likely refuse to grant the patent.[46] The usefulness or utility requirement has often been said to mean that the invention should have a factual use that can be seen and be of immediate use, not something whose use is speculative or of future use.[47]

6.3.3.4 Non-patentable subject matter

The invention must be part of the so-called "patentable subject matter" under the applicable law. In many African countries, scientific theories, mathematical methods, plant or animal varieties, discoveries of natural substances, commercial methods, or methods for medical treatment (as opposed to medical products) are not considered to be patentable subject matters.[48] Therefore, any invention relating to any of the above subject matters will not be granted a patent right because it is one of the non-patentable subject matters.

Non-patentable subject matters are:

- a scientific or mathematical discovery, theory, or method;
- a literary, dramatic, musical, or artistic work;
- a way of performing a mental act, playing a game or doing business
- the presentation of information or some computer programs;
- an animal or plant variety;
- a method of medical treatment or diagnosis;
- against public policy or morality;
- plant or animal varieties, or essentially biological processes for the production of plants or animals (other than microbiological processes and their products); or

45 Section 2(2)(c) of the Act.

46 This is for jurisdictions such as the USA, Japan, etc. where substantive examination is conducted.

47 JUSTIA, "Utility Requirement for Patents" (2023) https://www.justia.com/intellectual-property/patents/patentability-requirements/usefulness/#:~:text=The%20utility%20requirement%20often%20has%20been%20interpreted%20to,a%20speculative%20use%20or%20a%20possible%20future%20use Accessed 20 August, 2024.

48 Section 1(4) of the Act.

- inventions the publication or exploitation of which would be contrary to public order or morality (it is understood for the purposes of this paragraph that the exploitation of an invention is not contrary to public order or morality merely because its exploitation is prohibited by law);[49]
- principles and discoveries of a scientific nature are not inventions for the purposes of this Act.[50]

Smith noted on non-patentable subject matter in South Africa that an invention that comprises a discovery, a scientific theory, a mathematical method, a literary, dramatic, musical, or artistic work, or any aesthetic creation, a scheme, rule, or method for performing a mental act, playing a game, or doing business, a program for a computer, or the presentation of information cannot be patented in terms of the South African Patents Act.[51] This requirement is obtainable in most African countries' patent systems.

For improvement patents, the law requires that if the invention constitutes an improvement upon a patented invention, it must also be new, result from inventive activity, and be capable of industrial application.[52]

6.3.4 *Procedures and documentations for patent grants in Nigeria*[53]

The Patents and Designs Act recognises two types of patent registrations in Nigeria: the PCT or Conventional Patent and Non-conventional Patent. There are different types of patent applications which are complete, provisional, additional, and divisional patent applications. In a complete patent application, the inventor/applicant is required to provide the complete details of their invention. The provisional application allows the inventor or applicant to submit a brief description or an abridged version of the patent document. An additional patent, on the other hand, is filed when the inventor discovers further usefulness in a patented invention, and the divisional patent relates to situations where there exist more than one invention in a patent.[54]

In Nigeria, the patent application is filed at the Patents & Designs Registry, either electronically through the online platform or manually

49 Section 1(4) of the Act.
50 Section 1(5) of the Act.
51 Smit and Van Wyk, "South Africa Patent Exclusions in Intellectual Property" www.svw.co.za Accessed 12 August 2024.
52 Section 1(1)(b) of the Act.
53 Please note that similar procedures are applicable in most African countries.
54 Bayya Subba Rao, "An Overview of Patent System" (2014) AnOverviewofPatent.pdf Accessed 22 August, 2024.

through the IPAS (Automated Industrial Property System) filing system.[55] Based on experience, I would usually recommend filing electronically as an acknowledgement notice can be generated immediately, and there are no issues of misplaced files. Other inadequacies experienced with the manual patent filing procedure are delays, mislaid official files, bureaucratic procedures, payment verification time lag, costs of reconstituting misplaced files/documentation, etc.

Upon filing a patent application online, the acknowledgement notice is generated instantly; then, an acceptance notice is printed after the examination and acceptance by the patent examiners. Applicants are then required to print the patent documents in triplicate and submit them at the patent office for further review and patent grant. For applications filed using the IPAS system, upon submission of the manual application letter along with the patent documents (i.e. specifications, description, claims, priority documents, PCT publication pages, etc.), the application is received at the patent's front office. Payment is required to be confirmed prior to any action by the accounts unit. Upon approval, the acknowledgement is printed, and then the application is directed to the examiners for examination and acceptance, after which the Letters Patent is issued to the applicant.

6.3.4.1 *Requirements/procedure*

An application for the grant of a patent is made to the Registrar of Patents & Designs, and it consists of: [56]

- A petition or request for a patent with the applicant's full name and address (an address for service in Nigeria if the applicant resides outside Nigeria).
- A specification or description of the relevant invention with any appropriate plans and drawings. The description is expected to disclose the relevant invention in a manner sufficiently clear and complete for the invention to be put into effect by a person skilled in the art or field of knowledge to which the invention relates. Please note that the specification shall describe the relevant invention in a manner sufficiently clear and complete for the invention to be put into effect by a person skilled in the art or field of knowledge to which the invention relates.

55 The Federal Ministry of Industry, Trade and Investment, in collaboration the World Intellectual Property Organisation (WIPO), introduced the IPAS system in Nigeria to provide a world-class upgrade, automation, and transparency filing system in Nigeria on 28 January 2014.

56 Section 3(1) of the Act.

- A claim(s). The claim or claims shall define the protection sought and shall not go beyond the limits of the said description. The claim or claims are required to define the protection sought and shall not go beyond the limits of the said description.[57] The scope of the protection conferred by any patent is determined by the terms of the claims as interpreted by the patent description (and the plans and drawings, if any).[58]
- Where appropriate, a Deed of Assignment or a declaration signed by the true inventor requesting that he be mentioned as such in the patent and giving his name and address, or in the absence of this, where the applicant is not the inventor.
- If the application is made by an agent, a signed Letter of Authority or Power of Attorney, also known as a Form 2 (legalisation or certification of the signature of a power of attorney shall be unnecessary; a simple signature is acceptable); and
- Certified true copy of the priority document(s) [where the applicant seeks to avail himself of a foreign priority in respect of an earlier application made in a country outside Nigeria]. If a PCT application, then a copy of the publication page with the supporting documents.

It is important to note that a patent application shall relate to only one invention; this means that an applicant cannot validly obtain a patent grant in Nigeria and most jurisdictions for more than one invention in one application. However, it is possible to include in the application in connection with the invention:

a) claims for any number of products, for any number of manufacturing processes for those products, and for any number of applications of those products, and
b) claims for any number of processes, and for the means of working those processes, for the resulting product or products and for the application of those products.[59]

Patent applications in Nigeria and most African countries are examined for conformity with formality and not substance.[60] This simply means that, as far as the documentation is complete, the patent would normally be granted. Section 4(2) and (4) of the Patents & Designs Act provides that:

> (2) Where the examination mentioned in subsection (1) of this subsection shows that a patent application satisfies the requirements of

57 Section 3(2) of the Act.
58 Section 6(2) of the Act.
59 Section 3(3) of the Act.
60 Section 4(1) of the Act.

> section 3(1) and (3) of this Act, the patent shall be granted as applied for without further examination and, in particular, without examination of the questions – (a) whether the subject of the application is patentable under section 1 of this Act; (b) whether the description and claims satisfy the requirements of section 3(2) of this Act; and (c) whether a prior application, or an application benefiting from a foreign priority, has been made in Nigeria in respect of the same invention, and whether a patent has been granted as a result of such an application.
>
> (4) Patents are granted at the risk of the patentee and without guarantee of their validity.

There is no doubt that the specific requirement of the above provision is that patents in Nigeria should be granted without substantive examination and confirmation of their validity or patentability. Equally important is the understanding that the primary reason for patent examination is to ensure that the patent applications satisfy the tripartite patentability criteria stated above and that the patent inventions granted are for the public good. The provision raises issues about the quality of patents granted in the country, and it also creates a legal environment where low-quality patents can proliferate, potentially stifling innovation and undermining the credibility of the patenting system at large.[61] Therefore, it is recommended that we explore legal reforms to address these flaws by introducing either substantive or hybrid patent examination procedures, particularly in certain high-priority sectors such as medicine, medical and health gadgets, and engineering equipment and procedures, as is obtainable in some countries.[62] This will help to improve the overall quality of patents granted in Nigeria.

Patent applications can be made by anyone, not necessarily the inventor, and the first-to-file concept is practised in Nigeria and most African countries. Earlier, some jurisdictions, such as the USA, practised the first-to-invent system, which later changed to the first-to-file system.

6.3.5 Contents of a patent grant certificate

A patent grant certificate would usually contain the patent registration number, applicant's name, title of the invention, filing date, sealing date,

61 K.M. Waziri and S. Gwom, "Examination of Form Not Substance: Rethinking the Patent Examination Process in Nigeria." ResearchGate Publications, https://www.researchgate.net/publication/353015350_Examination_of_Form_Not_Substance_Rethinking_the_Patent_Examination_Process_in_Nigeria Accessed 4 January 2025.

62 Ibid.

the issuing authority, name and signature of the Patent Registrar, Priority and/or PCT information (if applicable).

6.3.6 Duration

Patent grants are generally for a limited period of time, typically 20 years from the filing date of the patent application, with annual renewal payments in most jurisdictions, such as Nigeria.[63] United States of America, ARIPO, Ghana, South Africa, Kenya, etc.[64] However, in Morocco, patent duration is 10 years from the filing date, which is renewable for 10 years within 6 months before the expiry or 6 months after the expiry date with the payment of a default fee.[65] Similarly, patent duration in Rwanda is 20 years from the filing date for a 10-year registration term, with a 60-day opposition term.[66]

A patent is valid for 20 years from the filing date in Nigeria and is renewable every year. If the prescribed annual fees are not duly paid before the due date, a grace period of six months is allowed for the payment of the fees. However, if the fees and any prescribed surcharge are not paid within the grace period, the patent shall lapse, and its expiration shall be registered and notified.

6.4 Compulsory licensing

The concept of compulsory licensing is one of the most debated provisions of patent laws, both in Nigeria, Africa, and other parts of the world. Compulsory licensing can significantly affect a patent holder's exclusive patent rights and is usually tied to public health and safety issues, as it grants licences for a patented invention based on its non-availability and/or non-affordability to the populace.[67]

In India's Nexavar case, the controller general of patents granted a compulsory licence to an entity known as Natco Pharma to produce and sell another company's (i.e. Bayer AG's) patented products for the anti-cancer

63 Section 7(1)(2) and (3) of the Act.

64 B&P Associates, "Patents in Ghana" www.bpaghana.com; MOORE IP, "Patents in South Africa: General Information." www.moorepatent.co.za; Patenting in Kenya, https://www.kenyaengineer.co.ke/patenting-in-kenya/ Accessed 1 August 2024.

65 ABOUNAJA Intellectual Property, MOROCCO | Trademark, Patent and Copyright | ABOU NAJA.

66 "Rwanda Patents, Patent Registration in Rwanda" www.svw.africa Accessed 2 August 2024.

67 Pankaj Musyuni, "Compulsory Licensing: Law, Challenges and Strategies," *LexOrbis*, LEXOLOGY, https://www.lexology.com/library/detail.aspx?g=8efb1c00-65cd-4d66-8925-5ece8f8f2551 Accessed 15 August 2024.

drug sorafenib tosylate (Nexavar). Sorafenib tosylate is an important medication for treating kidney and liver cancer in patients.[68] It was discovered that Nexavar was not only sold at exorbitant prices which were not affordable for most patients, it was also not reasonably available to patients, in addition to the fact that the drug was produced outside of the country. Bayer AG challenged the above decision of the Intellectual Property Appellate Board (IPAB), the Bombay High Court, and the Supreme Court, which decided against Bayer AG. It was noted that the compulsory licensing was duly granted against Bayer AG based on these grounds:

a. an inadequate supply of the patented drug within the country;
b. a high price that was not affordable for the citizens; and
c. non-working of the patented drug in India.[69]

In some other cases, the government rejected the requests for compulsory licences, such as the Ministry of Health being denied a compulsory licence request in Roche's Herceptin case.[70] Also, LEE Pharma's request for the grant of a compulsory licence for the Saxagliptin drug, which was owned by Bristol Myers Squibb (assigned to AstraZeneca), was disapproved because the applicant had failed to provide evidence and satisfy the grounds set out in Section 84(1) of the Act.[71]

Unlike in India and some other countries, it seems that there is yet no record of Indigenous compulsory licence grants in modern-day Nigeria, which is arguably not unconnected to the stringent procedural requirements of the law examined below. Prior to the enactment of the Patents & Designs Act, in the case of *Rhone – May & Baker v. Lodeka Pharmacy*,[72] the Federal Ministry of Health authorised the defendant to supply the patented drug on its behalf, and the claimant's argument that the United Kingdom (UK) Patents Act does not apply to Nigeria was upheld by the trial court while rejecting the defendant's contention that the alleged infringement of the plaintiff's patents was in furtherance of the use authorised by the government by the provisions of section 46(1) UK Patents Act of 1949, which provides that:

68 Ibid.
69 Ibid. These are the grounds set out in section 84(1) of the Indian Patents Act 1970.
70 Ibid.
71 Ibid.
72 (1965) LLR 9 cited in Gabriel Omoniyi, "Compulsions: Prospects for Mandatory Licensing of Patents in Nigeria," Lelaw Barristers & Solicitors, https://www.mondaq.com/nigeria/patent/1078088/compulsions-prospects-for-mandatory-licensing-of-patents-in-nigeria Accessed 7 January 2025.

> Notwithstanding anything in this Act, any Government department, and any person authorised in writing by a Government department, may make, use and exercise any patented invention for the services of the Crown in accordance with the following provisions of this section.[73]

Further to the foregoing and following the low record of medical supply and high costs, both drugs and other health gadgets at the surge of the COVID-19 pandemic between 2020 and 2022, this would have prompted public interest in obtaining compulsory licences on the mass production of the vaccines, drugs, and other essential items needed to save lives and property in Nigeria. On the procedure to obtain a compulsory licence in Nigeria, the Act provides that a person may apply to the Federal High Court (the "Court") for the grant of a compulsory licence, which is to be made upon expiration of three years after the grant of a patent or four years after the filing of a patent (whichever period last expires) based on any of the following grounds:

- That the patented invention is capable of being worked on in Nigeria and it has not been worked on;
- That the working on the patent in Nigeria does not meet the demand for the product;
- That the working on the patent in Nigeria is being hindered by the importation of the patented invention; and
- That the Patentee refused to grant a patent licence on reasonable terms and the establishment or development of industrial activities in Nigeria is unfairly and substantially prejudiced.[74]

It is important to note that a compulsory licence may be granted where working on another patent subsequently granted will amount to a breach of the initial patent.[75] The licence, in this case, would be granted on the basis that it is necessary to develop the latter patent provided that the industrial purpose served by the two patents is different and the latter invention constitutes a substantial improvement on the former. Also, a compulsory licence will not be granted in respect of a patent if the patentee satisfies the court that his or her actions in relation to the patented invention are justifiable in the circumstances, but he or she shall not be held to have satisfied the court if he or she merely shows that the patented invention is freely available for importation into Nigeria.[76] Notably, an

73 Ibid.
74 The First Schedule to the Act.
75 The First Schedule to the Act.
76 Ibid.

applicant for a compulsory licence is required to show to the court that he or she requested a contractual licence from the patentee on reasonable terms, which was refused.[77]

In Nigeria, the applicant is required to provide a guarantee that he/she will exploit the invention; the licence is non-exclusive, and the licensee cannot grant a further licence to a third party. Compulsory licences can also be withdrawn on certain terms as stipulated in the law. There are arguments that compulsory licences prevent patentees from enjoying the fruits of their labour. However, there are views that the greater good of the masses is paramount and should be placed before the individual patentee's exclusivity needs.[78]

It is important to note that the grant of a patent does not permit the patentee or patent owner to proceed to commercialise the invention if parts of it are covered by the patents or inventions of third parties; doing so could result in patent infringements.

6.5 Conventions and treaties

The Paris Convention (PC) and Patent Cooperation Treaty (PCT) play critical roles in patent grants around the globe, including Nigeria and Africa. The Paris Convention provides for priority claims relating to patent applications filed in any of the convention member states. The Treaty is instrumental for single filing and examination procedures, and it provides economic benefits during filings in addition to saving time and resources.[79] Several international treaties apply to African countries, including Nigeria, such as the Paris Convention for the Protection of Industrial Property, Stockholm, ARIPO; the Convention establishing the WIPO, World Trade Organisation (WTO) on trade-related aspects of intellectual property rights (TRIPS) agreement; and the Patent Cooperation Treaty (PCT).[80] On the other hand, there are recognised regional patent offices, which include:

1. The African Regional Intellectual Property Organisation (ARIPO), also known as the Harare Protocol on Patents and Industrial Designs, provides for a single deposit patent for 22 English-speaking African countries designated by the patentee. The countries include Botswana, The Gambia, Cape Verde, Eswatini, Ghana, Kenya, Lesotho, Liberia, Malawi, Mozambique, Namibia, Rwanda, São Tomé & Príncipe, Sierra Leone, Seychelles, Sudan, Swaziland, Tanzania, Uganda,

77 Ibid.
78 Pankaj Musyuni, ibid.
79 Bayya Subba Rao, "An Overview of Patent System" (2014) AnOverviewofPatent.pdf.
80 Ibid., B&P Associates.

Zambia, and Zimbabwe.[81] Somalia is also a member of ARIPO but cannot be designated at this time, and Nigeria and South Africa are not yet members of ARIPO. The implication is that if an inventor requires patent protection in Nigeria or South Africa, they will have to file a separate patent application in each country, unlike other African countries that are members of ARIPO, which can file a single patent application and obtain registration in multiple jurisdictions; this comes with high-cost implications, security risks, time consumption, and cross-border jurisdictional legal issues.[82] The ARIPO is said to have been effective in many innovative additions to its member states, such as organising training and seminars, identifying and supporting initiatives that promote the development of the region's IP ecosystem, in addition to assisting national efforts to harness the abundance of local innovative and creative resources[83]. Access to funding issues, expertise retention, low awareness among the citizenry, government support, etc., are some of the identified challenges of the organisation, which have greatly hindered the achievement of its seemingly ambitious goals, which include pooling financial and human resources and seeking technological advancement for the economic, social, technological, scientific, and industrial development of the African State.[84]

2. The Organisation Africaine de la Propriété Intellectuelle (OAPI). The OAPI provides for a single deposit patent for 17 French-speaking African countries, including Benin; Burkina Faso; Cameroon; Central African Republic; Chad; Republic of Congo; Cote d'Ivoire; Comoros; Equatorial Guinea; Gabon; Guinea; Guinea-Bissau; Mali; Mauritania; Niger; Senegal; and Togo.[85] The European Patent Office (EPO) receives patent requests and covers up to 40 European countries designated by the patentee.[86] African countries are not members of the EPO, although some arrangements, such as a patent deposit system, are made with a few African countries.

81 Íbid., Moore Intellectual Property.

82 Íbid.

83 "ARIPO's Drive to Strengthen Africa's Innovation Ecosystem," *ARIPO*, https://www.aripo.org/success-stories/aripos-drive-to-strengthen-africas-innovation-ecosystem-5035 Accessed 6 January, 2025.

84 Ibid.; https://www.aripo.org/public/#:~:text=The%20African%20Regional%20Intellectual%20Property%20Organization%20%28ARIPO%29%20is,human%20resources%20and%20seeking%20technological%20advancement%20for%20econ Accessed 6 January, 2025.

85 Íbid.

86 Íbid.

6.6 Conclusion

Inventions and patent grants are no doubt important economic indicators to be taken seriously by Nigeria and, indeed, African countries for their continued development. It is apparent that, prior to the advent of the Western schemes, Africans and Nigerians did not have structured and recognised or coordinated approaches to identifying and protecting Indigenous inventions, which were said to be a major attraction for the colonialists. It is not untrue that Nigeria and most African patent systems seem to be "independent", but the legal framework and systems are still largely based on the laws that were framed based on the colonial governments. There has been no radical change from the origins of these laws, and it has no doubt been a limiting factor for the development of these nations.

Nigeria and African nations' legislatures and stakeholders must look toward a drastic shift from the footprints of the colonial masters. China recently introduced a scheme that encouraged invention and inventiveness, which resulted in numerous patent filings across the globe from China and the Chinese, and this has no doubt contributed to the progress of China from a developing country to an emerging economy soon to become part of the developed economies.

How can African countries emerge when we are largely reliant on the support, existing laws and ideas of our past colonialists? There is an urgent need to give the subject matter of innovation, invention, and patenting greater attention in Nigeria and Africa to enhance stable, steady, and speedy intellectual and economic development. Indeed, African country law and policymakers should take patent systems seriously, given the increasingly important role that knowledge plays in national and global economic growth. It is therefore important that all hands are on deck, including the government, stakeholders, individuals, companies, and non-governmental organisations, to support African innovation and intellectual property rights in order to drive economic development and address national, regional and global challenges like earth degradation, climate change, etc.

7 Decolonisation of methods of medicine production and patents in Nigeria

The dilemma of colonial mentality on traditional medicine

Ayoyemi Lawal-Arowolo andAdesoji Kolawole Adebayo

7.1 Introduction

Colonisation is not limited to the enclosure of the physical commons. It transcends into the knowledge commons as well.[1] The enclosure of the knowledge commons, apart from appropriations, includes the altering of traditions, customs, or practices of the colonised to conform to that of the coloniser. Condemning the use of traditional medicine as witchcraft or black magic was corroborated in the drafting of laws against its practice or use during colonisation.[2] The perception of traditional medicine as diabolical is outdated; rather, "it is simply the utilisation of the benefits of natural products including plants, animals, and mineral substances. The mode of treatment is supported by indigenous beliefs, practical skills, and experiences handed down from generation to generation."[3] This contemporary view of traditional medicine provides a better picture of its essence in the past and the present.

The impact of such a tale on the mentality of Nigerians is resilient, and it is referred to as colonial mentality. This type of mentality is the mental dominance of Eurocentric perspectives in a non-European setting such as Nigeria, after colonisation, resulting in cultural inferiority and internal

1 Mehtab Khan, "<c>Traditional Knowledge and the Commons: the Open Movement, Listening, and Learning" </c>https://creativecommons.org/2018/09/18/traditional-knowledge-and-the-commons-the-open-movement-listening-and-learning/ accessed 28 May 2024. "The doctrine of discovery, which was used to legitimise and expand colonisation, held the assumption that indigenous peoples were "uncivilised" and hence could not own property like European settlers. Therefore, the land and knowledge of indigenous peoples were seen as part of the commons, open for 'discovery' and appropriation."

2 J.O. Ezekwesili-Ofili and A.N.C. Okaka, "Herbal Medicines in African Traditional Medicine" in Phillip F. Builders, *Herbal Medicine*, 30 January 2019, DOI: 10.5772/intechopen.80348.

3 Muhammed Majed et al., "The Pursuit of Natural Medicine – A Current Perspective" in Dilip Ghosh, Diana Bogueva, R. Smarta, *Nutrition Science, Marketing Nutrition, Health Claims, and Public Policy* (Academic Press 2023) 173–192, 175.

DOI: 10.4324/9781003602989-8

racial oppression.[4] Nigerians entrenched in Western ideas and philosophies are regarded as "colo mentals," those submerged in colonial mentality. Eradicating colonial mentality through the process of decolonisation, particularly in this situation, mentally, should aid the development, utilisation, and institutionalisation of traditional medicine in Nigeria. Decolonisation opposes colonialism and colonial mentality in institutions and systems of government. It demands traditional knowledge systems known to communities and advocates for rebuilding culture to interrogate the impact of colonialism on the psyche of the colonised and those free from colonisation (cultural, psychological, and economic freedom) but trapped in the mentality.

Foreigners struggled with accepting the novelty or originality of intellectual properties based on traditional medicine knowledge systems and the existence of communal rights similar to modern intellectual property rights, an instrument designed for an industrial capitalist society. They "were not interested in traditional healing methods and did not bother with regulating these methods during colonisation. This lack of interest was a reflection of the European practice of superiority over African regions as colonised regions."[5] Ironically, many orthodox medicines are based on traditional medicine knowledge. Some of these medicines include aspirin, artemisinin and more; they are referred to as landmark drugs.[6] Presumably, there would not have been a breakthrough in these cases without the existence of traditional medicine knowledge to depend upon; however, there could have been, through purely modern scientific laboratory-based methods of medicine discovery. "Traditional medicine is sometimes seen as pre-scientific...What is less known, however, is its contribution to modern science and medicine, and a long history of traditional products and practices being translated into effective treatments for health conditions."[7]

World Health Organization (WHO) confirms that traditional medicine has been in existence for hundreds of years before the development of

4 Decena, Ashley M., "Identity, Colonial Mentality, and Decolonizing the Mind: Exploring Narratives and Examining Mental Health Implications for Filipino Americans" (2014) (Masters Thesis), Smith College, Northampton, MA. https://scholarworks.smith.edu/theses/769.

5 Ayoyemi Lawal-Arowolo and Yinka Olomojobi, "Intellectual Property Rights, Orthodox Medicine and Traditional (Medicine) Knowledge Systems." (2020) 42 (12) *E.I.P.R*, 834.

6 World Health Organization (WHO), "Traditional Medicine Has a Long History of Contributing to Conventional Medicine and Continues to Hold Promise" (10 August 2023) https://www.who.int/news-room/feature-stories/detail/traditional-medicine-has-a-long-history-of-contributing-to-conventional-medicine-and-continues-to-hold-promise accessed 3 March 2023.

7 World Health Organization (WHO), "Traditional Medicine has a Long History of Contributing to Conventional Medicine and Continues to Hold Promise" (10 August 2023) https://www.who.int/news-room/feature-stories/detail/traditional-medicine-has-a-long-history-of-contributing-to-conventional-medicine-and-continues-to-hold-promise accessed 3 March 2023.

modern scientific medicine, and it is still in use without adverse effects on the users if used properly.[8] A parallel utilisation and institutionalisation of orthodox and traditional medicine in the healthcare system of Nigeria is the beginning of curbing negative perspectives of traditional medicine. The past cannot be wiped away, but the present requires a cheaper, accessible, and reliable means of curing and preventing ailments.

The historical and cultural significance of the use of traditional medicine in various traditional communities cannot be disregarded due to its benefits when used appropriately, as it was in the past. It is part of Nigeria's cultural heritage, passed on from generation to generation with newer developments by each generation. Religion also plays a huge role in undermining traditional medicine as a recognised means of healthcare in Nigeria. Even though many use traditional medicine,[9] it is often subjected to secrecy. The situation is different in some jurisdictions that are known for their utilisation of traditional medicine, including traditional Chinese medicine (TCM), traditional Indian (Ayurveda) medicine, and traditional Arabic (Unani) medicine.[10]

There are different categories of traditional medicine in Nigeria,[11] including herbal (use of plants for healing) and spiritual (incantations for medicinal purposes).[12] There are pharmaceutical industries and research institutes involved in the production of traditional medicine as well, thereby providing a contemporary means of producing and distributing traditional medicine:

8 World Health Organization (WHO), "Traditional Medicine Has a Long History of Contributing to Conventional Medicine and Continues to Hold Promise" (10 August 2023) https://www.who.int/news-room/feature-stories/detail/traditional-medicine-has-a-long-history-of-contributing-to-conventional-medicine-and-continues-to-hold-promise accessed 3 March 2023. I.A. Oreagba, K.A. Oshikoya, and M. Amachree, "Herbal Medicine Use among Urban Residents in Lagos, Nigeria." (2011) 11 *BMC Complement Altern Med.*, 117. DOI: 10.1186/1472-6882-11-117. PMID: 22117933; PMCID: PMC3252251. "Despite the widespread use of herbal medicines globally and their reported benefits, they are not completely harmless. The indiscriminate, irresponsible or non-regulated use of several herbal medicines may put the health of their users at risk of toxicity."

9 Juan José Maldonado Miranda, "Medicinal plants and their traditional uses in different locations" in Rouf Ahmad Bhat, Khalid Rehman Hakeem, and Moonisa Aslam Dervash, *Phytomedicine* (Academic Press 2021) 207–223.

10 Ibid.

11 S. Li, S. Odedina, I. Agwai, O. Ojengbede, D. Huo, and O. I. Olopade, "Traditional Medicine Usage among Adult Women in Ibadan, Nigeria: A Cross-Sectional Study." (2020) 20(1) *BMC Complement Med Ther.*, 93. Doi: 10.1186/s12906-020-02881-z. PMID: 32192455; PMCID: PMC7083039.

12 Mahdi Yousefi and Khosro Shafaghi, "Saffron in Persian traditional medicine" in Alireza Koocheki and Mohammad Khajeh-Hosseini (eds), *Saffron Science*, Technology and Health (Woodhead Publishing 2020) 393–404. Spiritual traditional medicine is also called non-medication therapies, "carried out primarily without the use of medication as in the cases of acupuncture, manual therapies, and spiritual therapies."

> Reported uses for traditional medicine (TM) include cancer, diabetes, HIV, and hypertension ... Parents often treat their children with traditional medicine, with documented uses for epilepsy, asthma, and sickle cell ... immigrants from Nigeria often bring their traditional beliefs to their new country of residence.[13]

It is apparent from this quotation that the use of traditional medicine to cure contemporary health issues is high among Nigerians at home or abroad.

Intellectual property laws do not expressly accommodate provisions on the protection of traditional medicine in Nigeria. However, there are provisions for the expression of folklore in the Copyright Act, though it does not suffice as a protection mechanism.[14] In the Act, forms of expressing folk medicine are not expressly protected as related rights.[15] In this chapter, folk medicine is perceived as folk poetry because it is a form of spiritual healing that requires incantations, a common practice in traditional healing. Incantation for healing is poetry, but it was not often fixed in the past and does not fulfil copyright requirements; rather, it fits into the related rights domain. The requirement of fixation is a hindrance to the protection of aspects of folk medicine as copyright since incantation is primarily orally transmitted or distributed. The digital era, however, caters for the fixation of incantations when they are recorded or documented. Overall, this form of healing is based on spiritual deliverance with incantations and other religious performances, different from traditional medicine that is dependent on plants and other resources from nature that involves grinding, mixing, extracting, and more. Both complement each other in the traditional healing process. In some situations, there might be a need for both at the same time or one.

In some communities, the method of producing medicine is transmitted through artwork, such as painting, carving, sculpting and moulding with clay. In this situation, the requirement of originality and fixation is apparent, yet recognition is not given to this form of fixing traditional medicine production. It is merely seen as folk art. The display of healing or the process of healing is also protectable as performance. A radical paradigm shift has been proposed in dealing with the suitability of copyright

13 S. Li, S. Odedina, I. Agwai, O. Ojengbede, D. Huo, and O. I. Olopade, "Traditional Medicine Usage among Adult Women in Ibadan, Nigeria: A Cross-Sectional Study." (2020) 20(1) *BMC Complement Med Ther.*, 93. Doi: 10.1186/s12906-020-02881-z. PMID: 32192455; PMCID: PMC7083039.

14 Copyright Act of Nigeria 2023, Federal Republic of Nigeria Gazette, Volume 110, No 56, A179-243

15 Ibid. Section 74(5).

protection for traditional knowledge as it relates to expressions of folklore. It is argued that the "adoption of an indigenous-inspired understanding of copyright exclusivity whereby the public interest is a central justification for this exclusivity rather than an exception to it."[16] Simply, copyright protection should take into consideration different groups of people in the South and their forms of creativity as protectable by revamping copyright law.

Other aspects of intellectual property law in Nigeria do not expressly protect traditional medicine even though symbols (trademarks), ornaments (industrial design), secrecy (trade secrets), and agricultural products, including medicinal plants (geographical indications), are used in the practice of traditional medicine. Some jurisdictions in Africa have specific laws on the protection of traditional knowledge regarded as sui generis; these include provisions on intellectual property law and more. Kenya has acted in an exemplary manner with the inclusion in its Constitution of the protection and preservation of traditional knowledge, the drafting of policies on the same matter, and establishing The Protection of Traditional Knowledge and Cultural Expression Act 2016:

> The Act aims "to provide a framework for the protection and promotion of traditional knowledge and cultural expressions" in Kenya, giving effect to Articles 11, 40 and 69(1)(c) of the Constitution of 2010. It vests "ownership" of TK in local and traditional communities and recognises individuals or organisations entrusted with the custody or protection of TK in accordance with customary law and practices. It employs the notion of "ownership" as applied in IP, which may be elusive and quite problematic.[17]

South Africa has also adopted a similar approach to Kenya and seeks a suitable protection framework for traditional knowledge through enacting *sui generis* laws and drafting policies.[18] A quotation which emphasises the need to seek protection in various forms for traditional knowledge is as follows:

16 Jade Kouletakis, "Decolonising Copyright: Reconsidering Copyright Exclusivity and the Role of the Public Interest in International Intellectual Property Frameworks." (2022) 71(1) *GRUR International*, 24. Doi: 10.1093/grurint/ikab099

17 Francis Kariuki, "Protecting Traditional Knowledge in Kenya: Traditional Justice Systems as Appropriate Sui Generis Systems." *WIPO-WTO Colloquium Papers*, 2019, 59.

18 Margo A. Bagley, "Toward an Effective Indigenous Knowledge Protection Regime: Case Study of South Africa" (December 2018) CIGI Papers No. 207, 3. "South Africa's legal and policy approaches to Indigenous knowledge and Indigenous biological and genetic resource protection largely derive from the framework provided by the CBD and its Nagoya Protocol."

> South Africa's cultural and genetic resource protection scheme has several components that, when fully implemented and operationalised, could operate together to achieve superior economic, cultural and sustainable outcomes ... and, importantly, to provide protection for Indigenous knowledge and Indigenous biological resources.[19]

Conversely, there are jurisdictions expressly providing for the protection of traditional knowledge in existing aspects of intellectual property laws. In China, patent law protects new traditional medicine-based products, methods of process, and new uses of traditional medicine, including herbal preparations, extracts from herbal medicines, foods containing herbal medicines, and methods for preparing herbal formulas.[20] Regardless of the existence of Chinese patent law on traditional medicine, knowledge holders might face challenges in satisfying the requirement to apply for a patent. The traditional process of producing medicine might not satisfy the novelty requirement in seeking patent protection.

> Due to the differences between perceptions about TMK from a traditional Chinese perspective and a "Western" legal perspective, an IP framework could be an unsuitable legal framework for the protection of TMK in China's unique cultural and historical context. The "round peg in a square hole" analogy illustrates this conflicting situation.[21]

Viewing this quotation from the perspective of colonial mentality and decolonisation, it might not necessarily be a round peg in a square hole, but what is needed is for aspects of intellectual property law to accommodate different knowledge systems and avoid being rigidly Eurocentric in perspective. It can be one cap that fits many.

Perhaps China should be commended for taking a bold step in attempting to eradicate the inferior/superior hierarchy, harboured by colonial mentality through the addition of traditional medicine in the Patent Act, thereby attempting to decolonise the Patent Act. Traditional medicine is not merely an act of the past but the present and the future. Holders of traditional medicine knowledge can easily fulfil the patent requirements in many situations. The Patent Act in Nigeria has remained the same for five decades and caters for an era that no longer exists. However, the good and

19 Ibid., 4.

20 World Intellectual Property Organization, "Intellectual Property and Traditional Medical Knowledge." Background Brief No. 6.

21 Nan Xia, "Intellectual Property Protection of Traditional Medical Knowledge in China's Context: A Round Peg in a Square Hole" (2023) 31 *Medical Law Review* 359 https://doi.org/10.1093/medlaw/fwad006 Advance access publication, 5 April 2023.

the bad of the Nigerian situation regarding the status of the Patent Act will be discussed subsequently.

The Patent Act of Nigeria adopts the formal rather than the substantive system of protection. It does not require the technicalities of the latter. However, the formal nature of the Act has not encouraged seeking patent protection for traditional medicine in comparison to the Patent Act in China. Even though it is expressly stated in the Act in China and not in Nigeria, the Act can accommodate the protection of traditional medicine due to the system adopted. Between 2011 and 2021, there were 45,411 Traditional Chinese Medicine Patents.[22] "The retail trade revenue of traditional Chinese and Western pharmaceuticals in China has decreased since 2017. In the most recently reported month in 2023, the retail sales figure in China amounted to about 68 billion yuan."[23] The revenue generated from traditional Chinese medicine by indigenous pharmaceutical industries is beneficial to the economy of the country without a doubt. Nigeria can benefit as well if the development of traditional medicine is promoted as a means of dealing with health issues as well as making an income through intellectual property.

The focus on the eradication of colonial mentality is to benefit maximally from Nigeria's rich traditional medicinal plants and knowledge systems. The use of these resources nationally to cater for different health situations has become imminent. Even though these resources have been depended on for centuries for healthcare in traditional communities, they remain valuable. The development of traditional medicine aligns with the new trend of sustainable innovation, suitable for Nigeria's development agenda and the African continent.[24] The impact of colonial mentality on the development of traditional medicine for use in the healthcare system of Nigeria is critically reviewed. The role patent law plays in the recognition of the value of traditional medicine in Nigeria and the implications of decolonisation are examined. The concept of colonial mentality can benefit from the concept of decolonisation in the sense that such mentality can be free from its colonial influence to rely on its traditional knowledge.

22 Wenyi Zhang, "TCM Patent Applications in China 2011–2021" (13 February 2024) https://www.statista.com/statistics/1235301/china-traditional-chinese-medicine-tcm-patent-applications/ accessed 6 March 2024.

23 Wenyi Zhang, "Monthly Retail Sales of Pharmaceuticals in China 2011–2023" (13 February 2024) https://www.statista.com/statistics/226906/trade-revenue-of-medicine-in-china-by-month/ accessed 6 March 2024.

24 CRS in Action, "Sustainable Innovation: A Solution to Africa's Poverty" ttp://csr-in-action.org/sustainable-innovation-solution-to-africas-poverty-2/ accessed 15 February 2023.

7.2 Health issues and traditional medicine in Nigeria

> In the pre-colonial, there were no hospitals in Africa. Herbalists or traditional medicine practitioners (TMPs) carried out the task of providing remedies to relief patients of their health challenges.[25]

Nigerians are faced with many health issues across different ages, social statuses, and regions.[26] Different illnesses or diseases claim lives in Nigeria daily at a higher rate in comparison to developed countries or, from a regional perspective, continents. The poverty level or rate of economic development in Nigeria is often associated with the availability of medicines to cure or curb these diseases. While there is easy access to traditional medicine, it is rated inferior in comparison to the superiority of orthodox medicine, which is imported. The majority of people in Nigeria cannot afford to buy modern medicine imported from developed countries, given their low income.[27]

There is limited government support for research, development and utilisation of traditional medicine, often linked to:

> Colonial suppression evidently seen in some beliefs and practices of foreign religions, on one hand, and absolute lack of patriotism and political will of the government and carefree attitudes of most African medical scientists of all categories, on the other hand.[28]

Nigeria's history influences the present regarding the perception of traditional medicine as inferior to orthodox medicine.

Traditional medicine took a back seat after colonisation, and the orthodox became the alternative. "Traditional African medicine has been in existence long before Western medicine found its way into Africa, and this is what African ancestors survived on when they were faced with all manner of illnesses."[29] In traditional communities or rural areas, traditional medicine is consulted first, and if it fails for some reason, they try Western

25 Ayoyemi Lawal-Arowolo and Yinka Olomojobi, "Intellectual Property Rights, Orthodox Medicine and Traditional (Medicine) Knowledge Systems." (2020) 42(12) *E.I.P.R*, 833.

26 Omoleke I.I. and B. A. Taleat "Contemporary Issues and Challenges of the Health Sector in Nigeria." (2017) 5(4) *Research Journal of Health Sciences* 212.

27 G.M. Adebo and S.D.Y. Alfred, "Gender Dimension of Herbal Medicine's Knowledge and Practice in Ekiti and Ondo States, Nigeria." (2011) 5(8) *Journal of Medicinal Plants Research*, 1283, available at http://www.academicjournals.org/JMPR accessed 7 July 2023.

28 Evaristus Emeka Isefi, "Decolonising Contemporary African Primary Health Care System: A Philosophical Proposition." (2022) 12(1) *Philosophy and Praxis*, 181–182.

29 Evaristus Emeka Isefi, "Decolonising Contemporary African Primary Health Care System: A Philosophical Proposition." (2022) 12 (1) *Philosophy and Praxis*, 181.

medicine. Traditional medicine can fail due to adulterations and quacks, just as orthodox medicine can fail due to counterfeits and quacks as well. It is worth mentioning that in the past, communities knew those who had expertise in traditional medicine. It was a spiritual and respected profession that no one dared to copy to avoid taboos.

During the COVID-19 pandemic, it became more apparent that research and development of a new type of medicine is expensive. In addition, patent protection limits access to the invented medicine in developing and poorer countries of the South. The vaccines cost an arm and a leg for African countries. Nigeria did not receive enough supplies for approximately 200 million people, and many were not vaccinated. Apart from the short supply due to costs, many Nigerians were not convinced that orthodox medicine was the sole solution and relied on traditional medicine or herbs to maintain their health.

The Nigerian government did not expressly support the use of traditional medicine during COVID-19 due to its silence on usage and advocacy for vaccination.[30] Nigeria's silence is contrary to the existence of at least a hundred traditional medicine plants with potential therapeutic value in the treatment of COVID-19, which individuals indulged in.[31] Ethiopia and a couple of other African countries explored this option.[32] Thousands of people received herbal medicines in China, while others depended on mainstream antiviral drugs. The situation in China during COVID-19 and after serves as best practice for the Nigerian government regarding the health of citizens in terms of development, provision of necessary medical facilities, and adequate medicines to promote the quality of healthcare

30 Cheluchi Oyemelukwe-Onuobia, Ayoyemi Lawal-Arowolo, and Emmanuel Chinaka Emmanuel, "Patents, Access to COVID-19 Vaccines and Medicines, and Traditional Medicine: A Dilemma for African Countries." (2020) 42 (9) *E.I.P.R*, 574–575.

31 Polydor Ngoy Mutombo et al., "Experiences and Challenges of African Traditional Medicine: Lessons from COVID-19 pandemic." (2022) *BMJ Global Health*. http://dx.doi.org/10.1136/bmjgh-2022-010813. Attah A. F., Fagbemi A.A., Olubiyi O., Dada-Adegbola H., Oluwadotun A., Elujoba A., Babalola C.P., "Therapeutic Potentials of Antiviral Plants Used in Traditional African Medicine With COVID-19 in Focus: A Nigerian Perspective." (2021) 12 *Front Pharmacol.*, 596855. http://dx.doi.org/10.3389/fphar.2021.596855.

32 Polydor Ngoy Mutombo et al. "Experiences and Challenges of African Traditional Medicine: Lessons from COVID-19 Pandemic." *BMJ Global Health*. http://dx.doi.org/10.1136/bmjgh-2022-010813 2. "With limited access to conventional health products and amid a deadly global pandemic, some Africans turned to the use of traditional therapies such as herbal medicines, one of the few therapies to which they had easy access. This is not unprecedented, as the use of traditional medicines in Africa has been reported recently for patients with AIDS symptoms in Malawi, South Africa, Uganda and Zimbabwe and as the main source of healthcare for mental illnesses in Uganda … More recently, in the context of infectious diseases with some similarity to COVID-19, Ebola survivors in West Africa appeared to turn to herbal medicines not only for treatment but also to fill the gaps in conventional healthcare services."

delivery.[33] The abundance of herbs and roots is an advantage that should be maximised.[34]

7.3 Exploring the term "traditional medicine"

The term traditional medicine is adopted in this work rather than alternative medicine as a system of healthcare in Nigeria.[35] In some terrains, the term alternative or complementary is most appropriate, taking into consideration their background. Alternative medicine is used interchangeably with traditional medicine or complementary medicine in Nigeria, and it includes traditional medical practices from Asian countries. The composition of the society and the number of people (approx. 200 million, the largest population in Africa)[36] reliant on traditional medicine on a daily basis for healthcare makes the term most appropriate in this chapter. The title "traditional medicine practitioner" is also adopted. This term is broad enough to accommodate all aspects of healers. The use of the word peoples rather than people highlights those at the communal level in need of better healthcare. They are regarded as the majority in Nigeria. The production process and distribution network for traditional medicine in Nigeria is divided into five categories in this chapter:

(1) Spiritual traditional medicine practitioners combine the usage of herbs, incantations, and divination for medicinal purposes. They are often found in villages or rural settings; some are known to reside in the cities, while others live outside Nigeria to cater for the needs of Africans in the diaspora. They perceive illnesses in two ways: the physical (illnesses you can see and treat) and the metaphysical (illnesses you cannot see, which are of the spirit and require a diviner).[37]

33 S.B. Lugar, "The Right to Health in Nigeria and Its Impact on Citizens' Access to Medical Care." (2022) 67 *Journal of African Law*, 4–5.
34 T.D. Popoola, "West African Medicinal Plants and their Constituent Compounds as Treatments for Viral Infections, Including SARS-CoV-2/COVID-19." (2022) 30 *Daru Journal of Pharmaceutical Science*, 191–210, https://www.ncbi.nlm.nih.gov/pmc/articles /PMC9043090 />accessed on July 2023.
35 Haidan Yuan et al., "The Traditional Medicine and Modern Medicine from Natural Products" (2016) 21(5) *Molecules* https://www.ncbi.nlm.nih.gov/pmc/articles/PMC6273146 accessed 15 July 2023.
36 J.O. Ezekwesili-Ofili and A.N.C. Okaka, "Herbal Medicines in African Traditional Medicine" *Herbal Medicine*, 2019, https://www.intechopen.com/chapters/64851 accessed 15 July 15, 2023.
37 J.O. Ezekwesili-Ofili and A.N.C. Okaka, "Herbal Medicines in African Traditional Medicine" in Phillip F. Builders, *Herbal Medicine,* 30 January 2019. Doi: 10.5772/intechopen.80348.

(2) Traditional medicine practitioners relying solely on herbs are categorised into various areas of specialisation found both in the villages and cities as well as rural and urban areas. Herbal medicine is a prominent aspect of traditional medicine with a specialism in the use of herbs to treat health issues. It encompasses a thorough knowledge of the medicinal properties of indigenous plants and the pharmaceutical steps necessary in turning such plants into drugs such as the selection, compounding, dosage, efficacy, and toxicity.[38] There are two prominent categories:
   (a) Herbalist specialising in the use of plants or extracts from plants to treat illnesses.
   (b) Herbalists (mostly women) specialising in medicines for children and women.[39] This category of herbalist is not recognised enough as contributing to the vast knowledge of traditional medicine even though many people consult them for healing children. Research conducted on traditional medicine practitioners in Ekiti State in Nigeria shows that herbal medicine practitioners are mostly elderly women with low educational status, while the male gender is often more educated and recognised more in the communities.[40]
      (c) Herbal medicine hawkers are mostly women, and they are seen on the streets hawking their medicine. Research was carried out on this category of herbalists, and it was discovered that:

> All the herb sellers were trained informally. More than half of them (80%) were trained by their nuclear families, some by their extended family. This indicates that Indigenous knowledge about plants and their medicinal values are still kept in families and passed down from generation to generation.[41]

The opportunities to learn about modern ways of plant collection, preservation, and the processing of raw materials, dosage, formulation, packaging, labelling, and marketing of their products are apparent in the research.[42]

38 Ibid.

39 O.O. Goodman, S.O. Adejoh, A. Adeniran, A.C. Emechebe, and Y.A. Kuyinu, "We Love Orthodox Medicine but Still Use Our 'Elewe omo': Utilisation of Traditional Healers among Women in an Urban Community in Nigeria" (2022) 11(1) *J Family Med Prim Care*, 215–223. Doi: 10.4103/jfmpc.jfmpc_1302_21. Epub 2022 Jan 31. PMID: 35309609; PMCID: PMC8930113.

40 G.M. Adebo and S.D.Y. Alfred, "Gender dimension of herbal medicine's knowledge and practice in Ekiti and Ondo States, Nigeria." (2011) 5(8) *Journal of Medicinal Plants Research*, 1285 http://www.academicjournals.org/JMPR accessed 14 July 14, 2023.

41 O.R Omobuwajo, G.O Alade, and A Sowemimo, "Indigenous Knowledge and Practices of Women Herb Sellers of Southwestern Nigeria" (2008) 7 3 *Indian Journal of Traditional Knowledge* 505..

42 Ibid.

Nevertheless, the method of production and distribution is slightly more modern; they soak various herbs and fruits in a large bowl with water or alcohol, display them in bottles, and sell them to their customers in small plastic bags. They are patronised mostly by low-income earners. It is claimed these herbal remedies are (a) effective in curing typhoid, malaria, headache, dysentery, and rheumatism, amongst other illnesses, (b) available and affordable, (c) fear of fake and expired medicine is limited, and (d) there are hardly any cases of side effects.[13]

(d) Herbal medicine ingredient retailers or distributors sell plants, animals, and insects in different forms for herbal preparations.[44]

(3) Traditional bone setters are often needed in Nigeria due to the regular occurrence of road and work accidents. "In Nigeria, the traditional bone setters, perhaps more than any other group of traditional caregivers, enjoy high patronage and confidence by the society."[45] Their clientele vary across different ages, educational backgrounds, and economic statuses. Community opinions on healing in most situations are positive regarding the treatment of bone injuries.[46] While some will approach them immediately after an incident, others resort to them when orthodox medicine is believed to be failing them or has indeed failed them.

Problems with traditional bone setting arise when those who lack the required skill or knowledge of treating the patient are involved.[47] Some patients are worse off when attend to by fake bone setters, and orthopaedic surgeons are sometimes faced with the problems caused by these bone setters in treating fractures.[48] Again lack of regulation has been identified

43 Duke Oreva, Agbo: "5 Reasons Why This Herbal Mixture Should be Preferred to Orthodox Medicine" *Pulse*, 17 July 2017 https://www.pulse.ng/lifestyle/beauty-health/5-reasons-why-agbo-should-be-preferred-to-orthodox-medicine-id7004542.html accessed 16 July 16 2023.

44 Violet Elohor Ikolo, "Perception of Traditional Medicine Practitioners towards Formal Information Sources in Delta State." (2022) 27(1) *Ghana Library Journal* 61.

45 A.A. Dada, W. Yinusa, and S.O. Giwa, "Review of the Practice of Traditional Bone Setting in Nigeria." (2011) 11(2) *Africa Health Sciences*, 262–265. Available at https://www.ncbi.nlm.nih.gov/pmc/articles/PMC3158503/ accessed July 2023.

46 L.O. Thanni, "Factors Influencing Patronage of Traditional Bonesetters." (2000 July–September) 19(3) *West Afr. J Med.*, 220–224

47 J. Ogunlusi, I. Okem, and L. Oginni. "Why Patients Patronize Traditional Bone Setters." (2006) 4(2) *The Internet Journal of Orthopedic Surgery*. https://ispub.com/IJOS/4/2/11045 accessed 16 May 2024.

48 Ibid.

as a major cause of these problems. When compared to other regions, there is a structure in place that often times ensures the patient is in good hands.

(4) Traditional medicine psychiatrists have expertise in treating and managing patients with mental illness.[49]
(5) Traditional medicine surgeons carry out minor surgical procedures on male and female patients.[50]
(6) Herbal Medicine pharmaceutical companies have adopted a modern approach to the manufacturing and distribution of traditional medicine. Father Anselm Adodo's vision of preserving the knowledge of African traditional medicine resulted in the establishment of Pax Herbal Clinic and Research Laboratories in 1996. Pax Herbal is one of the largest manufacturers and research laboratories of herbal medicinal products in Africa:

> Embedded in the philosophy of Communitalism, Pax herbals' integral enterprise model has put the interest of the local community at their centre, showcasing a healing force for people, Nigerian society and Africa.[51]

Even though Pax Herbal is having an impact informally on healthcare in Nigeria, the federal government has not recognised its impact officially or promoted its activities in healthcare delivery nationally.

(7) Research institutes at the federal and state levels are involved in the development of herbal medicine. The National Institute for Pharmaceutical Research and Development (NIPRD), established in 1987, is the main institution at the federal level with functions relating to traditional medicine.[52] These functions include undertaking research and development on drugs and biological products from indigenous natural resources and other science and technology methodologies.[53] Investigations and consequent applications are conducted in the areas of evaluation, preservation, purification, standardisation, safety, and rational utilisation of traditional medicine.[54]

49 Violet Elohor Ikolo, "Perception of Traditional Medicine Practitioners towards Formal Information Sources in Delta State." (2022) 27(1) *Ghana Library Journal* 61.
50 Violet Elohor Ikolo, "Perception of Traditional Medicine Practitioners towards Formal Information Sources in Delta State." (2022) 27 (1) *Ghana Library Journal*, 61.
51 Pax Herbal, "About Us" https://www.paxherbals.net/about-us/ accessed 4 April 2024.
52 National Institute for Pharmaceutical Research and Development https://niprd.gov.ng/about-us/ accessed 4 April 2024.
53 Ibid.
54 Ibid.

> The Institute depends on indigenous knowledge of medicinal plants as a basic step during discovery. This knowledge greatly reduces the number of plants being screened intensively and increases the potential for success...the indigenous knowledge of these people is a highly valuable human cultural resource and should be carefully safeguarded and considered.[55]

1 The value of traditional medicine to the Institute is seen in this quotation. Basically, it makes drug discovery easier since they have been pre-discovered by traditional medicine practitioners from various communities.

Methodologies for quality assessment of biological products, orthodox and herbal medicines, including their raw materials, are developed.[56] Ethno-botanists or traditional medicine practitioners in the Institute are involved in revealing the medicinal use of plants or the development of traditional medicine. Advanced technology in the production of medicine has enabled extractions from biological sources, labelling them as products of biotechnology.[57] These generic biopharmaceuticals are already in the markets (including Nigerian markets) protected by patents.

The world is turning to biological resources for medicine. The perception is that medicine based on biological resources is a better option for sustainable development. In going bio, biomedicine or biotechnology does not make the process of producing medicine nor the technology adopted cheap. "The biomedical research system is under enormous pressure as it has become far more diverse ... and has become increasingly costly to maintain.".[58] Indeed, there is a convergence between biology, medicine, and technology, giving rise to the terminologies biomedicine and biotechnology, amongst others. The originators of health innovation for the future are still troubled by the future of health and technology and the escalating costs of producing new medicines.[59] The health status of Nigeria can only

55 Adeola Jegede, "Historical Perspectives and Protection of Traditional Medicine Practitioner's Knowledge in Drug Development: NIPRD's Experience" in Ayoyemi Lawal-Arowolo and Dorcas A. Odunaike, *Human Rights, Intellectual Property, the Environment and Arbitration: From Nigeria to the Global* (Princeton Press 2023) 361.

56 National Institute for Pharmaceutical Research and Development https://niprd.gov.ng/about-us/ accessed 4 April 2024.

57 Gary Walsh, *Pharmaceutical Biotechnology: Concepts and Applications* (Wiley 2007) 1.

58 Biomedicine and Health Innovation SYNTHESIS REPORT (OECD November 2010).

59 Biomedicine and Health Innovation SYNTHESIS REPORT (OECD November 2010). "Health innovation involves various players having interconnected roles with a combination of the following phases: i) identification of need, ii) research and development, iii) commercialization, iv) delivery, and v) diffusion. Health innovation is tightly connected

be muddled up in all these uncertainties if it does not become a major player in the production of medicines for the people through a cheaper but effective means.

With the situation in the West, the people of Nigeria remain reliant on developed and, to an extent, developing nations for biotechnology transfer as well as biomedicine. First, it was the availability of medicine; now, it is the availability of medicine and technology. Counterfeiters, quack medical practitioners, and deceptive traditional medicine practitioners (an ill person's worst nightmare) have capitalised on the situation in Nigeria, creating chaos in the health status of the nation. "The era 1985-2000 in Nigeria has heralded the regime of faking and quackery … the present situation is alarming in the West African sub-region, including Nigeria … there may be more fake than genuine drugs in circulation."[60]

Even though traditional medicine is readily available and Nigerians indulge in its usage, the production process in most cases is underdeveloped. It is not given enough recognition to be regarded as a means of improving the quality of life and generating income as an intellectual property:

> The stiff opposition to traditional medical practice from official quarters has not whittled down its level of patronage by the people simply because it was developed in response to the dictates of their environment. Consequently, it is affordable, accessible and considered efficacious by the people.[61]

Inventions in traditional medicine are not directly linked to the patent system. Inexplicably, the same system has not been able to act as a capitalist tool in the discovery of medicine in Africa or be the catalyst for economic development, social, and cultural well-being. The balance between the development of traditional medicine as a form of innovation and public interest is practically nonexistent.

---

to the provision, uptake and use of new treatments: feedback from purchasers, providers and patients is essential in shaping the innovation process."

60 W.O. Erhun, O.O. Babalola, and M.O. Erhun, "Drug Regulation and Control in Nigeria: The Challenge of Counterfeit Drugs." (2013) 4(2) *Journal of Health & Population in Developing Countries*, 23–34. Doi: 10.12927/whp..17597

61 Toyin Adefolaju: "Traditional and Orthodox Medical Systems in Nigeria: The Imperative of a Synthesis." (2014) 2(4) *American Journal of Health Research*, 118–124 http://www.sciencepublishinggroup.com/j/ajhr accessed 15 May 2023.

7.4 Colonial mentality in the realm of traditional medicine production in Nigeria: decolonisation where art thou?

The mentality of Nigerians regarding traditional medicine should be decolonised for its promotion and development. Colonial mentality restricts the resolution of issues from an Afrocentric perspective. Nigerian languages are prohibited at all school levels due to colonial mentality. The English language is the approved official language of the country, while Nigerian languages are termed vernacular. Many children can barely speak Nigerian languages. The disadvantage of this situation is that many traditional knowledge systems and traditional medicine are linked to a Nigerian language in transmitting them from generation to generation. Colonial mentality "is a deeply embedded mindset that feels like the only norm to the perpetrators. But it is a corrosive belittling of all 'the other' as being lesser. Implicit in colonialism are racism, patriarchy, and excess individualism or egotism."[62] "Colo mentals" believe there is no way out of the situation except through the ways of those who colonised them before independence, in this situation: the British.

The feeling of superiority held by the colonialists is passed on to indigenes in the colonies and further transmitted down for generations, resulting in what exists presently. The colonialists are no more, but their mentality lives on in the minds of the people in the territories they colonised. Fela Anikulapo Kuti, a legendary musician, sang about colonial mentality:

> If you say you be colonial man (if you are a colonial man). You don be slave man before (you have been a slave man before). Them don release you now (you are released). But you never release yourself (but you do not release yourself). I say you fit never release yourself (I say you may never release yourself) Colo-mentality (colonial mentality). E be say you be colonial man (it seems you are a colonial man).[63]

He rejected Western ideas and philosophies through his music. Fela believed African thoughts were tarnished because of colonial control and there should be a cleansing:

> Fela … argues that despite direct and physical implementations of colonialism ending, as colonial superpowers began to leave the continent as

62 David Trubridge, "The Colonial Mindset is Deeply Embedded and Persists Today," *The Guardian*, October 2021 https://www.theguardian.com/world/2021/oct/01/the-colonial-mindset-is-deeply-embedded-and-persists-today> accessed 22 May 2024.

63 Lyrics, "Colonial Mentality" https://www.lyrics.com/lyric/964438/Fela+Kuti/COLONIAL +MENTALITY#google_vignette accessed 15 May 2024.

> early as 1957, that the minds of African people were still stuck in the psychological bondage of the colonial mentality.[64]

Foreign ideas and ideals are internalised by an average Nigerian in the hope of aligning with the superiority of the Western world. This mindset belittles traditional knowledge systems in Africa. The people look down upon themselves, which results in the abandonment of their ways of life:

> The thing wey black no good (Black things are not good) – Na foreign things them dey like (They like foreign things) – No be so? (He be so!) (Is it not so – It is so) … Them Judge him go put white wig (They judge him with white wig on) – And jail him brothers away (And jail their brothers) – No be so? (He be so!) (Is it not so – It is so).[65]

A connection exists between colonial mentality and the utilisation and institutionalisation of traditional medicine in Nigeria. The suppression of the phenomenon of black consciousness through colonial mentality makes the development of traditional medicine superfluous.[66] "Colo mentals" are quick to display their foreign adopted cultural heritage of orthodox medicine and laws:

> Every people in whose soul an inferiority complex has been created by the death and burial of its local cultural originality – finds itself face to face with the language of the civilising nation … He becomes whiter as he renounces his blackness, his jungle.[67]

It appears from this quotation that decolonisation should be a means to renounce colonial mentality and the whiteness attached to it. It challenges Eurocentric perspectives, thereby challenging colonial mentality and, in this situation, orthodox notions of medicine. Such a challenge is required in providing traditional medicine as a worthy option for healthcare in Nigeria. The thoughts of Nigerian traditional medicine practitioners will be excavated and there will be continuity of traditional medicine practice in combating diseases or illnesses of the past and present.

64 Ajibola Bodunrin, "Introduction – Colonial Mentality in The Decolonization of Fela Kuti: A Mediation on the Creation of Afrobeat" (April 2019) https://medium.com/the-decolonization-of-fela-kuti-a-meditation-on/introduction-the-colonial-mentality-aaeef3c17fa1 accessed 30 March 2024.

65 Lyrics, "Colonial Mentality" https://www.lyrics.com/lyric/964438/Fela+Kuti/COLONIAL+MENTALITY#google_vignette accessed 15 May 2024.

66 C. Ogunyemi and B. Fela, "Kuti's Consciousness: African Cosmology and the Re-configuration of Blackness in Colonial Mentality." (2021) 19(4) *African Identities*, 487–501. Doi: 10.1080/14725843.2020.1803793 accessed 22 May 2024.

67 Frantz Fanon, *Black Skin, White Mask* (Pluto Press 1967) 18.

Decolonisation is expected to douse the impact of colonisation on traditional medicine and the mentality of people in regions where traditional medicine originated. Colonisation brought with it:

> The introduction of Western medicine and culture gave rise to "cultural-ideological clash" which had hitherto created an unequal power-relation that practically undermined and stigmatised the traditional health care system in Africa because of the over-riding power of the Western medicine.[68]

It is this mentality that transcends generations from the time of colonisation to the present in Nigeria, still causing damage to the development of traditional medicine that should be crushed. There are claims that herbalists attempted to cleanse their mode of healing from the stigma brought to it by colonisation.

A first-of-its-kind protest to decolonise traditional medicine happened in 1922, where the protesters rejected marginalisation and the lack of legal recognition of traditional medicine.[69] The Federal Government of Nigeria has taken steps to recognise traditional medicine through the Ministry of Health, the National Institute of Pharmaceutical Research and Development (NIPRID), and the National Council on Health (NCH), among others. A major step was the establishment of the Nigeria Natural Medicine Development Agency (NNMDA) to promote the practices and products of traditional medicine in Nigeria, with the possibility of integration into the healthcare system.[70] In 2023, a colloquium was organised by NNMDA, still on the issue of integrating traditional medicine into the healthcare system. There were suggestions on how NNMDA could move forward to realise the benefits of traditional medicine rather than continue to go around in circles. A statement made by the agency shows desperation in conquering the dilemma faced by seeking collaborations with those who have practical expertise through a fellowship programme:

> NNMDA is not unaware of the colonial mindset that traditional medicine in Nigeria is not "international"; we are rather visioned by the reality that majority of our people depend on this means of healing, and to move the discussion from the computers to the shelves in accordance with presidential directive and ministerial charge, we are calling on

68 A. A. Abdullahi, "Trends and Challenges of Traditional Medicine in Africa." (2011) 8(5 Suppl) *Afr J Tradit Complement Altern Med.*, 115–123. Doi: 10.4314/ajtcam.v8i5S.5. Epub 2011 Jul 3. PMID: 22754064; PMCID: PMC3252714.

69 Ibid.

70 Ibid.

> global scholars to join us as we convert our academic knowledge to practical relevance through our newly established NNMDA Fellowship.[71]

A collaboration between NNMDA and 16 professors was announced in August 2024.[72] The development of a traditional medicine database and training of traditional medicine practitioners is projected for 2025. The irony of the situation is that traditional medicine practitioners at the communal level are not often considered in these projects. While the agency is advocating for the use of traditional medicine in healthcare on one hand, it is attempting to do so from a non-African/Nigerian perspective and continues to disregard the knowledge and skills of traditional medicine practitioners at the communal level. It is perceived from the perspective of modern technology and techniques revolutionising the progression of drug discovery from medicinal plants and monitoring and maintain the quality of traditional formulations and mechanism for its formulation.[73]

The customs or practices of traditional communities as they relate to traditional medicine knowledge and production, from the past to the present, are crucial to its integration into healthcare in this era. It should involve a collaboration of both types of technology, the medicine production process, and knowledge system. Recognition of traditional technology in medicine production is key. Considering Nigerian languages in training traditional medicine practitioners is indeed a step in the right direction. Involving local governments is also a good initiative. It is believed that "if the nation were to focus on it to develop traditional medicine in different local governments, there would be at least 100 different traditional recipes, processes, and services in each local government."[74] Language is important in passing on medicinal knowledge systems of a traditional nature, considering Nigeria's cultural background. Traditional languages for producing medicine were used in different regions across Nigeria.

71 Tolu Aiyebusi, "FG Reiterates Support to Advance Traditional Medicine" (2024) *News Agency of Nigeria*, https://nannews.ng/2024/09/10/fg-reiterates-support-to-advance-traditional-medicine/ accessed 18 January 2025. "The NNMDA Call for Transformational R&D Fellowship Awards" includes the above quotation https://nnmda.gov.ng/wp-content/uploads/2024/01/NNMDA-Fellowship-Call-1-Copy-Editable.pdf

72 Lateef-Ibrahim Animashaun, "NNMDA Collaborates with 16 Professors to Revolutionise Natural Medicine" (2024) *Voice of Nigeria* https://von.gov.ng/nnmda-collaborates-with-16-professors-to-revolutionise-natural-medicine/ accessed 18 January 2024.

73 Tolu Aiyebusi, "FG reiterates support to advance traditional medicine" (2024) *News Agency of Nigeria*, https://nannews.ng/2024/09/10/fg-reiterates-support-to-advance-traditional-medicine/ accessed 18 January, 2025.

74 Samuel Omowunmi, "Traditional Medicine at the Core of Universal Health Coverage – NNMDA Reveals" (2024) *Voice of Nigeria* https://von.gov.ng/traditional-medicine-at-the-core-of-universal-health-coverage-nnmda-reveals/ accessed 18 January, 2025.

The efforts to establish a regulatory body for traditional medicine, expressed in a Bill, are yet to become law.[75] The National Association of Nigerian Traditional Medicine Practitioners is keen on the passing of the Traditional Complementary and Alternative Medicine Council Bill into law for effective and efficient practice.[76] NANTMP has been able to achieve "global recognitions with interactive and fruitful engagements" with "various foreign embassies like the People's Republic of China and India," again "working on an exchange program with some foreign embassies like China, India and the republic of Switzerland."[77] The Bill will provide for the organisation, administration, protection, and regulation of traditional medicine practice. The major aim of establishing the Council is to improve the usage of traditional medicinal plants and herbs and promote a synergy between traditional and orthodox medicine. The synergy is based on using modern knowledge in orthodox medicine to promote the production of traditional medicine and bring it to an impressive standard.

Nevertheless, the superior/inferior saga remains in the form of a colonial mentality in Nigeria. The gap between orthodox medicine practitioners and traditional medicine practitioners has grown due to distrust, thereby affecting the process of the coming together of the two forms of healthcare systems in Nigeria and creating delays in the regulation of traditional medicine. The reluctance to accept traditional medicine in the health system is often apparent in discussions:

> Nigerian medical students have reservations about the integration of TM into the mainstream of health care provision in the country. This is an indication that not much is being done in medical schools to encourage the teaching of TM as they keep unfolding in some parts of the world.[78]

Decolonisation of traditional medicine is required to reshape and enable the participation of traditional medicine practitioners that establish true

75 Traditional Medical Practitioner Commission Bill 2003. It appears the Bill was revisited in 2017 as a Bill for an Act to provide for the establishment of the Traditional Medicine Council of Nigeria; it has also passed the third reading in the House of Representatives. https://www.vanguardngr.com/2017/03/bill-regulate-promote-traditionalmedicine-nigeria-passes-2nd-reading/ accessed 17 July 17 2023.

76 Salihu Ali, "Association Calls on Tinubu to Sign Traditional Complementary Medicine Bill" (2024) *Voice of Nigeria*, https://von.gov.ng/association-calls-on-tinubu-to-sign-traditional-complementary-medicine-bill/ accessed 18 January, 2025.

77 Ibid.

78 A.A. Abdullahi, "Trends and challenges of traditional medicine in Africa." (2011) (5 Suppl) *Afr J Tradit Complement Altern Med.*, 115–123. Doi: 10.4314/ajtcam.v8i5S.5. Epub 2011 Jul 3. PMID: 22754064; PMCID: PMC3252714.

partnerships between both methods of medicine production and regulators in the healthcare system.

7.5 Traditional medicine production from grass to grace through decolonisation and patent registration in Nigeria

Traditional medicine production exists across tribes in Nigeria; there are three distinct regions in Nigeria, including the Igbo, Hausa, and Yoruba. Earning an income empowers them financially to enhance their drug-making process, including the purchase of land for medicinal plant farming, which has become a gradual trend in Nigeria, and basic equipment to make their practice easier, such as grinding machines, mixers, traditional medicine clinics, and more.[79] Worth mentioning is the view that experiments on various plant species by random sampling to extract bioactive ingredients for medicinal purposes are possible without consulting traditional medicine practitioners, a process perceived as purely scientific.[80] When traditional medicine practitioners are involved in revealing the medicinal use of plants or the development of herbal medicine, the process of experiments is faster.

Traditional medicine practitioners are conversant with the application of natural resources, sometimes with incantations to produce the required medication. This form of application can be rationalised, explained, and investigated scientifically, similar to the willow plant, which led to the discovery of aspirin.[81] The technique of empirical observation in their act of curing illnesses is adopted. They do not stop at observation but carry out experiments as well. Consequently, through experiments, the potency of plants for curing various and diverse illnesses is invented.[82] The difference between the sequence of preparation of traditional medicine by a traditional medicine practitioner at the communal level and a scientist at the national level or in another developed jurisdiction is minimal.

79 Chukwuma Muanya, "How Traditional Medicine Can Fund Nigeria's Yearly Budget," *The Guardian*, 31 January 2023 https://guardian.ng/news/how-traditional-medicine-can-fund-nigerias-yearly-budget/ accessed 28 May 2024.

80 A.R. Abubakar and M. Haque, "Preparation of Medicinal Plants: Basic Extraction and Fractionation Procedures for Experimental Purposes." (2020) 12(1) *J Pharm Bioallied Sci.*, 1–10. Doi: 10.4103/jpbs.JPBS_175_19. Epub 2020 Jan 29. PMID: 32801594; PMCID: PMC7398001.

81 C.N. Fokunang et al., "Traditional Medicine: Past, Present and Future Research and Development Prospects and Integration in the National Health System of Cameroon"" (2011) 8(3) *Afr J Tradit Complement Altern Med.*, 284–295. doi: 10.4314/ajtcam.v8i3.65276. Epub 2 April 2011. PMID: 22468007; PMCID: PMC3252219

82 E. Ernst, "Herbal Medicines: Where is the Evidence?" (2000) 321(7258) BMJ, 395–396. Doi: 10.1136/bmj.321.7258.395. PMID: 10938031; PMCID: PMC1127780.

This minimal difference is obvious in comparing the process of production. The latter is a mere modification or translation of the former. The former carries out research and results in a different language and environment understandable to a non-Westerner. In order to make this view clearer, the biological names of plants differ based on language. *Lawsonia inermis* is known as *Lalle* in Northern Nigeria, and its common name is *Henna, Henne (F)*.[83] Apart from using the leaves for cosmetic purposes, it treats leprosy, dermatitis, fever, and trauma.[84] Without a doubt, the Western scientific process is conducted in contemporary laboratories and technologies such as biotechnology, while traditional methods have remained the same for generations, a more simplified process devoid of advanced technology.

As earlier mentioned, traditional medicine can lead for the discovery of orthodox medicine for a substantial patent application in the United States. A patent application (no. 452,902) was filed by Shaman Pharmaceuticals on 19 December 1989, claiming the invention of a biologically active compound (*dioscoretine*) isolated from (*Dioscorea dumetorum*).[85] It is useful as a hypoglycaemic agent with a pharmaceutical composition for the treatment of diabetes mellitus.[86] *Dioscorea dumetorum* is commonly known commonly in traditional Nigerian communities as yellow yam.[87] Traditional medicine practitioners or herbalists have used yellow yam for generations to treat diabetes, using it as a topical anaesthetic and more. In this situation, the use of yellow yam has existed for years. Medicine is produced from yellow yam using traditional methods, prior to those produced using Western scientific methods to cure the same ailments. Various studies have corroborated the medicinal use of yam generally to promote healthcare and cure many ailments in Africa as well as Asia and now in Western countries.[88]

Western science is seen as deserving of a substantial patent in another jurisdiction due to the method adopted. The language and scientific terms play a huge role in its acceptance as worthy of a patent application since scientific research is perceived as validating the efficacy of traditional

83 N.R. Mshana et al. (eds), *Traditional Medicine and Pharmacopoeia: Contribution to the Revision of Ethnobotanical and Floristic Studies in Ghana* (Organization of African Unity/Scientific, Technical and Research Commission 2000) 393–394.

84 Ibid.

85 Ibid.

86 Ibid.

87 Ibid.

88 H.K. Go, M.M. Rahman, G.G. Kim, C.S. Na, C.H. Song, J.S. Kim, Kim, and H.S. Kang, "Antidiabetic Effects of Yam (Dioscorea batatas) and Its Active Constituent, Allantoin in a Rat Model of Streptozotocin-Induced Diabetes." (2015) 7(10) *Nutrients* 8532–8544. Doi: 10.3390/nu7105411. PMID: 26501316; PMCID: PMC4632431.

medicine as opposed to the traditional process. There is a view that Western scientific research tears apart everything non-Western but scientific by denying the principles of traditional medicine knowledge systems because the methods and the languages are unknown to them:

> Enzymes, raw materials, amino acids, chlorophyll, aromas ... can act as catalyst for the so called active ingredient in any healing substance. In fact, they may be the very things that make it possible for the active agent to act at all! Isn't nature, with all its complex biochemistry, wiser than we who possess only a fragmentary knowledge of her mysterious and infinite interactions?[89]

Regardless of the claim of absence of Western scientific processes in traditional medicine, the presence of the non-western scientific process is enough for the formal patent system to register traditional medicine inventions. The patent system in Nigeria can accommodate both the formal and the substantive as a means of modifying the patent system to recognise the epistemological foundations of traditional medicine knowledge. Patents issued in an examining system are stronger than those in a registration system which is dependent on formal processes. Better traditional medicine methods are accommodated without subjecting those with such knowledge to the technicalities of the substantive process. The registrar in the patent office in Nigeria examines the patent application to determine if it satisfies statutory requirements, which include completion of the form, payment of appropriate fees, and relates only to one invention; the patent is likely to be granted without enquiry as to its novelty, inventiveness and industrial applicability or whether the specification sufficiently discloses the invention.

The patent value of traditional medicine in Nigeria has not been rigorously investigated in connection with rising health issues, declining health facilities, and the availability of drugs. However, some scholars preach caution in overestimating the patent value of traditional medicine in Western countries in their quest for drug discovery.[90] Indeed, such countries have the technology to discover new drugs without involving traditional medicine, even though it makes discovery faster and easier if they

89 Elizabeth Kafaru, "Promotion of African Traditional Medicine and Medicinal Plants" in Robert N. Mshana and Mbaye Ndoye (OAU/STC 1999) *African Traditional Medicine and Medicinal Plants* (Proceedings of the 6th Inter-African Symposium on African Traditional Medicine and Medicinal Plants 17–19 May 1996, Kampala, Uganda, OAU/STRC 1999) 5.

90 Graham Dutfield, "A Critical Analysis of the Debate on Traditional Knowledge, Drug Discovery and Patent Based Biopiracy." (2011) 33(4) *European Intellectual Property Review*, 237–243.

do. Traditional medicine is perceived in present-day drug discovery as a portion of an enormous reserve of available knowledge and scientific information.[91] The game is different in Nigeria; thus, the value of traditional medicine should be hyped to create awareness, recognition, and development of traditional medicine in healthcare and as patents. It is the only option available that is indigenous to Nigeria.

In Nigeria and other developing and least developed countries, there is limited access to scientific knowledge, whereas there is an abundance of biological resources and traditional knowledge on how to use these resources.[92] The facilities and equipment to perform expensive random testing of plants are not easily accessible in comparison to traditional methods of discovering and producing drugs. Despite indigenous industrial pharmaceutical capacity to produce orthodox drugs, it is not enough to cater for the needs of the people, thus leading to the importation of drugs.[93]

Indigenous pharmaceutical companies producing traditional medicine are not as sophisticated in the methods adopted for the discovery and production of medicine as developed countries. The means of medicine production differ in some ways. They have the means to adopt some modern technology to support production. Pax Herbal is a scientific laboratory for researching, testing and manufacturing traditional medicine.[94] Universities and NIPRD have relied on scientists to carry out research generally and ethnobotanists or traditional medicine practitioners who conduct research using different methods. NIPRD attempts to recognise the expertise of traditional medicine practitioners and reinforce their importance by providing compensation for their knowledge of medicine production. However, developing a compensation scheme has been a challenge for NIPRD. The most challenging and difficult issue faced is how to provide reciprocal benefits and the mechanisms adopted for individuals and communities to receive befitting compensation at the right time.[95]

91 Ibid.

92 S. Li, S. Odedina, I. Agwai, O. Ojengbede, D. Huo, O.I. Olopade, "Traditional Medicine Usage among Adult Women in Ibadan, Nigeria: A Cross-Sectional Study." (2020) 20 *BMC Complementary Medicine and Therapies* https://www.ncbi.nlm.nih.gov/pmc/articles/PMC7083039/ accessed 17 May 2024.

93 W.O. Erhun O.O. Babalola, and M.O. Erhun, "Drug Regulation and Control in Nigeria: The Challenge of Counterfeit Drugs." (2001) 4(2) *Journal of Health & Population in Developing Countries* 23.

94 T.A. Owolabi, D. Osaretin, and B. Eyinayan, "Bioactive composition and TLC profile data on Pax Herbal Malatreat Tea," (2022) 6 *Drug Analytical Research* 35–36 https://www.researchgate.net/publication/362457590_Bioactive_composition_and_TLC_profile_data_on_Pax_Herbal_Malatreat_Tea accessed on 17 May 2024.

95 Adeola Jegede, "Historical Perspectives and Protection of Traditional Medicine Practitioner's Knowledge in Drug Development: NIPRD's Experience" in Ayoyemi Lawal-

The connection between traditional medicine and patent law in Nigeria is not expressly stated or easily identifiable. NIPRD has developed phytomedicines for common illnesses, including sickle cell, HIV/AIDS, malaria, diabetes, and tuberculosis, among others. NIPRISAN, a drug for sickle cell, was developed and patented by NIPRD; it is not often that inventions indigenous to Nigeria are patented. This view is reflected in the number of available patent registrations over the years.

> The uniqueness of the NIPRISAN case is that the project was initiated and executed by African scientists working in Africa at a time when international provisions for benefit sharing regarding commercial products derived from indigenous medical knowledge were unavailable. A Memorandum of Understanding (MOU) was developed by the Institute for research collaboration with the traditional medicine practitioner … It was a unique development because it was regarded as the first of its type globally and has been adopted by both the WHO and the World Intellectual Property Organization (WIPO).[96]

In the MOU, the patent, which is obtained by NIPRD, is jointly owned. Indeed, this situation is not a common one in Nigeria; as stated in the quotation, it is unique and should be applauded. More is expected from NIPRD since there has not been another success story like the NIPRISAN case. Most researchers in Nigeria are unaware of the patent regime or how it works. The essence of the patent regime as a reward mechanism or means of providing incentives to inventors is not well grounded in the Nigerian environment. While traditional medicine practitioners continue to produce drugs at a low level and, in most cases, adopt an indigenous process of production, they are not reliant on patents to protect their rights.

The challenges faced by research institutes are not related to the registration of patents; rather, it is the funding of research activities. These research institutes do not generate enough income from internal resources to supplement government funding. Consequently, research institutes conduct research at a slow pace in comparison to their Western counterparts. The challenges faced by universities are similar to those of research institutes. Other challenges include inconsistent government policies on funds allocated for research, lack of interest in local R&D results by the industry,

---

Arowolo and Dorcas A. Odunaike, *Human Rights, Intellectual Property, the Environment and Arbitration: From Nigeria to the Global* (Princeton Press 2023) 361.

96 Adeola Jegede, "Historical Perspectives and Protection of Traditional Medicine Practitioner's Knowledge in Drug Development: NIPRD's Experience" in *Ayoyemi Lawal-Arowolo and Dorcas A. Odunaike, Human Rights, Intellectual Property, the Environment and Arbitration: From Nigeria to the Global* (Princeton Press 2023) 363–364.

poor industry–academic linkage, lack of adequate support for SMEs, and apathy of financial institutions such as banks to invest in R&D activities.[97]

Technicalities should not affect the value of the knowledge of the production of traditional medicine. The irony is that those who do not understand the methods or speak the language of a traditional medicine practitioner will find their methods technical or foreign. Acceptance of plurality in knowledge production will resolve the issue of disregard for traditional medicine knowledge and methods of production. The patent system should accommodate various methods of production of medicine as long as they are a discovery or rediscovery of methods of healing.

7.6 Conclusion

Recognition and regulation can promote traditional medicine on the one hand and reduce imposters or quacks in the field of traditional medicine practice on the other hand. The trade in counterfeit orthodox medicines can be curbed if there are authentic biologically based products produced through inexpensive procedures; thus, making them affordable. Decolonisation of colonial mentality, as well as the methods of production of traditional medicine in the healthcare system, is a means of providing healing options in Nigeria. The impact of colonisation on the minds of Nigerians regarding the production of traditional medicine should be eradicated. Awareness of the utilisation and institutionalisation of traditional medicine can serve as a means of eradicating colonial mentality through various programmes by Federal, State, and Local Governments. The benefits of traditional medicine in the healthcare system can also be expressed through policy frameworks and dispersion of decision-making. Basically, the goal should be the reconfiguration of the healthcare system to accept both forms of medicine production as valuable systems of healing. The challenges of healing people in Nigeria will remain if options are not created and the superior/inferior hierarchy persists.

The economic situation in the country and restrictions in accessing orthodox medicine make the recognition and regulation of traditional medicine crucial. The dilemma of disregard or secrecy surrounding the use of traditional medicine at the national level can be suppressed by decolonising colonial mentality. Those at the communal level publicly indulge in its usage, but there is still a need for regulation to avoid inappropriate use and discourage quacks from the practice of traditional medicine. A balance

97 K. Osemene, M. Ilori, and A. Elujoba, "Assessing the Commercialisation of Herbal Medicine Research and Development Outputs in Nigeria." *The Nigerian Journal of Pharmacy* 2011

in the perception and benefit of traditional and orthodox medicine in the healthcare system is required to move forward in Nigeria.

Patent protection reinforces the value of traditional medicine. It is a means of expressly authenticating its safety, efficacy, and quality. The method of medicine production is protectable by registration of patents in Nigeria through the formal rather than the substantive system. There should be more awareness of the benefit of applying for patents for traditional medicine. Patent law in Nigeria has not explicitly included or excluded traditional medicine. However, the registration process, as it is can accommodate traditional medicine as patentable, as long as it meets the requirements for registration. Traditional medicine has remained resilient, and indeed, it is time to formally integrate it into Nigeria's healthcare system, recognising both the traditional and modern methods of production.

8 A comparative study of African and Western mediation cultures with a focus on the music industry

Seun Lari-Williams

8.1 Introduction

The Chief[1]

In a foreign land, far from home,
an African chief stood all alone,
His brightly colored robes a stark contrast,
to the dull grey walls of a waiting room in Paris
His head adorned with feathers and beads,
a symbol of his status and his people's needs,
Wrapped in his kente cloth, he braved the icy breeze,
but his skin felt frozen, as though it would freeze
A dispute had brought him to this foreign land,
a sacred song had been abused by a rock band.
But at the mediation, he felt out of place,
the customs were foreign, and he couldn't read their face
Looking at the mediator was a sign of disrespect,
So, he kept his eyes lowered, to the mediator's neglect.
They thought him uninterested and disengaged,
While he was just following an age-old adage
He listened intently, he nodded his head,
but they misunderstood, and thought he agreed instead.
They spoke of justice, of what was right,
but to him, their ideas seemed out of sight
They spoke of strange laws, of contracts signed,
but to him, all these seemed rather unkind.
He missed his home, where the sun knew his face,
and his head knew the laws and customs in every case
The biting cold outside mirrored the chill in his heart,

1 The Chief (https://mediate.com/wp-content/uploads/2023/04/The-Chief-1.pdf) accessed 9 February 2025.

DOI: 10.4324/9781003602989-9

for he knew that justice was not served from the start.
He left the place, feeling lost and alone,
for his culture's ways were utterly unknown

If I do say so myself, the above poem illustrates the cultural chasm that can exist in dispute resolution when traditional African approaches clash with Western practices. Indeed, Alternative Dispute Resolution (ADR) has gained significant prominence,[2] with mediation touted as "the single most powerful tool in the ADR movement …"[3] However, as the world continues to evolve into a global village propelled by the digital revolution (leading to an increased ease in conducting international transactions or being involved in international private disputes),[4] mediators increasingly find themselves involved in resolving disputes that arise between people of diverse cultural backgrounds.[5] Issues arising from this include the fact that the conception of conflict and of ways to resolve conflict are not universal.[6] Mediation practices can vary significantly based on cultural contexts,[7] and culture affects both how individuals experience and approach conflict. It creates "the mental and emotional structures through which people understand their actions and those of others in the conflict."[8] As such, it might seem surprising, but the rituals that frame the mediation – the preliminary

2 Report of the European Law Institute and the European Network of Councils for the Judiciary 2018.

3 Roberta Baruch Bush and Joseph P. Folger, "The Promise of Mediation: Responding to Conflict Through Empowerment and Recognition," at Xi (1994) cited in Peter K. Yu, "Toward a Nonzero-Sum Approach to Resolving Global Intellectual Property Disputes: What Can We Learn from Mediators, Business Strategists, and International Relations Theorists." *U. Cin. L. Rev.*, 70 (2002), 569.

4 David Throsby, "The Music Industry in the New Millennium: Global and Local Perspectives" Paper prepared for The Global Alliance for Cultural Diversity, Division of Arts and Cultural Enterprise, UNESCO, Paris, October 2002.

5 John Barkai, "What's a Cross-Cultural Mediator to Do – A Low-Context Solution for a High-Context Problem" (2008) *Cardozo J Conflict Resol*, 10 (2010), 43.

6 Sally Merry, "Disputing Without Culture." 100 HARV. L. REV. 2057, 2063 (1987) ("Disputing ... is cultural behaviour ...").

7 Carrie J. Menkel-Meadow "Cross-cultural disputes and mediator strategies (September 26, 2022). Chapter 2" in The Routledge Handbook of Intercultural Mediation, Edited By Dominic Busch, Forthcoming by Routledge, 2023, available on Taylor & Francis eBooks, 2022, UC Irvine School of Law Research Paper No. 2022-33, Available at https://ssrn.com/abstract=4230372

8 Lorig Charkoudian and Ellen Kabcenell Wayne, "Fairness, Understanding, and Satisfaction: Impact of Mediator and Participant Race and Gender on Participants Perception of Mediation," *Conflict Resol. Q.*, 28 (2010), 23.

exchanges and the concluding ceremonies – can be even more crucial than the mediation itself in certain cultural settings.[9]

When disputes involving parties from different cultures arise, and mediation is recommended, it would seem self-evident that the effects of these differences in cultures on the process and perception of mediation as a method of dispute resolution should be taken into account. However, cultural norms, values, communication styles, and legal traditions – which all play a role in shaping how mediation is understood and practised in different parts of the world – are often overlooked. For example, it has been observed that the European Code of Conduct for Mediators, issued by the European Commission, makes no reference to cultural sensitivity and competency.[10] Notwithstanding, such differences in the understanding of what mediation entails bear fundamental significance for how disputants evaluate the process and outcome of mediation and their perception of justice in that regard.[11]

A conversation about mediation cultures is important for many reasons, chief of which is that a common goal in all cultures in discussions of conflict is the pursuit of some form of justice (even in mediation).[12] This concept encompasses several components: the equitable distribution of outcomes (distributive justice), the fairness of decision-making procedures (procedural justice), and the justness of interpersonal interactions and information exchanges among involved parties (interactional justice).[13] These components significantly impact the extent to which parties accept or contest decisions, as well as their inclination towards cooperation,

9 Nokukhanya Ntuli, "Africa: Alternative Dispute Resolution in a Comparative Perspective," *EBSCOhost*, 2018, https://openurl.ebsco.com/contentitem/doi:10.24193%2Fcsq.22.3?sid=ebsco:plink:crawler&id=ebsco:doi:10.24193%2Fcsq.22.3 (accessed 10 Feb 2025).

10 Lisa Blomgren Amsler, Janet Martinez, and Stephanie Smith, "Dispute System Design: Preventing, Managing, and Resolving Conflict" (30 May 2020). Lisa Blomgren Amsler, Janet K. Martinez, and Stephanie Smith, *Dispute System Design: Preventing, Managing, and Resolving Conflict.* (Stanford University Press 2020), 102; "European Code of Conduct for Mediators." https://e-justice.europa.eu/63/EN/eu_rules_on_mediation accessed 24 September 2023. However, Amsler et al. observed that the World Bank handbook for the assessment and implementation of commercial mediation discusses the importance of cultural sensitivity in depth.

11 John Barkai, "What's a Cross-Cultural Mediator to Do? A Low-Context Solution for a High-Context Problem." *Cardozo Journal of Conflict Resolution*, 10 (2008), 43–89. Available at https://ssrn.com/abstract=1434165

12 Adrian Pop, "Traditional Approaches in Alternative Dispute Resolution: A Brief Overview." *Conflict Studies Quarterly*, 7 (2014), 34–48

13 Ibid.

withdrawal, or conflict. Moreover, the perception of justice is profoundly shaped by the cultural milieu.[14]

This chapter uses the music industry as a case study for compelling reasons. This industry epitomises a dynamic sector where individuals, regardless of their geographical origins or backgrounds, can seamlessly participate in a global business environment, all thanks to the digital age.[15] As a result, disputes arising from international collaborations and copyright infringements are prevalent, and parties may find themselves in mediation. This inclusivity and accessibility render the music industry an excellent illustration of the challenges and opportunities inherent in cross-cultural mediation. However, while this chapter focuses on the music industry, the impacts of its analysis and the insights provided extend beyond this specific context. They can be effectively adapted and applied to a wide range of fields and industries, emphasising the universal relevance of culturally sensitive mediation techniques. In this regard, the practical importance of culturally sensitive mediation is underscored by dispute resolution initiatives undertaken by international dispute resolution providers such as the International Mediation Institute, JAMS, the International Chamber of Commerce, and the World Intellectual Property Organisation (WIPO), including those in partnership with national IP offices.[16] To fully realise their potential, such projects should prioritise the development of culturally sensitive mediation training programmes, the creation of adaptable ADR guidelines that recognise local approaches to mediation, and the active documentation of successful cross-cultural mediation practices in the copyright field.

Recognising that neglecting cultural disparities can significantly hinder the success of mediation, this chapter compares African mediation techniques to Western approaches to mediation. In essence, it inquires how mediators can best "fit the forum to the folks" when such folks are from different cultures. This chapter contributes to the ongoing debate about the cultural appropriateness and effectiveness of Western-style mediation techniques in resolving disputes in non-Western or cross-cultural contexts while focusing on the music industry. It highlights the need for a more nuanced and culturally sensitive approach to promoting mediation in the music industry, providing insights into how mediation can be effectively

14 Ibid.

15 Brian A. Benko, "Russia and Allofmp3.com: Why The WTO And WIPO Must Create a New System for Resolving Copyright Disputes in The Digital Age." *Akron Intellectual Property Journal*, 1(2) (2007), Article 4. Available at https://ideaexchange.uakron.edu/akronintellectualproperty/vol1/iss2/4

16 "Mediation and Arbitration for Copyright Disputes in Nigeria" https://www.wipo.int/amc/en/center/specific-sectors/ipoffices/nigeria/index.html accessed 5 May 5, 2024.

integrated into African cultural and legal systems to resolve copyright disputes. It notes, however, that Africans do not share a common culture but have cultures that are particularistic and based on high levels of cultural and linguistic diversity. While this chapter highlights the importance of culturally sensitive mediation, it has some limitations. It relies on theoretical comparisons and anecdotal examples rather than empirical data, which future research could address. Additionally, its broad contrast between "African" and "Western" mediation simplifies regional differences. The critique of institutions like WIPO also lacks discussion on legal constraints that may limit reform.

Following this introduction, this chapter is divided into three parts. The first part discusses the features of African and Western mediation approaches, highlighting significant differences. It considers African cultures, with a particular emphasis on the Yoruba, one of the biggest African ethnic groups with a population of around 47 million people, concentrated in the southwestern part of Nigeria and extending to nations including Benin, Togo and Ghana.[17] The second part discusses the role of cross-cultural mediators and the mediation techniques they could adopt in the resolution of international music copyright disputes. The third part concludes the chapter by highlighting the roles of institutions in encouraging culturally sensitive mediation.

8.2 Comparing Western and African mediation cultures

The history of mediation in Western culture is well-documented,[18] but mediation has also been a longstanding tool for settling disputes in Africa,[19] deeply intertwined with the preservation of cultural norms and traditional values.[20] The Nigerian Supreme Court, in the case of *Okpwuru v. Okpokam*,[21] highlighted this historical practice, emphasising its rootedness

17 Yoruba, *Encyclopaedia Britannica*.

18 C.H. Mayer, "Mediation as a Global Phenomenon" in *Intercultural Mediation and Conflict Management Training* (Springer 2020). https://doi.org/10.1007/978-3-030-51765-6_9

19 Julia Ann Gold, "ADR through a Cultural Lens: How Cultural Values Shape Our Disputing Processes," *J Disp Resol* (2015), 289.

20 Hezekiah O. Adeosun, "Indigenous Knowledge Systems and Dispute Resolutions: The Yoruba Example" in Munyaradzi Mawere and Samuel Awuah-Nyamekye, *Between Rhetoric and Reality: The State and Use of Indigenous Knowledge in Post-Colonial Africa* (2015), 241–259.

21 ^{(1998) 4 NWLR (pt 90) 554 at 586}; see also Jacqueline Nolan-Haley, "Mediation and Access to Justice in Africa: Perspectives from Ghana." *Harv Negot L Rev*, 21 (2015), 59.

in pre-colonial times and its enduring significance in contemporary society. Justice Oguntade noted:

> In the pre-colonial times and before the advent of the regular court, our people certainly had a simple and inexpensive way of adjudicating disputes between them. They referred them to elders or a body set up for that purpose. The practice has over the years become strongly embedded in the system that they survive today as custom.

This is contrary to the situation in Western culture, where ADR methods in recent times have been generated as a response to the difficulties and deficiencies associated with court proceedings.[22] Litigants grew tired of confrontations in the courtroom, and many sought a more cost-effective avenue for justice. Some were simply in pursuit of forums that offered a less rigid and formal setting than traditional courts.[23] Accordingly, while Western mediation might be an additional option ("alternative"), in Africa, historically, mediation has been the primary way to resolve disputes, while litigation is the true alternative.[24] In this section, I highlight the respective distinctive characteristics of Western and African approaches to mediation from the perspectives of the definition of mediation, models of mediation, and cultural influences on dispute resolution.

8.3 The definition of mediation

To begin with, it is important to note that how the term "mediation" is defined varies across cultures. According to the EU Mediation Directive, "mediation" means a structured process, however named or referred to, whereby two or more parties to a dispute attempt by themselves, on a voluntary basis, to reach an agreement on the settlement of their dispute with the assistance of a mediator.[25] This definition provided by the EU Mediation Directive encapsulates the prevailing Western approach to mediation. It emphasises a structured process wherein disputing parties, of their own volition, strive to come to an agreement with the guidance of a mediator. This implies a significant degree of party autonomy in the resolution process. In contrast, many traditional African societies may place

22 Carlo Osi, "Understanding Indigenous Dispute Resolution Processes and Western Alternative Dispute Resolution: Cultivating Culturally Appropriate Methods in Lieu of Litigation." *Cardozo J Conflict Resol*, 10 (2008), 163.

23 Ibid.

24 Dmitry Maleshin, "Chief Editor's Note on Mediation in the BRICS Countries." *BRICS Law Journal*, 4(2) (2017), 4–5.

25 Article 3(a), Directive 2008/52/EC of the European Parliament and of the Council of 21 May 2008 on certain aspects of mediation in civil and commercial matters.

less emphasis on the parties taking the lead. Instead, they may attribute a more directive role to the mediator, reflecting diverse perspectives on the mediator's involvement in the process.[26] For example, mediation to the Yorubas implies coming before elders whose roles go beyond merely "assisting" the parties. The mediators usually focus on ensuring that peace and harmony reign supreme in society.[27] Consequently, a Yoruba person might define mediation as a process in which respected elders or mediators take an active and directive role (though not formally binding) in guiding discussions between disputing parties, with the primary goal of restoring and maintaining peace and harmony within the community.

8.4 Models of mediation

Further distinctions between Western and African mediation techniques can be analysed through the lens of mediation models. There are various approaches to mediation, with facilitative, evaluative, and transformative mediation being the three main styles recognised in the literature.[28] Each approach has its own strengths and weaknesses, and different cultures tend to prefer one type over the other. Facilitative mediation is perhaps the most popular style in which the mediator acts as a facilitator and assists the parties in finding a mutually acceptable solution to their dispute. It is a non-directive approach that focuses on facilitating communication between the parties and helping them to identify their underlying interests but does not offer any opinions or recommendations on the merits of the case.

In contrast, evaluative mediation is a more directive approach. It involves a mediator who provides recommendations and feedback after evaluating the strengths and weaknesses of each party's case.[29] The mediator may provide an assessment of what the outcome would likely be if the case went to trial and may suggest a settlement that is consistent with the evaluation. Transformative mediation, on the other hand, is based on communication and relational theory. It allows the parties to determine their own direction and supports the parties' own opportunities for perspective-taking, deliberation, and decision-making rather than simply resolving

26 Ken Ahorsu & Robert Ame, "Mediation with a Traditional Flavor in the Fodome Chieftaincy and Communal Conflicts." 1 *Afr. Conflict & Peacebuilding. Rev.* 1 (2011) 6, 7, cited in Jacqueline Nolan-Haley, "Mediation and Access to Justice in Africa: Perspectives from Ghana." *Harv Negot L Rev*, 21 (2015), 59.

27 A.T. Ajayi and L.O. Buhari, "Methods of Conflict Resolution in African Traditional Society." *African Research Review*, 8(2) (2014), 138–157.

28 Zumeta Z, "Facilitative Mediator Responds." *J. Disp. Resol.* (2000) Available at https://scholarship.law.missouri.edu/jdr/vol2000/iss2/8

29 Harold Abramson, "Selecting Mediators and Representing Clients in Cross-Cultural Disputes." *Cardozo J. Conflict Resol.*, 7 (2006), 253.

the dispute. The mediator focuses on building trust and understanding between the parties, with the goal of empowering the parties to develop their own solutions to the dispute.[30]

In addition to the foregoing, there is a less popular approach to mediation (in the Western context). This has been described as "evaluatively directive mediation."[31] It can be distinguished from evaluative mediation in that the latter only refers to the power to offer an evaluation, not the power to persuade or pressure the parties to accept the evaluation. Furthermore, there also exists what has been categorised as "Wisely Directive and Authoritatively Directive Mediation."[32] Here, disputing parties are accustomed to turning to a "wise" third party for definitive answers, who will assertively guide them towards a solution. A Wisely Directive mediator thoroughly investigates the dispute, assesses it, and formulates and advocates for solutions based on the wisdom for which they were chosen. This wisdom may be influenced by local cultural norms, religious values, or the mediator's age, legal expertise, or position of leadership and authority.[33] Parties anticipate receiving concrete answers and are open, if not eager, to adopt them. There is minimal consideration for safeguarding party self-determination. Consequently, although the role of the wise third party may be termed "mediation," they effectively operate as a quasi-adjudicator, imposing a resolution on the parties.

While Western mediators may lean more towards facilitative[34] or evaluative mediation, African societies such as the Yoruba tend to fall within the Wisely Directive and Authoritatively Directive Mediation model. Traditional mediators typically belong to the local elite, garnering respect from the community due to their deep understanding of the local culture. They excel at resolving disputes within the cultural framework and may include religious or political appointees, village elders, or individuals known for their conflict-resolution skills. In some cases, especially in the past, the mediator may be a trusted friend of both parties, enjoying mutual confidence from each side. An illustrative example of this approach can be found in what may be the most famous mediation case in Nigeria's creative industry, which occurred in 2016 between Nigerian record label bosses Olamide and Don Jazzy. While the details of the process remain confidential (as is the case with most mediations), the dispute was swiftly resolved

30 Ibid.

31 Harold Abramson, "Selecting Mediators and Representing Clients in Cross-Cultural Disputes." 7 *Cardozo J. Conflict Resol.*, 7 (2006), 253.

32 Ibid.

33 Ibid.

34 Jacqueline Nolan-Haley, "Mediation and Access to Justice in Africa: Perspectives from Ghana." *Harv Negot L Rev*, 21 (2015), 59.

through mediation with the assistance of billionaire Aliko Dangote.[35] In this case, while the parties and the mediator are from different cultures in Nigeria (indeed, they each represent the three major ethnic groups in Nigeria), this case underscores the fact of the constancy of the role of elders and respected individuals in dispute resolution across cultures.[36] If the parties had rejected the mediator's attempt to resolve the dispute, there would have been a lot of criticism and social pressure from both the Nigerian music industry and the general populace as to why the parties were being difficult.

8.5 Hofstede and cultural influences on disputing styles in Western and African mediation

An important lens through which Western and African mediation techniques can be analysed is through cultural features that influence disputing style. Before exploring what these features are, it is important to provide a working definition of culture. Kenneth Cloke defines culture as "a set of understandings, interpretations, and expectations regarding our environment."[37] According to Hofstede, these cultural features encompass a spectrum of dimensions, including individualistic versus collectivist tendencies, universalist versus particularist approaches to rules, as well as varying attitudes towards power dynamics and hierarchy.[38] Furthermore, differences in communication styles, time perception, and responses to uncertainty also play pivotal roles in shaping how disputes are approached and resolved within different cultural contexts.[39]

While Western culture has often been described as individualistic,[40] the prevalent characteristic of African cultures is their inclination towards

35 Vanguard Newspaper, "How Dangote Reconciled Don Jazzy, Olamide," *Vanguard News*, 12 January 2016. Available at https://www.vanguardngr.com/2016/01/how-dangote-reconciled-don-jazzy-olamide/ accessed 19 September 2023.

36 It has also been found that Gambians prefer evaluative mediators and that weak disputants may best be served by evaluative, directive mediation. See Jacqueline Nolan-Haley, "Mediation and Access to Justice in Africa: Perspectives from Ghana." *Harv Negot L Rev* 21 (2015), 59.

37 Kenneth Cloke, *Mediating Dangerously: The Frontiers of Conflict Resolution* (Jossey-Bass, A Wiley Company 2001), 24.

38 G. Hofstede, "Dimensionalizing Cultures: The Hofstede Model in Context." *Online Readings in Psychology and Culture* (2006).

39 Carrie Menkel-Meadow, "Mediating Multiculturally: Culture and the Ethical Mediator" Georgetown Public Law and Legal Theory Research Paper No. 12-061 (2011).

40 A.O. Akinola and U. O. Uzodike, "Ubuntu and the Quest for Conflict Resolution in Africa." *Journal of Black Studies*, 49(2) (2018), 91–113. https://doi.org/10.1177/0021934717736186

collectivism.[41] This implies that individuals identify strongly with their communities, such as family, clan, or village. In conflicts, the interests of the collective group are often intertwined with personal interests. Resolving a dispute, therefore, transcends the individual and becomes a communal endeavour, where the harmony and well-being of the larger social unit are of paramount importance.

In the context of the philosophy of Ubuntu, which emphasises the interconnectedness of all individuals, the inclination towards collectivism in African cultures aligns seamlessly. Ubuntu recognises the fundamental unity of people and stresses the importance of communal well-being. This resonates with the notion that in conflicts, personal interests are intertwined with those of the larger community. In this way, resolving disputes becomes a communal effort, reflecting the core principles of Ubuntu, where the harmony and welfare of the collective hold utmost significance.[42]

Furthermore, Western cultures are generally deemed universalistic, while African cultures exhibit more particularist tendencies in their approach to rules and norms.[43] This implies that solutions are not solely derived from a universal set of rules but are tailored to fit the unique dynamics of the situation. Flexibility and context-dependency are key elements in the latter approach, allowing for a nuanced understanding of the specific circumstances and relationships involved.

In terms of attitudes towards power dynamics and hierarchy, African cultures may vary, but they often emphasise communal decision-making and respect for elders or authority figures. Decisions in disputes frequently involve consultations with community leaders or other influential figures.[44] Their authority is derived not only from their age and experience but also from their deep knowledge of the community's customs, traditions, and history. This contrasts with Western mediation, where mediators are typically professional practitioners with formal training in conflict resolution but may lack the cultural and historical knowledge that elders possess.

41 Jacqueline Nolan-Haley, "Mediation and Access to Justice in Africa: Perspectives from Ghana." *Harv Negot L Rev.*, 21 (2015) 59.

42 A.O. Akinola and U.O. Uzodike (2018). "Ubuntu and the Quest for Conflict Resolution in Africa." *Journal of Black Studies*, 49(2), 91–113. https://doi.org/10.1177/0021934717736186

43 J. Opute, D. Hack-Polay, and M. Rahman, "Resisting Global Universalistic Practices – the Endurance of Culture and Particularism in African HRM." *Journal of Work Applied* Management, 12(1) (2020), 55–68. https://doi.org/10.1108/JWAM-11-2019-0032

44 Julia Ann Gold, "ADR through a Cultural Lens: How Cultural Values Shape Our Disputing Processes." *J Disp Resol* (2005), 289; Kariuki, Francis, Conflict Resolution by Elders in Africa: Successes, Challenges and Opportunities (July 9, 2015). Available at https://ssrn.com/abstract=3646985 or http://dx.doi.org/10.2139/ssrn.3646985

In specific African cultures, gender representation poses a significant challenge, particularly in contexts like oil-bearing communities in Nigeria, where the responsibility for managing intra-communal conflicts arising from oil exploitation falls on entities like the Community Development Association (CDA) and the Traditional Elders' Council (TEC). Led by the *Enogie* or *Odionwere*, the TEC assumes a pivotal role in providing overall leadership within these communities.[45]

Additionally, communication styles in many African cultures are characterised by high-context communication, which relies on shared experiences and unspoken cues. Sub-Saharan Africans place importance on non-verbal cues, context, and implicit meanings in communication, significantly influencing how conflicts are addressed.[46] In considering perceptions of time, African cultures in this region tend to exhibit a more flexible outlook, valuing the present moment and relationships over strict adherence to schedules. This perspective can impact the pace and urgency with which disputes are addressed. Patience and a willingness to engage in extended dialogue may be key elements in the mediation process. Lastly, responses to uncertainty within Sub-Saharan African cultures are marked by adaptability and creativity. Given the dynamic and unpredictable nature of many African contexts, there is often a higher tolerance for uncertainty. This adaptability proves to be a valuable asset in resolving disputes that arise in diverse and complex social environments.

8.6 Features of Western and African approaches to mediation

The Western approach to dispute resolution is defined by several distinctive features.[47] It places a premium on confidentiality, ensuring that the details of the dispute remain private.[48] The process is exclusively tailored to the involved parties,[49] offering a space where they can address their concerns without external interference. This approach steers clear of spiritual or

45 Samuel Osagie Odobo, "Nigeria: Oil Exploitation and Conflict Transformation in Edo State." *Conflict Studies Quarterly*, 22 (2018), 62–80.

46 Olugbenga Ebenezer Oloidi, "Philosophical Analysis of Verbal and Non-Verbal Communications in Yoruba Ethical Culture" in Desmond Onyemechi Okocha, Muhammad Yousaf, and Melchizedec J. Onobe, *Handbook of Research on Deconstructing Culture and Communication in the Global South* . (IGI Global 2023), 116–125. https://doi.org/10.4018/978-1-6684-8093-9.ch008

47 Sharon Press and Ellen E. Deason, "Mediation: Embedded Assumptions of Whiteness?" *Cardozo J Conflict Resol* 22 (2021), 453.

48 See, for example, Article 15 of the WIPO Mediation Rules on confidentiality.

49 See, for example, Article 10 of the WIPO Mediation Rules, which provides that "The mediation shall be conducted in the manner agreed by the parties, including meetings by telephone, videoconference or using online tools."

ceremonial elements such as oaths. Furthermore, the Western approach is also characterised by a gender-neutral stance. Professional mediators, proficient in conflict resolution techniques, are integral to this approach. It is often more formalised, regulated, and institutionalised, potentially necessitating a written agreement. In many instances, a mediator is appointed by either a court or a private organisation. The ultimate aim is to achieve a win-win outcome that leaves all parties feeling satisfied and resolved.[50]

African customary mediation is more informal and relies heavily on traditional customs, beliefs, and social norms to resolve conflicts, and it usually does not require a written agreement. The specific roles of customary mediators vary depending on traditions, circumstances, and personalities and may include applying pressure, making recommendations, giving assessments, conveying suggestions on behalf of the parties, emphasising relevant norms and rules, envisioning the situation if an agreement is not reached, or reiterating the agreement already attained.[51] The following are some key features of African approaches to mediation:

8.6.1 *Reconciliation*

In many African dispute resolution systems, a significant cultural value is placed on reconciliation. Customary authorities emphasise the restoration of harmony within the community, fostering consensus, and finding common ground among conflicting interests. As part of the process, an offending party might be asked to offer an apology, either to the community as a whole or to a specific individual before any settlement is reached.[52]

8.6.2 *Influence of indigenous knowledge systems in dispute resolution: use of proverbs*

Indigenous knowledge systems are a body (or bodies) of knowledge of the indigenous people of particular geographical areas that they have survived on for a very long time and have originated locally and naturally.[53] Among the Yoruba, indigenous knowledge systems, such as proverbs and poetry,

50 Claude-Hélène Mayer, "Background to Mediation." (2020). Doi: 10.1007/978-3-030-51765-6_8.

51 T.A. Ajayi and L.O. Buhari, "Methods of Conflict Resolution in African Traditional Society." 8(2), Serial No. 33 (2014), 138–157.

52 Jacqueline Nolan-Haley, "Mediation and Access to Justice in Africa: Perspectives from Ghana." *Harv. Negot. L. Rev.* 21(59) (2015).

53 Hezekiah O. Adeosun, "Indigenous Knowledge Systems and Dispute Resolutions: The Yoruba Example" in Munyaradzi Mawere and Samuel Awuah-Nyamekye, *Between Rhetoric and Reality: The State and Use of Indigenous Knowledge in Post-Colonial Africa* (2015), pp. 241–259.

play a vital role in the resolution of conflicts or disputes. Fadipe noted that in Yoruba peace-making justice, the objective is to mediate disagreements and misunderstandings that may weaken kinship ties or social cohesion or have the potential to escalate into a genuine breach of peace. Notions of seniority, as well as hierarchies within relationships such as between husbands and wives, chiefs and subjects, parents and children, and even between genders, often inform the process of adjudicating disputes.[54]

Somc Yoruba proverbs that have been established and sanctioned by custom for the resolution of disputes include the following:

- What qualifies one to live with others makes one qualified to advise one another;
- Fighting each other does not mean one wants the other dead;
- If one does not forget the incident of the previous day, one may likely not see anyone to play with;
- If dirt is removed from an eye, one shows the dirt to the eye for it to know that it was indeed dirty.

8.6.3 Neutrality

The concept of neutrality is not universally accepted across all cultures. In many cultures in sub-Saharan Africa, during customary mediation, a mediator is expected to take a more directive approach.[55] They are expected to seek a shared solution rather than acting as an impartial third party.[56] In Ghana, there is the concept of qualified neutrality, which is practised in order to establish a new relationship among the parties when there is power asymmetry among them.[57] In The Gambia, it has been found that "mediators actively direct the mediation discussions and express their opinions."[58] The Ghana ADR Act also appears to allow for directive behaviour as it

54 Hezekiah O. Adeosun, "Indigenous Knowledge Systems and Dispute Resolutions: The Yoruba Example" in Munyaradzi Mawere and Samuel Awuah-Nyamekye, *Between Rhetoric and Reality: The State and Use of Indigenous Knowledge in Post-Colonial Africa* (2015), pp. 241–259.

55 Jacqueline Nolan-Haley, "Mediation and Access to Justice in Africa: Perspectives from Ghana." *Harv. Negot. L. Rev.*, 21(59) (2015).

56 E.E. Uwazie, *Alternative Dispute Resolution in Africa: Preventing Conflict and Enhancing Stability*. Vol. 16. (Africa Center for Strategic Studies, 2011).

57 Ken Ahorsu and Robert Ame, "Mediation with a Traditional Flavor in the Fodome Chieftaincy and Communal Conflicts." 1 *Afr. Conflict & Peacebuilding. Rev.*, 6, 7 (2011) cited in Jacqueline Nolan-Haley, "Mediation and Access to Justice in Africa: Perspectives from Ghana." *Harv. Negot. L. Rev.*, 21(59) (2015).

58 Jacqueline Nolan-Haley, "Mediation and Access to Justice in Africa: Perspectives from Ghana." *Harv. Negot. L. Rev.*, 21(59) (2015).

empowers mediators to "formulate the terms of a possible settlement and submit them to the parties for their consideration."[59]

These cultural expectations of the mediator's role and the mediation process differ significantly from the Western-inspired models for standards of conduct for mediators, which generally assume the value of neutrality as an overarching principle.

8.6.4 Confidentiality

Further, in Western mediation discourse, mediation processes are confidential, while in Africa, the whole community is involved at different levels in resolving any conflict that has the potential to threaten community cohesion.[60] In the Yoruba culture, kola nuts are broken and passed around for everyone present to eat as a way of celebrating the resolution of the conflict. Palm wine or gin is also poured in libation. These actions help to reinforce the terms of the reconciliation.[61]

8.6.5 Self-determination

The individualistic notion of party self-determination is also in tension between customary and modern dispute resolution.[62] The Western approach holds out self-determination as the controlling principle of mediation. This means that the parties involved in a dispute have the ultimate say in how the dispute is resolved. In traditional African societies, mediation and negotiation are seen as a way to maintain harmony within the community. The individual is not seen as separate from the group, and their rights and duties are defined by the group. As a result, African mediators often focus on finding an "honourable compromise" that preserves the interests of both parties and upholds the honour of the community.[63] Further, while the free will of the parties is an essential element of mediation in the Western approach, the African customary approach allows mediators to take the initiative in starting a mediation.

59 Alternative Dispute Resolution Act, Act 798, § 81(1) (2010), cited in Nolan-Haley (2016).

60 Adeoye O. Akinola and U.O. Uzodike, "Ubuntu and the Quest for Conflict Resolution in Africa." *Journal of Black Studies* 49(2) (2018), 91–113.

61 T.A. Ajayi and L.O. Buhari, "Methods of Conflict Resolution in African Traditional Society." 8(2), Serial No. 33, (2014), 138–157.

62 Jacqueline Nolan-Haley, "Mediation and Access to Justice in Africa: Perspectives from Ghana." *Harv. Negot. L. Rev.* 21(59) (2015). Available at https://ir.lawnet.fordham.edu/faculty_scholarship/1251

63 Ibid.

8.6.6 *The role of the elders*

As stated above, elders play a key role in dispute resolution in traditional African settings.[64] For example, among the Zulu people of South Africa, disputes are often resolved by the induna, a traditional leader who is respected for his wisdom and impartiality. The induna not only mediates the dispute but also ensures that the resolution is consistent with the community's values and traditions.[65] Amongst the Yorubas in West Africa, the conflict resolution process places significant emphasis on the role of the *agba*, which signifies more than just an elder; it encompasses qualities of reflection, discernment, and the ability to critically assess presented data. As Lawrence Bamikole notes,[66] an *agba* engages with information thoughtfully, considering its implications and motives. Additionally, an *agba* embodies attributes like courage, kindness, tolerance, and selflessness. This makes them a revered model and leader within the Yoruba community. Notably, ancestors are also considered agba, contributing their wisdom to the conflict resolution process due to their perceived greater insight and experience. Concerning the role of the elder in Kenyan customary settings, Kenyatta notes:

> The function of an elder, both in his own family group and in the community, is one of harmonising the activities of various groups, living and departed. In his capacity of mediator his family group and community in general respect him for his seniority and wisdom, and he, in turn, respects the seniority of the ancestral spirits.[67]

8.6.7 *The role of spirituality and rituals*

One of the most distinctive features of African mediation is the incorporation of spiritual and ritualistic elements, which are often absent in Western mediation practices. In many African cultures, mediation is not merely a secular process but is deeply intertwined with spiritual beliefs and

64 Kariuki, Francis, "Conflict Resolution by Elders in Africa: Successes, Challenges and Opportunities" (July 9, 2015). https://ssrn.com/abstract=3646985 or http://dx.doi.org/10.2139/ssrn.3646985

65 Ingrid Palmary, "Traditional Leaders in the eThekwini Metropolitan Region: Their Role in Crime Prevention and Safety Promotion," Centre for the Study of Violence and Reconciliation and Midlands Women's Group, 2004.

66 L. Bamikole, "An Indigenous Yoruba Socio-political Model of Conflict Resolution." *Philosophy Study*, 3(2) (2013), 144–152 cited in Adrian Pop, "Traditional Approaches in Alternative Dispute Resolution: A Brief Overview." *Conflict Studies Quarterly*, 7 (April 2014), 34–48.

67 J. Kenyatta, *Facing Mount Kenya: The Tribal Life of the Gikuyu* (Vintage Books 1965), 255.

practices. For instance, among the Yoruba, mediation sessions often begin with prayers or invocations to ancestral spirits, seeking their guidance and blessings for a peaceful resolution.[68] The breaking of kola nuts in Igbo culture is not just a symbolic act but is believed to invoke the presence of the ancestors, who are considered active participants in the mediation process.[69] This spiritual dimension adds a layer of solemnity and legitimacy to the proceedings, reinforcing the authority of the mediators and the commitment of the parties to abide by the resolution.

In contrast, Western mediation is typically secular, focusing on rational negotiation and legal frameworks. The absence of spiritual elements in Western mediation reflects the broader secularisation of Western societies, where religion and spirituality are often relegated to the private sphere. However, this secular approach can sometimes be perceived as lacking in depth or moral authority by parties from cultures where spirituality plays a central role in conflict resolution.

8.6.8 *The role of the community in African mediation*

Another key feature of African mediation is the involvement of the community in the dispute resolution process. Unlike Western mediation, which is often conducted in private and involves only the disputing parties and the mediator, African mediation is a communal affair. The community plays an active role in the process, offering support, witnessing the proceedings, and sometimes even participating in the decision-making. This communal involvement is rooted in the collectivist nature of African societies, where the well-being of the individual is seen as inseparable from the well-being of the community.

For example, among the Igbo people of Nigeria, disputes are often resolved in the presence of the entire village, with elders and community leaders playing a central role in mediating the conflict. The community's presence serves as a form of social pressure, encouraging the parties to reach a resolution that is acceptable to all. This communal approach not only ensures that the resolution is fair and just but also reinforces social cohesion and solidarity.

In Western mediation, the emphasis is on privacy and confidentiality, with the process typically involving only the disputing parties and the

68 Isola Olusola, "Rhetoric of Conflict Settlement in Yoruba Traditional Societies" (2020). Available at https://www.academia.edu/49560760/RHETORIC_OF_CONFLICT_SETTLEMENT_IN_YORUBA_TRADITIONAL_SOCIETIES?utm_source=chatgpt.com, accessed 9 February 2025.

69 Ikenna Ukpabi Unya, "The Historical Significance and Role of the Kola Nut among the Igbo of Southeastern Nigeria."

mediator. While this approach has its advantages, particularly in protecting the privacy of the parties, it can sometimes lead to a sense of isolation and disconnection from the broader community. In contrast, the communal nature of African mediation fosters a sense of belonging and collective responsibility, which can be particularly effective in resolving disputes that have broader social implications.

8.7 Cross cultural mediation of intellectual property disputes: a case study of the music industry

In this section, using the music industry as a case study, we aim to provide a concise explanation of the dynamics involved in music copyright disputes. We also examine the crucial role of mediators who navigate cross-cultural disputes within this industry, along with intellectual property institutions that design dispute resolution processes specifically tailored for resolving music copyright disputes.

International music copyright disputes encompass different facets. These disputes often arise from disagreements over ownership, usage, and distribution rights of musical works across borders. Common issues include unauthorised sampling or reproduction, disputes over royalty distribution, and conflicts arising from collaborative works involving artists from different cultural backgrounds. For instance, in 2009, Cameroonian singer Manu Dibango sued Michael Jackson and Rihanna for copyright infringement of his song "Soul Makossa," alleging that they had used elements of it without permission or credit in "Wanna Be Startin' Somethin'" and "Don't Stop the Music," respectively. The cases were settled out of court.[70] Similar cases have occurred in recent years involving well-known artists such as Shakira for the official song for the 2010 FIFA World Cup, "Waka Waka," composed by the Cameroonian band Zangalewa. Another example is the case of Timbaland and Jay-Z's song "Big Pimpin'," which sampled the song "Khosara Khosara," composed by the famous Egyptian composer Baligh Hamdi.[71]

The advent of digital platforms and the ease of sharing music online have introduced new dimensions to these conflicts, further complicating the resolution process. Cultural differences may exert a profound influence on the resolution of these disputes. These disparities encompass a range of elements, including worldviews, values, and communication styles (discussed above), all of which significantly shape the dynamics of negotiations and the overall dispute resolution process. Let's imagine the following scenario.

70 G. Velasquez, "No Credit Where Credit is Due: Exploitation in Copyright." *J Pat & Trademark Off Soc'y*, 99 (2017), 693.

71 Ibid.

In Lagos, Nigeria, an Afrobeats musician called Omoluabi from Ajegunle, a local community, finds himself entangled in a complex copyright dispute with a well-established international music label over a hit song. Omoluabi and the label attempt mediation to resolve their differences. However, cultural misunderstandings and differing mediation expectations become apparent. Omoluabi is used as a directive mediator, but the label insists on a neutral facilitator. Having been raised within the Yoruba culture and seeing how disputes are resolved in his community, he expects a mediator who would hold and express their opinions on the dispute. However, the label would consider it unethical and unprofessional for a mediator to express direct opinions on the merits. Among the many questions that arise are: which of the IP dispute resolution organisations may be able to provide mediation services that can address the foregoing differences? Going to any mediator who is bound to apply mediation rules steeped in Western mediation culture may not be the most fitting course of action.

Also, cultural disparities in communication styles can present significant challenges. High-context cultures, where much of the message is implied and relies on shared understanding, may interact differently in a mediation setting compared to low-context cultures, which tend to rely on explicit verbal communication.[72] These nuances in communication styles can lead to misunderstandings, misinterpretations, and even more conflicts during the resolution process. In our scenario, Omoluabi's respect for the *agba* might work against him. So, are there techniques that enable the mediator to probe beyond the legal aspects and address intercultural matters that might initially appear as a straightforward copyright dispute?

8.8 Strategies for culturally sensitive mediation: the role of the mediator

Evidently, both the Western and African approaches to mediation have their own merits and demerits. For instance, evaluative mediation, which is a common feature of the African approach, may be preferred in scenarios where one of the parties is in a disadvantaged position, such as in terms of knowledge, power, or resources. This is because the mediator can provide guidance, information, and an assessment of the case, which can help level the playing field and lead to a more equitable resolution.

In the context of the music industry, evaluative mediation may be particularly relevant in cases where one party, often an artist from a local community, has less power, resources, or bargaining leverage compared to a more established international music label. In such cases, the mediator

72 John Barkai, "What's a Cross-Cultural Mediator to Do – A Low-Context Solution for a High-Context Problem." *Cardozo J Conflict Resol* 10 (2008) 43.

can help the artists to understand their legal rights, assess the strengths and weaknesses of their case, and negotiate a fair and equitable resolution that takes into account the cultural and economic value of their intellectual property.

In mediating cross-cultural disputes, the core task of the mediator would be to build upon pre-existing dispute resolution systems and connect to local customs and values.[73] For music copyright disputes with musical, cultural heritage as the subject, such pre-existing dispute resolution systems could be with local chiefs and village elders as repositories of culture.

Specific steps by the mediator in the mediation process could set the tone right. For instance, it has been suggested that especially if one of the parties is not aware of or does not appreciate the importance of cultural differences, a soft, Socratic method approach of teaching through questions asked by the mediator could be very effective.[74] LeBaron advised that mediators should be conscious of their own lenses and advocate that all parties reflect upon their own perceptions.[75]

Mediators must avoid assuming a universal adherence to Western values and cultures among all parties and should acknowledge that cultural complexities can significantly affect cases. They should engage in open discussions with the parties to clearly define their roles in alignment with the parties' expectations.[76] Additionally, mediators should acquire a thorough understanding of the cultural dynamics at play among the involved parties and strive to accommodate both cultural perspectives throughout the mediation process. Mediators have also been recommended to employ elicitive/transformative approaches. Here, disputants ideally have a say not only in the substance of discussions and agreements but also in the overall process. Transformative mediators diverge from a rigid, staged model and instead permit the disputants to actively shape the process.[77]

73 Nolan-Haley, J., "Mediation and Access to Justice in Africa: Perspectives from Ghana." *Harv. Negot. L. Rev.* 21 (2015).

74 Barkai, John "What's a Cross-Cultural Mediator to Do – A Low-Context Solution for a High-Context Problem" (2008) 10 *Cardozo J Conflict Resol* 43.

75 Michelle LeBaron, "Transforming Cultural Conflict in an Age of Complexity" in *Berghof Handbook for Conflict Transformation*, 30 March 2001.

76 Carrie J. Menkel-Meadow, "Cross-Cultural Disputes and Mediator Strategies (September 26, 2022). Chapter 2" in The Routledge Handbook of Intercultural Mediation, Edited By Dominic Busch, Forthcoming by Routledge, 2023, available on Taylor & Francis eBooks, 2022 , UC Irvine School of Law Research Paper No. 2022-33. Available at https://ssrn.com/abstract=4230372

77 Mark Davidheiser, "Mediation and Multiculturalism: Domestic and International Challenges." *Beyond Intractability*, January 2005. Available at https://www.beyondintractability.org/essay/mediation_multiculturalism accessed 27 September 2023.

8.8.1 The importance of cultural intelligence in mediation

One of the most critical skills for a cross-cultural mediator is cultural intelligence (CQ), which refers to the ability to function effectively in culturally diverse settings. Cultural intelligence encompasses four key dimensions: cognitive, emotional, physical, and behavioural.[78] A mediator with high CQ can navigate the complexities of cross-cultural disputes by understanding the cultural norms, values, and communication styles of the parties involved.[79] For example, in the case of Omoluabi and the international music label, a mediator with high CQ would recognise the importance of respecting the Yoruba tradition of involving elders in dispute resolution while also addressing the label's preference for a neutral, facilitative approach.

Cultural intelligence also involves the ability to adapt one's mediation style to suit the cultural context. For instance, in high-context cultures like those in Africa, where communication relies heavily on non-verbal cues and implicit meanings, a mediator might need to pay closer attention to body language, tone of voice, and other subtle signals. In contrast, in low-context cultures like those in the West, where communication is more explicit, the mediator can focus on the verbal content of the discussions.

8.8.2 The role of trust-building in cross-cultural mediation

Trust is a cornerstone of successful mediation, and building trust across cultural boundaries can be particularly challenging. In many African cultures, trust is often established through personal relationships and communal ties. For example, in the Yoruba culture, trust is built through shared experiences, mutual respect, and the involvement of respected community leaders. A mediator working in this context might need to invest time in building rapport with the parties, perhaps by participating in local customs or rituals, such as breaking kola nuts or pouring libations, to demonstrate respect for the culture.

In contrast, in Western cultures, trust is often built through professionalism, transparency, and adherence to formal procedures. A mediator working with a Western party might need to emphasise their qualifications, experience, and adherence to ethical standards to gain trust. Balancing

78 Thomas Rockstuhl, Stefan Seiler, Soon Ang, Linn Van Dyne, and Hubert Annen, (2011). "Beyond General Intelligence (IQ) and Emotional Intelligence (EQ): The Role of Cultural Intelligence (CQ) on Cross-Border Leadership Effectiveness in a Globalized World." *Journal of Social Issues*, 67. Doi: 10.1111/j.1540-4560.2011.01730.x.

79 Gabriela Gonçalves and Cátia Sousa, "Cultural Intelligence in Intercultural Mediation" in *The Routledge Handbook of Intercultural Mediation*, 2022.

these different approaches to trust-building is a key challenge for cross-cultural mediators.

8.8.3 The role of intellectual property-related institutions in encouraging culturally sensitive mediation

8.8.3.1 Transnational mediation organisations

The clash between different cultural approaches to mediation presents significant challenges. However, transnational mediation organisations are beginning to tackle these issues. For example, the International Mediation Institute (IMI) has established criteria to certify mediators in a set of standards and skills for "intercultural competence."[80] But not enough concern is shown within the field of intellectual property mediation, particularly.

8.8.3.2 WIPO Arbitration and Mediation Center

For instance, the World Intellectual Property Organization (WIPO) unwittingly promotes Western-style mediation to resolve music copyright disputes – even where such disputes occur in African countries. On 14 July 1967, during a special convention held at the Stockholm Revision Conference, WIPO was formally established. WIPO's overarching mission is to advance the creation, dissemination, use, and safeguarding of intellectual creations through international cooperation. In pursuit of this mission, WIPO established the WIPO Arbitration and Mediation Center in 1994. This entity offers various avenues for private parties to address intellectual property disputes, including mediation, arbitration, and expedited arbitration. For these procedures to be implemented, both parties must willingly opt for them. This voluntary submission can be achieved either by incorporating a clause in a contract or through a mutual agreement to employ WIPO's dispute resolution mechanisms.[81]

WIPO organisation recently concluded an agreement with the Nigerian Copyright Commission (NCC), enabling WIPO to extend mediation services to the latter. This development is noteworthy for various reasons. First, it recognises the efficacy of mediation, offering a swifter alternative to often overburdened courts. Second, WIPO's wealth of expertise and resources bolsters its capacity to mediate effectively. WIPO boasts a

80 International Mediation Institute, "Criteria for QAP Intercultural Competence." Available at https://imimediation.org/orgs/cag-icc/ accessed 25 September 2023.

81 Brian A. Benko "Russia and Allofmp3.com: Why The WTO And WIPO Must Create a New System for Resolving Copyright Disputes in The Digital Age." *Akron Intellectual Property Journal*, 1(2) (2007), Article 4. Available at https://ideaexchange.uakron.edu/akronintellectualproperty/vol1/iss2/4

global network of mediators, including professionals based in Nigeria. Furthermore, even if both parties are Nigerian, there is no impediment to selecting a foreign mediator from WIPO's roster, affording parties the freedom to choose a mediator who best suits their needs.

However, WIPO's list of mediators arguably favours mediators trained in Western-style mediation, potentially excluding grassroots-level practitioners who use non-Western styles in mediation. Therefore, mediators versed in cultural mediation techniques, who factor in cultural elements such as ethnicity and religion, may be overlooked by WIPO's approach. This issue is further exacerbated by the insistence on formal qualifications for mediators.

Furthermore, although WIPO's effort to include mediators familiar with the diverse cultures and religions of the parties involved must be acknowledged, nonetheless, its Mediation Rules could potentially limit the applicability of local mediation techniques, including the imperative of neutrality and self-determination. Article 8 of the WIPO Mediation Rules provides that "the mediator shall be neutral, impartial and independent." As seen in Part I, this approach may be unfamiliar to some African cultures where the mediator might be expected to hold and express their opinions (at least to some extent) on the dispute.[82] As a result, mediators might not be fully equipped to handle disputes that arise in such contexts. In addition, due to its emphasis on confidentiality,[83] the Rules do not provide for the recording or publication of information about the mediation process or the settlement reached. This lack of transparency could limit the ability of other parties to learn from mediation processes and potentially improve cross-cultural mediation efforts. There should be an option to waive confidentiality.

Moreover, the Rules do not contain provisions that address cultural differences in communication styles and decision-making processes, which are crucial in cross-cultural mediation. During the 2017 WIPO Mediators Meeting Exchange of Best Practices, the issue of cross-cultural issues in mediation was discussed. David Perkins, a WIPO Arbitrator and Mediator, argued that cultural differences have "all but ceased to exist" over the last two decades, at least in terms of international business. Perkins attributed this to the increasing universality of music, film, fashion, food and lifestyle.[84] However, this statement oversimplifies the complex cultural and

82 J. Nolan-Haley, "Mediation and Access to Justice in Africa: Perspectives from Ghana." *Harv. Negot. L. Rev.*, 21 (2015), 59.

83 See Article 15 of the WIPO Mediation Rules, which provides: "No recording of any kind shall be made of any meetings of the parties with the mediator."

84 David Perkins, "Cross-Cultural Issues in Mediation and Arbitration Exchange of Best Practices," Geneva, Switzerland, 24 March 2017. Available at https://www.slideshare.net

communication differences that still exist in cross-cultural mediations. Indeed, there may be some degree of cultural convergence in certain areas of globalised business; it is important to recognise and respect cultural differences in the mediation process to ensure fair and effective dispute resolution. As such, cross-cultural factors are still very much an issue.

This chapter therefore proposes a re-evaluation by mediation institutions in promoting culturally sensitive mediation, especially for IP disputes as they easily involve international parties. They could do this by placing less emphasis on Western-centric approaches. Instead, they should give room for the flexibility that cross-cultural mediation requires. For instance, WIPO can leverage its existing relationship with local collecting societies to, when necessary, involve traditional mediators (even if only to serve as advisers).

8.8.3.3 Local collecting societies

Local collecting societies play a crucial role in mediating music copyright disputes, particularly when disputes arise between local artists and international music labels. These organisations, such as the Musical Copyright Society Nigeria (MCSN), are deeply embedded in the cultural and legal frameworks of their respective countries, making them well-positioned to address disputes that require a culturally sensitive approach.

Unlike international organisations that may approach copyright disputes primarily from a legalistic perspective, local collecting societies understand the intersection of copyright law with indigenous practices, communal ownership traditions, and the informal methods of dispute resolution prevalent in many African societies. As a result, they often employ hybrid mediation approaches that integrate formal legal principles with customary conflict resolution mechanisms.

One of the key challenges in cross-cultural mediation is balancing international copyright norms – such as those established under the Berne Convention for the Protection of Literary and Artistic Works – with local cultural perspectives on artistic ownership and creative labour.[85] To address this challenge, organisations like the MCSN can serve as intermediaries that ensure culturally appropriate resolutions while upholding legal standards. For instance, when disputes arise between Nigerian artists and international record labels, the MCSN could collaborate with traditional

/MatthewRushton7/crosscultural-issues-in-mediation-and-arbitration accessed 25 September 2023.

85 Chidi Oguamanam, "Local Knowledge as Trapped Knowledge: Intellectual Property, Culture, Power and Politics." 11 *Journal of World Intellectual Property* 29–57 (2008). Available at SSRN: https://ssrn.com/abstract=2283297

mediators – such as village elders, religious leaders, or respected musicians – who possess a deep understanding of local customs and artistic heritage. This collaboration helps build trust between disputing parties and ensures that resolutions respect both legal principles and cultural expectations. Beyond direct mediation, local collecting societies also play a crucial role in shaping policies that bridge the gap between international copyright frameworks and local artistic traditions. This advocacy is crucial in preventing future disputes by creating frameworks that reflect the realities of local artists. Similarly, the role of local collecting societies extends to public awareness campaigns that educate artists and record labels about their rights and obligations. By ensuring that artists like Omoluabi fully understand their legal standing, these societies help reduce the likelihood of cross-cultural disputes arising in the first place.[86]

8.9 Cross-cultural mediation and dispute system design

Cross-cultural mediation is an essential component of effective dispute system design (DSD), particularly in the realm of music copyright disputes, whether they occur online or offline. DSD encompasses the strategic planning and implementation of processes and systems to prevent, manage, and resolve streams of disputes or conflicts.[87] The field of DSD has developed certain guiding principles for the resolution of disputes. They include fairness and disputants' satisfaction with the process and outcome.[88] When cultural nuances are not taken into account in the design of a dispute system, a critical aspect of fairness is potentially compromised. Culture profoundly influences how individuals perceive and navigate conflicts. Failing to consider these cultural dynamics risks creating a system that inherently disadvantages parties from certain cultural backgrounds. This can lead to resistance to mediation, dissatisfaction, and a perceived lack of fairness in the process.[89] Moreover, music copyright disputes often involve parties

86 O.M. Atoyebi, "The Roles of Collecting Societies in the Administration of Copyright in Nigeria," *Lawpavilion*, https://lawpavilion.com/blog/the-roles-of-collecting-societies-in-the-administration-of-copyright-in-nigeria/?utm_source=chatgpt.com accessed on 9 February 2025.

87 Lisa Blomgren Amsler, Janet Martinez, and Stephanie Smith, "Dispute System Design: Preventing, Managing, and Resolving Conflict" (30 May 2020). Lisa Blomgren Amsler, Janet K. Martinez, and Stephanie Smith, *Dispute System Design: Preventing, Managing, and Resolving Conflict* (Stanford University Press 2020), 7.

88 Ibid.

89 Carrie J. Menkel-Meadow, "Cross-Cultural Disputes and Mediator Strategies (September 26, 2022). Chapter 2" in Dominic Busch, *The Routledge Handbook of Intercultural Mediation* (Forthcoming: Routledge 2023), available on Taylor & Francis eBooks, 2022, UC Irvine School of Law Research Paper No. 2022-33, Available at SSRN: https://ssrn.com/abstract=4230372

from diverse cultural backgrounds, given the global nature of the music industry. In this industry, numerous stakeholders are involved in shaping the contours of dispute resolution systems.

These stakeholders encompass a wide spectrum of entities, including collective management organisations (CMOs),[90] entrusted with the task of collecting and distributing royalties on behalf of creators, record labels that serve as conduits between artists and the global music market, industry associations such as the Recording Industry Association of America (RIAA) and the International Federation of the Phonographic Industry (IFPI), and more. Incorporating cross-cultural mediation techniques into the design of music copyright dispute systems is not only a matter of fairness but also a practical necessity. It ensures that the system is equipped to handle disputes involving parties from diverse cultural backgrounds, ultimately leading to more satisfactory and equitable outcomes. This approach not only enhances the effectiveness of the dispute resolution process but also contributes to fostering stronger and more productive relationships within the music industry.

8.10 Conclusion

As the music industry becomes increasingly globalised, more and more disputes involving parties from an even wider range of cultural backgrounds arise. This trend is driven by the digital revolution, which has made it easier for artists from different parts of the world to collaborate, share, and distribute music across borders. However, this increased interconnectedness also brings with it a host of challenges, particularly when it comes to approaching the dispute resolution process. To address these challenges, dispute resolution systems must evolve to accommodate the growing diversity of the music industry. This means developing mechanisms that are not only legally robust but also culturally sensitive, ensuring that all parties feel that their cultural perspectives are respected and valued. In addition, these systems must be flexible enough to adapt to the rapidly changing cultural dynamics of the music industry, which is constantly being reshaped by technological advancements, shifting consumer preferences, and emerging artistic trends.

One of the most significant factors shaping the future of cross-cultural mediation in the music industry is technology. Digital platforms and tools are already playing a crucial role in facilitating communication and collaboration between artists, record labels, and other stakeholders from

90 In the EU, a key measure to improve the governance of CMOs is the publication of available dispute resolution mechanisms; see Article 21 of the Directive on Collective Management of Copyright and Related Rights and multi-territorial licensing.

different cultural backgrounds. For example, online mediation platforms can enable parties to resolve disputes without the need for costly and time-consuming travel, making it easier for artists in remote or underserved regions to access justice. However, the use of technology in cross-cultural mediation also presents challenges. For instance, while video conferencing can help bridge geographical distances, it may not fully capture the nuances of high-context communication styles, which rely heavily on non-verbal cues and implicit meanings. To address this, future mediation platforms may need to incorporate advanced features, such as real-time translation, sentiment analysis, and AI-driven cultural sensitivity tools, to ensure that all parties feel heard and understood.[91] For example, in the case of Omoluabi and the international music label, an online mediation platform might be a practical solution for resolving the dispute efficiently. However, the mediator would need to ensure that the platform accommodates the cultural preferences of both parties. For instance, the platform might need to include features that allow for non-verbal communication, such as video conferencing, to ensure that the high-context communication style of the Yoruba culture is respected.

Furthermore, as the music industry becomes more culturally diverse, the need for mediators with high levels of cultural intelligence (CQ) will become increasingly important. Mediators with high CQ are better equipped to navigate the complexities of cross-cultural disputes, as they can understand and adapt to the cultural norms, values, and communication styles of the parties involved. To develop a new generation of culturally intelligent mediators, it is essential to invest in comprehensive training programmes that focus on cross-cultural competence. These programmes should include modules on cultural awareness, communication skills, and conflict resolution techniques, as well as practical exercises that simulate real-world mediation scenarios. In addition, mediators should be encouraged to engage in continuous learning and professional development, as cultural dynamics are constantly evolving.

In addition, local collecting societies, such as the MCSN, will continue to play a crucial role in shaping the future of cross-cultural mediation in the music industry. These organisations are deeply embedded in the cultural and legal frameworks of their respective countries, making them well-positioned to address disputes that require a culturally sensitive approach. In the future, local collecting societies could take on a more proactive role in mediating disputes, particularly those involving international parties. For example, they could establish specialised mediation units that focus on cross-cultural disputes, staffed by mediators with expertise in both local

91 Seun Lari-Williams, "Agba: The Tailor-Made Mediator" 2025. Available at https://mediate.com/agba-the-tailor-made-mediator/ accessed 9 February 2025.

and international copyright law. These units could also collaborate with international organisations, such as the WIPO, to develop hybrid mediation approaches that integrate formal legal principles with customary conflict resolution mechanisms.

As the saying goes, "different strokes for different folks," and as Michelle LeBaron noted,[92] while we may not fully adopt another's cultural perspective, making a genuine effort to understand it is crucial. This endeavour fosters empathy and trust, facilitating authentic dialogue in various conflicts, whether personal or international. While mediation might indeed be an effective tool in resolving conflicts, and as ADR increasingly becomes synonymous with increased access to justice, the clash between different approaches to resolving disputes presents significant challenges. Therefore, it is essential to develop and adopt culturally sensitive mediation techniques that are better suited to the specific context and cultural dynamics of the parties involved. Elements of the different types of dispute resolution, including the traditional forms of reconciliation and the Western mediation approaches, can be integrated to reach this end. That said, it is also important to exclude harmful elements, such as gender imbalances found in some African cultures – in the context of mediation. Anthropologist Laura Nader acknowledges that methods like mediation serve various social functions and can both challenge and reinforce hierarchies.[93] So, by taking a balanced look at dispute resolution approaches and considering different cultures, we can see the potential of mediation in bridging African and Western approaches.

92 Michelle LeBaron, "Transforming Cultural Conflict in an Age of Complexity," *Berghof Handbook for Conflict Transformation*, 30 March 2001.

93 M. Davidheiser, "Harmony, Peacemaking, and Power: Controlling Processes and African Mediation." *Conflict Resolution Quarterly*, 23 (2006), 281–299.

Conclusion

From passive to active voice, or the start of a conversation with Africa

Jade Kouletakis

The history of intellectual property in Africa is heavily Eurocentric, defying the Afrocentric paradigm. Western requirements for the protection of intellectual property are contrary to the background of African communities but compatible with the background of societies in the West. In the West, it is generally accepted that technology plays a crucial role in the development of cultural industries and intellectual property law. For example, in the case of copyright, it was the invention of the printing press in the West that led to the requirement of originality and fixation for copyright protection. In contrast, Africa's creativity was primarily oral, even though original, meaning there was no historical requirement for fixation. In addition, the forms of fixation in existence then are not recognised by the copyright law regime today, for example, rock art for literary and artistic works and bronze sculpting for the same type of works. The development of creative industries in Africa is not linked to technology nor even values of a Western orientation, but rather to traditional knowledge-based ones that remain unrepresented in the literature – until now.

This book has sought to reposition the African countries away from the existing narrative that sees them as developing nations who exist on the periphery of – or so-called limitations and exceptions to – the norm of an intellectual property regime created to reflect and protect the position of the so-called developed nations. That they should hitherto be represented in this way makes sense given that the laws within which they must operate were made by the developed world for the benefit of the developed world. However, this book has sought to represent Africa in a new light as existing within the centre of the international intellectual property debate, not as an up-and-coming continent trying to keep pace with the West and its standards as seen in previous literature. It highlights Africa as a powerhouse of original, autonomous innovation, values, and traditions which predate the West's concept of intellectual property and are equally as valid today as they were pre-colonisation; at the very least, this book argues that they deserve the same legislative respect and academic consideration

DOI: 10.4324/9781003602989-10

as that of the system which has been imposed upon it through bloodshed and colonisation.

In drawing upon the historical development of the international intellectual property framework with a view to replacing its Eurocentric developmental narrative with that of an African-centred one, this book is the first collective piece to challenge the fundamentals of the current intellectual property framework. Unlike previous publications, this book is not concerned with the development, resourcefulness or success of Africa within the context of the West's concept of intellectual property rights. It does not seek to assess Africa against the gold standard of the West. As detailed by Dr Chime, the challenges experienced by Africa when it comes to implementing the current Western intellectual property framework – so detailed in literature – are oftentimes ignored. For example, a lack of rights awareness sometimes leads to those on the ground going without the legal protection they are entitled to, which means they are exploited and left with effectively no recourse to support themselves. Issues such as a lack of infrastructure, illiteracy, lack of electricity or loadshedding, and poor internet connectivity mean that those rights which might benefit the developing world in theory often transform into paper rights in reality. Instead of considering Africa as a "have not," this book seeks to provide a fresh platform upon which leading African thinkers coming from academia and practice may give voice to their wealth of knowledge about what Africa *does* have that the West does not. Where specific jurisdictions such as Nigeria or South Africa have been used as case examples, the principles within these chapters should not be seen as being limited to said jurisdiction – the principles transcend the example and are to be applicable across Africa. It represents the African experience of intellectual property from a pro-African perspective as shared by African authors – nothing about us without us.

It is hoped that, at the very least, this book will have challenged the veracity with which the reader might have held previously existing truths as they relate to the operation of intellectual property law. For example, it is generally agreed in the intellectual property community that the protection of intellectual property rights began with the passing of the Statute of Anne in 1710 in England. The academics and practitioners in this book hope to have persuaded the reader to reject this pseudo-fact. As Professor Lawal-Arowolo discusses, prior to the colonisation project, traditional peoples already had ways of protecting their intangible knowledge systems through custom. Dr Itanyi, speaking about the success of Nollywood, the Nigerian film industry, and how it relied on traditional tales and folklore, laments that in these traditional settings, stories were communally owned, storytellers were custodians rather than exclusive owners, and the concept of collective authorship was embraced. Unfortunately, in the wake of colonisation and a colonially borne international intellectual property regime, these principles have been eradicated and deemed in conflict with Western notions of exclusive ownership and individual authorship. Obiechine, offering a practice-based perspective as a patenting expert, details how even post-colonial Africans have been at the forefront of original thought and inventive processing, but oftentimes must see their value enjoyed by the Western world with little to no benefit being reaped by the African countries from whence they came. Obiechine points out the intellectual property systems in Africa might seem to be "independent," but their legal frameworks are still largely based on the ghosts of colonial governments.

Indeed, utilising a Western-based international intellectual property framework, and acknowledging that the national intellectual property laws of many African countries have their roots in colonisation, the "colo mentality" (as aptly described by Professors Lawal-Arowolo and Adebayo) of intellectual property law necessarily positions Africa as the passive receptor of Western norms, values and standards to which they must scramble to live up. The result of doing so is akin to joining a Blackjack table where the game has already begun and the House is playing with a loaded deck – the House will always win. For example, when South Africa attempted to amend its outdated Copyright Act 78 of 1978 and move from a system of fair dealing to one of fair use, it was threatened with trade sanctions from the European Union and America if it implemented such change. This lack of respect for the independence of Africa's people is still reflected legally, politically, and geographically through the colo mentality which lives on despite independence from colonisation supposedly occurring in the 20th century.

That Africa's traditions and innovations may not be readily reconcilable with the current Westernised intellectual property law framework is addressed by many an author in this book. As Professor Lawal-Arowolo rightly states, indigenous customary law is marginalised because it is not given recognition beyond the traditional communities from whence it came. This is the result of an inability of the current framework to recognise legal plurality, instead doggedly holding onto a so-called "universal" Western legal perspective. As a result, there have been arguments made by many to recognise indigenous customary law as it relates to intangible property rights through the creation of *sui generis* rights. These are intended to exist alongside intellectual property rights, with the intellectual property system remaining superior. They are "like intellectual property rights, but not quite." The concept of "separate but equal" is a dangerous one tinged with an infamous history. Separate but equal development has long been used to support ideologies whereby traditional African experiences have been treated as "behind" or "inferior" to that of historically colonising ways of seeing and experiencing the world, from the Supreme Court using it to legitimise the Jim Crow Laws in America to Prime Minister Hendrik Verwoerd using it to legitimise the system of Apartheid in South Africa. The natural result of separation can never be equality.

Instead, as proposed by Dr Kouletakis, an entire paradigm shift is needed whereby the international intellectual property community reconsiders the narrative around the "what," "why," and "how" of intellectual property's legal framework. In doing so, they argue that there ought to be a paradigm shift whereby the international intellectual property framework is required to have an inclusive (i.e. considering equally the interests of Africa and the West) rather than monolithic (i.e. Western) outlook. In the realm of copyright, Dr Kouletakis argues that this can be done by shifting the onus from being on users to evidence the need for access to copyright-protected works, to *the copyright owner* bearing the onus to justify their exclusive ownership of the work in the first instance with reference to the United Nation's developmental goals. Viewing the international intellectual property framework through the prism of the United Nation's developmental goals, it is posited, will allow for better representation of and protection for indigenous African customary law in the intellectual property law space. This is because those indigenous African communal practices and values can be broadly seen as in alignment with the United Nation's developmental agenda. In doing so, this paradigm shift will create a pluralistic framework in which Africa is accepted as offering its own unique solutions to intellectual property-related problems which European colonisers would not have recognised as legitimate and which the present Western intellectual property framework still does not recognise as legitimate despite the potential value that could be added to the West in doing so. Ezedum offers one such example of this in their unpacking of apprenticeship (*Igba boyi*), a system of knowledge transfer utilised in Igbo Land, Southeast Nigeria, in maintaining customs, practices and traditional knowledge to prevent them from becoming extinct. They do this by highlighting that the *Igba boyi* is currently the largest business incubator system globally, grooming young people to become established business owners and drawing links with how this might prove effective in the realm of technology transfer for patents. Lari-Williams, speaking from his experience in practice and as a PhD researcher at the University of Antwerp, also offers a critique of the effectiveness of Western-style mediation techniques in resolving disputes in non-Western or ever-increasing cross-cultural contexts relating to copyright. He argues for an African approach to mediation as it relates to non-Western or cross-cultural issues of copyright, such as the involvement of the community over individualism and the sharing of information with others over strict confidentiality. That recognising these indigenous

African customs and values could reap benefits both for Africa and the West is plain to see for any non-colo mentalist.

As the eminent Professor Dutfield states in the foreword for this book, "while [Africa's] rule-taker role largely reflects reality, change is in the offing." This book has indeed sought to humbly stoke the fires of such a change. It is hoped this book will provide a catalyst for others to challenge the current legal hegemonic discourse around intellectual property. It is hoped that the authors have been able to convince the reader that Africa ought to be regarded as an active contributor to a truly global intellectual property framework. This necessarily requires that the framework be changed so as to equally reflect the norms, values, and standards of Africa at an international level, and to afford Africans the independence with which to address their culture-specific concerns in the intellectual property context. Above all, it is hoped that this book will persuade the reader to see Africa as a potential rule-maker instead of the inept and inferior perpetual rule-taker dominant literature would have them believe.

Index

Note: Page numbers with "n" refers to footnote numbers

FSC
www.fsc.org
MIX
Papier | Fördert gute Waldnutzung
FSC® C083411

Kolibri 360 GmbH
Ferdinand-Jühlke-Straße 7
99095 Erfurt, Deutschland
produktsicherheit@kolibri360.de